WAYS OF STUDYING CHILDREN

WAYS OF STUDYING CHILDREN

An Observation Manual for Early Childhood Teachers

Revised Edition

Millie Almy
University of California at Berkeley
and
Celia Genishi
University of Texas at Austin

Teachers College, Columbia University
New York and London 1979

Library of Congress Cataloging in Publication Data
Almy, Millie Corinne, 1915-
Ways of studying children.

Includes bibliographies and index.
1. Child development. 2. Observation (Educational
method) 3. Group work in education. I. Genishi,
Celia, 1944-   joint author. II. Title.
LB1115.A44   1979   372.1'8   79-13881
ISBN 0-8077-2551-X

Designed by Romeo M. Enriquez
Illustration on cover by
Victor Juan Gorospe, aged 4 ½

1 2 3 4 5 6 7 8   87 86 85 84 83 82 81 80 79
Manufactured in U.S.A.

CONTENTS

FOREWORD

It is a great honor and privilege for me to write a foreword to this new edition of *Ways of Studying Children*. While it is not always clear what gives a book staying power across the vicissitudes of social change and educational mood swings, the qualities that have given this book its continued appeal are easy to discern. And this new edition, including the modifications, continues to reflect these qualities. It may be useful then to describe the features that, to me, have made this book a friend to teachers in the past, and which will continue to win it new friends in the future.

First of all, it is wise about children. There is, I believe, a child sense that is roughly analogous to our other senses, although it is of a somewhat higher order. Child sense gives to the teacher what vision gives to the painter, a perception of reality, which is at once both more concrete and more abstract than the perception of the ordinary person. The painter sees more concretely because he or she can dismiss societal frameworks and view reality in a more pristine, more naive way. Yet the painter also has a more abstract conception of his or her vision. This is true because the artist has an understanding of how the visual impression was produced and how it can be reconstructed.

Child sense is of the same order—it enables the teacher to see children outside the trappings of societal frames, in a direct and existential way. At the same time, that perception is coupled with a deeper understanding of the structures in which the behavior is rooted and from which it springs. Dr. Ruth Cunningham, whose work gave impetus to the first edition, Millie Almy, and Celia Genishi are all blessed with child sense as it is described here. This shows in the way they capture children in their descriptions and the way in which those descriptions are used to cap one or another principle of child development.

Secondly, the book has teacher sense. Understanding teachers is every bit as difficult as understanding children. It is a lesson that experimental psychologists, who freely prescribe classroom practice, have yet to learn. Teachers, too, have to be understood in their immediacy, in the existential totality of their classroom experience. But they also have to be understood as people who have their own lives, who must deal with their own parents, their own children, spouses, and so on. And also, they have to be seen as people who have to deal with administrators, with the parents of children not their own, and, not least of all, with ingrained societal stereotypes of their profession.

Here again the authors have succeeded in speaking to both facets of teacher life. And they have even given hints of paths to integration. My impression from reading the book is that teachers who read it will learn about themselves as well as about children. It will help them, I believe, to acquire or to improve their own child sense. But, equally important, it will further their attainment of teacher sense, a better understanding of themselves in the classroom and also outside it.

Finally, the third quality that gives this book its appeal is that it is nicely written with a style that is low key but never dull. The reader is never talked down to, but is carried along with the writers as they describe what they or others have done and observed. One has a sense of shared experience and healthy comradery. In this regard it is much more than a "manual" and reminds me rather of a teacher's handbook, to be kept in the desk for periodic rereading and reference.

I am sure there are many other qualities besides the ones that I have mentioned that have made this book a success in the past and will continue to make it so in the future. But the wisdom of child sense and teacher sense in this book, together with its comfortable style, will, of themselves, give it an abiding place on my shelf.

DAVID ELKIND
Chairman
Eliot-Pearson Department
of Child Study
Tufts University

PREFACE

The first edition of *Ways of Studying Children* was published in 1959. It was a compilation of the experiences of many teachers while working with the Horace Mann-Lincoln Institute of School Experimentation, Teachers College, Columbia University. The book described the various ways elementary and junior high school teachers collect evidence about how children behave, feel, and think. Most of the material had been collected by Dr. Ruth Cunningham and her associates, prior to her death in 1955. In writing the book I drew heavily on this material and on initial drafts prepared by Dr. Cunningham. I also added new material derived from my own experience in helping teachers understand children, particularly at the early childhood level.

In the lively two decades since the first edition, public education in the United States has been subjected to many new influences, including an increased emphasis on the importance of the early years. In 1959, preschool education for poor children was only beginning, and only on an experimental basis. Concern for better performance in mathematics and science, eventually to result in extensive curriculum revision, was already evident. Most educators, however, had yet to learn how the theory of Piaget could contribute to the understanding of such performance. Although the Supreme Court had declared segregation illegal in 1954, little had been done to implement the decision.

In the 1960s all this was to change. The Elementary and Secondary School Act of 1965 brought massive federal funding to many schools. Innovation became the watchword. Kindergarten enrollments increased substantially. Head Start, and other preschool programs for the poor, underscored the importance of early childhood education and parental involvement. Minority groups began to push for education more relevant to their needs and culture. Head Start and Follow Through programs were organized around "models" based on various theories of development and learning. Behavior theory predominated but Piaget was widely cited, and interest in Maria Montessori's theory revived. The technology of education burgeoned. Programmed texts designed for self-teaching and testing, workbooks, "packaged" programs for math, science, and social studies proliferated, as did various kinds of audiovisual materials.

The need to know the effects of these innovations and to maintain accountability for the spending of federal and state funds led to increased emphasis on evaluation. Those responsible for evaluation were pressed for "hard" data that could be neatly summarized and reported. Standardized tests, even for preschoolers, were widely used, and hundreds of new tests constructed.

The exuberant expansion of the sixties gradually was replaced by sober reassessment in the seventies. Initially, innovation—at least as measured by the available evaluation instruments—seemed not dramatically successful. The gains in achievement made by poor children who had participated in innovative preschool programs lessened as they moved into third and fourth grades. Research on Follow Through was severely criticized for methodological problems. Only toward the end of the decade were the long-term effects of some of the early "model" programs evident. Children who had participated in them were more likely than their peers to stay in regular school and not be shifted into special education classes. Although this was an important gain, it provided little assurance that preschool programs, either experimental or Head Start, can solve the problems of families beset by poverty. On the other hand, many teachers and parents involved in Head Start can testify that the program has had beneficial effects on children's health and nutrition, on parent-child relationships, and often on child and parental self-esteem.

Although somewhat less critical of Head Start than of other innovative programs, critics of public education continued to call for a return to the "basics." They wanted schools and early childhood programs to emphasize reading, writing, and arithmetic, with no "frills," and a continuation of standardized testing procedures.

Some influences on education in the seventies were progressive. Working mainly through the courts, various individuals and groups sought and received protection for certain of their rights. Parents received the right to examine all education records directly related to their children, to challenge any inaccurate or misleading information in them, and to be consulted and give consent about any possible disclosure of the records to a third party. Parents of children who are physically, mentally, or emotionally handicapped won the right to have them educated in the "least restrictive environment"; "mainstreaming" began for many of them. Some progress in changing classroom material with discriminatory views of minorities and women also came as state-adopted textbooks and other curriculum materials were examined for evidence of racism and sexism. As an increasing number of women, many of them mothers of preschool children and infants, found employment or returned to school, day care, varying greatly in quality, expanded. The stranglehold of standardized testing on the classification of students and on curricula was loosened somewhat by critiques coming from various national groups, by certain cases brought to state courts, and by legislation in a few states.

When we review the sixties and seventies, noting particularly the increasingly complex demands placed on teachers, we marvel that *Ways of Studying Children* continued to be used in so many classes by so many teachers. The evidence available suggests that it was valued for two reasons. First, it took a "whole child" approach, recognizing the interdependence of cognition and affect. Second, it saw teachers, along with children, as human beings who were developing and learning. The evidence also indicates that *Ways of Studying Children* may have been more widely used among early childhood teachers than among teachers at upper grade levels, even though many of its illustrations were drawn from those levels.

In revising the book, I have been fortunate to have the collaboration of Dr. Celia Genishi, whose teaching experience has included both early childhood and secondary education. We have agreed to focus the revision on early education and care, the area of greatest interest to both of us. In no other area is the teacher's effectiveness so closely tied to expertise in the ways of studying children. Although some of the ways of studying children and dealing with parents described in the book are relevant to infancy, our illustrative material comes from ages two through eight.

Those of our readers who were familiar with the first edition will note that not only have we added *early childhood* to the title, we have also included *observation*. Paying attention to what children do and say is essential in all the ways of studying children we describe.

The structure of the book essentially is the same as it was in the first edition. We begin with the meaning of child study for teachers, and move on to observation, the most basic way to study children. Chapter 3, which is completely new, deals with ways of studying children's thinking. Since the thought of the child and the thought of the adult differ in many ways, the study of children's thinking is important and challenging to teachers of young children. We apply Piaget's theory to this study.

In chapter 4, we discuss how teachers can talk with children and use more formal ways of asking children about themselves to gain a better understanding of them and their ways of learning. We are concerned not only with what children know, but also with how they feel, and how their knowledge and feelings are related.

Chapter 5 deals with the study of young children in groups. This topic, though not greatly stressed in recent years, is essential for the teacher of young children who wishes to promote social competence and responsibility.

We treat children's feelings and knowledge as they are spontaneously revealed in language, play, art, and movement in Chapter 6. Dr. Genishi offers new insights from current studies of children's language development.

Chapter 7 looks away from the children themselves to the various adults, primarily the parents, who know them and can aid in assessing their progress. Chapter 8 considers ways to document children's development and learning, and notes the limitation of tests for young children.

In chapter 9, directed specifically to the teachers who undertake child study, we emphasize the benefits to be gained in the process.

We are indebted to many people for assistance in the preparation of this revision. Professor Francis A.J. Ianni, Director of Horace Mann-Lincoln Institute for School Experimentation, graciously gave permission for us to retain the title of the book while altering its content and shifting its focus to early childhood education

The many teachers who contributed experiences to the first edition, while they worked with the institute, were not identified by name. We are grateful to them for the illustrations that are retained in this edition.

For other illustrations—both those that are included, and those that could not be used because of a lack of space—Dr. Genishi and I have drawn on the generous goodwill of our colleagues and of teachers who have been in our classes, or who have known us in other capacities. Sometimes as we visited classrooms, we saw checklists, charts, and other devices we thought looked very useful. We asked the teachers whether we might copy some of these. Sometimes teachers turned over files of their materials to us, telling us to take what we liked. Often we found that the same form was being used by several teachers. Early childhood teachers like to share good ideas and neither they nor we know who originated a particular form.

On some occasions we asked teachers who were keeping anecdotal records about their children, or who were documenting the children's progress with samples of their work, to furnish us with illustrations. Their contributions helped us to clarify certain points.

To protect the children's identities, we have changed their names. Because we are so often uncertain about who originated the ideas we have received from teachers, and in line with the policy of the first edition of *Ways of Studying Children*, we have not identified the teacher contributors in the text. We are pleased to identify them here.

In naming them, we hope we have not omitted any. In any event, we wish to express our appreciation to all who have helped us. In California, this includes: Florence Bradford, Terry Brock, Rebecca Burke, Amity Buxton, Pat Cox, Margaret Godwin, Kathleen Hurty, Keith Jordan, Barbara Keller, Jean Kelly, Mary Lee Luzmoor, Hermine Marshall, Minerva Mendez, Pat Monighan, Charles Muckelroy, Hannah Sanders, Jane Sandstrom, Barbara Scales, Carol Trimble, and Gloria Weng.

In Arizona, contributors were Jane Raph and Irene Zehr.

In Texas, they were Kent Alterman, James Barufaldi, Carol Berberian, Donna Bricker, Ellen Buell, Sheila Campbell, Alberta Castaneda, Anna Fell, Bonnie George, Victor Gil, Teresa Guerrero, Michael Henniger, Dan Kowalski, Mary Louise Serafine, Ann Sloper, John Smith, Carey Taylor, Frances Trahan, and Elizabeth Tucker.

Glendora Patterson helped us greatly by critiquing chapter 7.

Patrick Duffy provided bibliographic information on the Family Educational Rights and Privacy Act.

We also wish to acknowledge the publishers who gave us permission to reproduce copyrighted materials.

Barbara Scales and Richard Simonds, in California, and Howard Gold, in Texas, provided technical assistance on the reproduction of photographs.

Cheryl Liebling served as bibliographic assistant.

In California, typing was done by MaryAnn Luckenbill and Kathy Scully; in Texas, by Alita Zaepfel.

Our thanks go to all of them, for their expeditious assistance.

WAYS
OF STUDYING
CHILDREN

1 TEACHERS AND CHILD STUDY

This is a manual for early childhood teachers who want to teach as effectively as possible. It is for students who are just beginning to teach, as well as for those with years of experience. It is for teachers seeking answers to the recurrent and perplexing problems arising as they work with children. But we must warn you: this is not a book of answers. There are no recipes. You cannot find in the index a prescription for "classroom discipline" or a formula for meaningful social studies. Rather, this is a book describing ways of gathering information that can help provide answers. And since these answers will be based on evidence from your particular class, in your particular school, with its own community setting, it is likely that they will be more adequate for your situation and you than any ready-made answers would be.

The demands on all teachers are great. Early childhood teachers particularly find themselves caught between the trends and countertrends that are so pervasive in our society today. Whether early childhood teachers are employed in the public schools or elsewhere, current dissatisfaction with the schools touches all of them.

Great expectations for early childhood education were set during the 1960s. Today, many people believe that the early years are a prime time for learning, but few agree on the nature of the learning to be expected. Widespread concerns that the schools are not promoting early learning have led national funding agencies, state education departments, and local school systems to press for "accountability"—evidence that teachers are fulfilling their mandates for particular programs—at the early childhood level, as at other levels of education. Such procedures as setting behavioral objectives, monitoring their realization, and administering standardized achievement tests provide evidence that performance stan-

1

dards have been met. Some teachers like the clarity they see in these procedures. Others find them constraining and inadequate to the complexities of early development and learning.

Similarly, some teachers like "diagnosis and prescription" in teaching young children. Others note, as did one Head Start teacher working with handicapped children, "So much time goes into testing and then writing up the plan for teaching that the child gets less attention than was the case before we started the procedure."[1]

Many teachers find themselves caught between two levels of accountability. On the one hand, they confront the performance standards and attendant paperwork set by state departments and federal funding agencies. On the other hand, they experience considerable pressure, implicit or explicit, from parents and from the immediate community.

In our society the positive possibilities in cultural pluralism are only beginning to be understood. Conflict, openly expressed or lying just below the surface, often occurs in schools and centers serving the children of ethnic minorities, or children from families whose values differ from those of the middle-class "core" culture. To cope effectively with conflict, teachers need to understand many perspectives: their own individual perspectives and how they have been shaped by their sex, by their racial, ethnic, religious and social-class groups, by the ways they themselves have been brought up, and by their adult experiences; similarly, they need to understand the perspectives of people from different backgrounds with different experiences in growing up. Understanding of varied perspectives is essential both for effective work with parents and for the provision of instruction that meets the diverse needs of children.

Teachers of young children not only face the demands of our society but also the special complexities of teaching at this level. Much more is involved than may be apparent to the casual observer who notes how the teacher settles a play-time dispute, or helps a child to think through the sound and meaning of a new word. The teacher's knowledge of the children as individuals with different backgrounds, together with knowledge of the long and short-term effects of different teaching strategies—all this and more bear on every classroom episode.

Considering these demands and the expectations our society has for education, we might expect early childhood teachers to be rewarded with high social and financial status. They are not, mainly because of the way public schooling developed in this country. Much more reliance was placed on the textbook than on the teacher's professional skill. Today's proliferation of standardized tests, behavioral objectives, and performance standards reflects a continuing lack of belief in the teacher as a true professional.

Teachers in public schools have managed to improve their financial status somewhat through unionization. Early childhood teachers who work in child-care centers—publicly funded or proprietary—or in privately operated preschools, however, still are poorly paid. Their low pay reflects society's image of them as baby-sitters rather than as educators.

Early childhood teachers, as they try to improve financial status, do well to consider how they may also increase respect for the work they do. For example, we think that teachers who understand development and learning will be wary of curriculum and assessment procedures that are clearly "teacher proof." Mere opposition to such materials will not engender new respect. Demonstration of better ways of providing experience for children, of solving instructional problems, and of documenting children's progress is clearly required.

In this book we present a variety of techniques teachers can use to match their teaching to the needs and interests of the children and to monitor the effectiveness of their teaching.

The time and energy the teacher contributes to studying young children not only pays off in teaching effectiveness. Many teachers involved in such study have found that they gained more self-respect as they reflected more deeply on their work and assumed more responsiblity for solving their own teaching problems.

The methods this manual describes have been tested by teachers working in many schools and under varied conditions. The teachers who have tried these methods are convinced that many of the questions teachers raise about educational problems can be answered by using methods similar to those used in scientific research.

The steps in solving a problem are not so very different from one problem to another. Finding answers to problems—whether they deal with atomic energy or why Kate doesn't read—always involves certain basic steps.

Step 1. Identify the problem.
Step 2. Develop hunches about its cause and how it can be solved.
Step 3. Test one or more of the hunches.
  a) Collect data, evidence about the situation. Some hunches held initially or tentatively may have to be rejected when more of the facts of the situation are known. Hunches that seem reasonable after careful consideration become the hypotheses of scientific investigations.

   b) Try out the hunches in action. (The tryout may be in a test
   tube or a classroom.)
   c) See what happens (collect more data or evidence).
   d) Evaluate or generalize on the basis of evidence.

When such steps are used in the setting where the problem arises, by
the people who are involved in it, and the testing is done in the original
setting, the term "action research" is often applied.[2]

Such research has dealt with a wide range of problems. One group of
preschool teachers became interested in questions related to "dominion"
behavior—the ways children assert "mineness" in relation to space,
things, or people.[3] Their observations, pooled from a number of centers,
eventually led some of them to develop new teaching strategies for
dealing with different forms of child assertiveness. Another group of
preschool teachers, concerned about the ways parents of different ethnic
backgrounds regarded various aspects of the preschool and parent program, planned a study in which the parents were interviewed.[4] The
results gave them a much clearer picture of the parents' satisfactions as
well as their concerns. The teachers in a kindergarten-third alternative
school were interested in improving their assessment of children's language as expressed in dictation and writing. From a random sample of a
year's journals kept by the children, they eventually developed a set of
dimensions to aid them in appraising the children's language.[5]

Clearly, teachers do not tackle problems such as these without some
knowledge of child development and learning. Such knowledge is essential to the formulation of reasonable hunches about why children behave
as they do, and how we as teachers may influence their behavior. At the
same time, such understanding offers clues about the kind of evidence
necessary to verify our hunches.

Sometimes the evidence needed is relatively easy to gather. It may
involve little more than the careful collection of information about the
community, the number of working mothers, or the number of children
in family day care. But often the basic data and evidence have to do with
subtle factors that are difficult to measure, factors that involve individual
differences in personality and learning style. We believe that collecting
evidence about how children behave and think and feel can be of help to
teachers in developing increasing insight and understanding.

The techniques we report are the ones teachers tried as ways of
collecting evidence. We hope these techniques will help other teachers
seeking solutions to classroom problems and endeavoring to find better
means of evaluation.

As insight and understanding grow, so does artistry in teaching. Though we stress the methods of science, we do not underestimate the importance of the teacher's intuition and sensitivity. Please note this manual is not called "Techniques of Studying Children" or even "Methods of Studying Children." The emphasis is on ways of working and living with youngsters, on interpersonal relations and human understanding, not on devices designed to manipulate.

It is the teacher who determines the effectiveness of the ways of studying children described in this manual. Now and then teachers may try out many techniques, perhaps keeping elaborate and systematic records, without gaining much insight into children or finding many solutions to the problems they faced in their teaching. More often, teachers find that as they study children, they themselves change. Thus we often gain insight and understanding not only of the children but of ourselves as well.

But "understanding" alone, whether of the children or of ourselves, is not enough. The crucial question is whether such understanding improves the teacher's ability to help children learn, whether it facilitates provision of the experiences children need.

Teachers, as we have indicated, are subject to many demands. Does child study, which adds more demands on time and energy, pay off in greater effectiveness? Many teachers who have been involved in child study think it does.

CHILD STUDY: A PROFESSIONAL SKILL

Child study is only one of the many professional skills teachers need. Teachers also need to know how to set up an environment appropriate for learning, to organize a day with a balance between individual and group, strenuous and quiet activities, to engage a child's attention when necessary, to ask good questions. Conceivably, a teacher might master the ways of studying children described in this manual, and yet lack the ability to help children learn. Effective teachers not only have to appraise each child's behavior, thinking, and feeling, but also set up situations in which children will want to learn and are likely to learn effectively. They must know how to demonstrate the learning they expect, how to relate new learning to the child's previous experience, how to correct the child's mistakes, and so on. Child study can provide the teacher with many clues regarding such matters, but teaching involves knowledge and professional skills that are outside the realm of child study.

Child Study Isn't Really New

Whether you are a student entering the classroom for the first time, or a teacher with twenty years of experience, you are already involved in child study.

Teachers indicate that they have observed their children's behavior when they make statements appraising their status: "This class does better work in science than any other class I have had." "This group is really sharp. They'll be through their math workbooks by April."

Often teachers see beyond behavior to some of the feelings that lie beneath. One may say, "So many of these children seem so insecure. They're afraid to try new things."

Again, they comment on individual performance: "Gerald is having an unusual amount of difficulty with math." And again, they may go more into the area of children's feelings: "Sam seems antagonistic to George." "Rita is such an unhappy-looking youngster."

Similarly, teachers use their knowledge of children to appraise their progress. One may say, "Rupert has just blossomed. When he came he didn't know his colors. Now he can classify by color and shape at the same time." Another, in discouragement, comments, "Nine-tenths of this group haven't developed effective word-attack skills. They still guess, rather than think."

Consider what goes through teachers' minds as they think about each child at report card time, or as they prepare for a parent conference. Perhaps they have some records to examine—scores on tests or inventories, or their own notes on each child's performance. Whatever the nature of the records, the teacher also has a composite picture of each child's behavior. The teacher's assessment of the child's progress depends on what has gone into that picture. It is a matter of how intently the child's behavior has been studied and what has been inferred about his or her thinking and feeling.

Teachers often take their cues from children's behavior when they try to identify the sources of some problem. One notes that "Susan's aggressive ways *could* be a cover-up for feelings of inadequacy." Another, looking at the discrepancies between the material in the basal readers and the kinds of interests shown by the children, doubts that they can find any significant meaning in their reading.

But this, you may say, is what teachers do all the time. True. It is in this sense that there is nothing new in studying children. But the ways of studying children set forth in this manual go beyond a casual noting of children's responses. Child study is more than casual observation. The more carefully and systematically you observe children, the more thoroughly you look for evidence, the more inclined you are to want much more than a single incident as "proof," the closer you are to the kind of child study described in this manual. We stress how much child study teachers are already doing so that it will be clear that our proposals are not intended to add to teachers' professional burdens without also increasing their professional effectiveness.

Systematic Child Study Adds to Teaching Effectivenesss

Although the ways of studying children described in this manual build on what the teacher already does, these suggestions usually add to efficiency. Instead of trying to remember what may have been significant, the teacher learns to record details that are relevant to the problems of concern. Instead of hoping to gain the necessary evidence, the teacher learns how to look for it at strategic times and even to set up situations that are likely to produce it. Certain shortcuts that enable one to accumulate adequate evidence with a minimum of time and effort are learned. As the teacher gets to know the children better, moreover, he or she finds it easier to choose the teaching methods and materials that are most appropriate for them. Fewer mistakes are made in handling situations as they arise, and less time is wasted in trying ideas that don't work.

Systematic Child Study Reduces Teacher Bias

Like everyone else, teachers tend to see things from their own personal perspectives. Some teachers conclude that children are making satisfactory progress when they appear to be busy and attentive. Some teachers are prone to notice certain kinds of behavior and block out other kinds. Some only pay close attention to whatever disrupts classroom routine. Others are more concerned with symptoms of possible unhappiness.

When it comes to teaching methods, teachers may consider only the results that fit their personal preference. Such bias may be evident as early as the first weeks of student teaching. What kinds of results do students look for as they develop their own teaching methods? When the strategy they are trying is one they feel enthusiastic about, they are inclined to pay most attention to children's responses that confirm their views. Conveniently, and perhaps unconsciously, they ignore those reactions that suggest the children find the strategy confusing, or that they feel pressured by it. On the other hand, when a particular strategy isn't their own idea, but must be tried at the insistence of a supervisor or cooperating teacher, the possible negative effects are readily perceived.

And, quite frankly, in identifying problems, doesn't much the same thing happen? Do you have some favorite problems? Or, leaving you out, how about your colleagues? One sees most problems stemming from "emotional insecurity," another traces them to "poor home background," and still another blames them on "too little discipline."

The ways of studying children described in this manual are intended to eliminate some of this personal bias or to provide corrections for it. This, as we shall presently see, does not mean that the teacher can or should be completely objective. It does mean, however, that the children get a fairer break. They, their learning, and their concerns are seen not from a single point of view, but from many.

Systematic Child Study Depends on Evidence

Teachers learn to look for evidence relevant to the aspect of the child's behavior and learning of concern to them. At one level this is pretty simple. If, for example, the concern is with the children's reading ability, teachers study each child in a variety of reading situations to see how they are doing. They look for *valid* measures of reading ability. The facts that George appears to be well liked by the members of his class, he has been absent only twice during the year, his father and mother are divorced, and even that he made a good score on a first-grade intelligence test, do not provide evidence about his reading per se.

At another level, the question of what is valid evidence becomes more complex. For example, once it has been established on the basis of relevant evidence that a child is having real difficulty in learning to read, facts such as those mentioned about George may become relevant to the problem of finding the causes of the difficulty. They provide evidence about various aspects of the child's background and functioning that may be directly or indirectly involved in the reading problem.

Teachers who study their children systematically learn to look for evidence that is both valid and *reliable*. They are skeptical about evidence based on hearsay. They regard the evidence that comes from a single situation—whether it is a test, a drawing, or an episode of classroom or playground behavior—as tentative until they have seen it confirmed often enough to be regarded as typical.

They look for valid, reliable, and also *sufficient* evidence. For example, recognizing that emotional disturbance is often related to difficulties in reading, a teacher might fasten on the fact that a child was upset because the parents were divorced and conclude that it was a factor in poor reading. To do so would be to ignore the need for evidence of many other kinds—the child's vision and hearing, for instance, or the methods of teaching used with the child. (Just to highlight this complexity, we should note here that learning difficulties rarely have a *single* cause. The sources of the majority of such problems are many and interrelated.)

Finally, teachers learn, at least to some extent, to take their own individual biases and predilections into account when they evaluate the evidence they gather. Rather than striving for complete objectivity, they try to develop awareness of themselves as observers. If, for example, they record an episode in which two youngsters fight with each other, they will try to describe what happens as accurately as possible, but also may note how they themselves felt about it. If a teacher felt strongly sympathetic to one or the other of the youngsters, such feeling necessarily colors the observation. It seems fairer to acknowledge such bias than to attempt to ignore it.

THE TEACHER AND THE CHILDREN

What about the children? How do they feel about being studied? They, after all, come to a school or center (or are sent) to learn. We might say, especially in the case of older children, they come to study and not to be studied. Again, we return to the teacher. The skilled teacher is not unlike the skilled painter or musician. When such an artist's work is well done we are much more aware of *what* he or she has accomplished than of *how* it was done. So it is with the teacher. When he or she is skilled, the children do not feel that they are being studied. They only know that this teacher is different in some ways from others. If the youngsters were old enough to analyze how this teacher differs, they might note that the teacher listens more, talks less. Perhaps the activities the teacher provides are more varied, and perhaps they think more. Such a teacher seems to know when they need help and when they can go ahead on their own. They learn a lot. Possibly they would say that they feel comfortable with this teacher. They might specify that this teacher seems to understand how they feel about things. But they are not likely to comment on how it is that the teacher knows. The techniques used for studying them seem so much a part of the ongoing classroom procedure, so focused on their learning, that they are not unduly aware of them. Were the children more sophisticated, they would probably comment on the good rapport between themselves and the teacher.

Rapport is a subtle factor that exists when people feel in harmony with one another. It involves mutual liking, respect, and acceptance. There is no one way to establish rapport with children. One teacher gives a class a good many instructions and directions. Another is much more inclined to share decision-making. A third is inclined to gentle joking and humor, while the teacher next door is more inclined to be sober-faced and solemn. Yet all four enjoy good relationships with their children. All are trusted and liked.

These teachers, different as they are, share feelings of interest and appreciation for the youngsters they teach. Such positive feelings cannot be faked. Children are always sensitive to hypocrisy in adults. They see through behavior to the feelings underneath and respond as much to them as to what the teacher does.

This is why we say that mastery of the techniques of studying pupils doesn't necessarily make a good teacher. But it is surely clear that actually getting to know children better may lead to understanding, and this, in turn, to more positive feelings.

We place so much emphasis on rapport because we think good rapport is essential to good teaching under any circumstances, and also because a number of the methods of getting to know children better demand their active cooperation.

Children and adults protect themselves, if they can, from revealing their feelings when they are too painful or in situations where it may be risky to do so. As teachers, our goal is to *understand* children, not to disturb them. To attempt to force a child's reaction may negate the very thing we are hoping to achieve. Sometimes a technique that is intriguing and acceptable to most children is upsetting to a particular individual. Of course, such an individual should not participate, and if the apparent disturbance is marked and seems at all contagious, the technique should undoubtedly be abandoned completely. As a safeguard, teachers should refrain from opening up with children areas in which the teachers themselves would be unwilling to reveal feelings.

THE TEACHER'S INVOLVEMENT
AND LIMITATIONS

Many people believe that early childhood teachers have a rather positive view of the world (sometimes labelled "sweetness and light"). They seem more likely to see good traits than bad ones. If this is true, it probably is advantageous in most teaching situations since children appear to learn more effectively in an atmosphere of approval than they they do under criticism.

But an inclination to look on the bright side may be hazardous to teachers themselves. They may be prone to say "yes" to various proposals for the use of their professional time without critically considering the pros and cons. We ask that for the time being you doff your positive inclination toward child study and take a good look at what it involves for you.

Let's Be Realistic

Before you decide to launch into an intensive study of the children in your group, think about your current commitments. Consider the number of children you have in your group and the obligations you have in addition to teaching them. We believe it is fair to count your noonday lunch assignments, your committee responsiblities, the various funds and collections you handle—all that goes into your day as a teacher. We even think it is fair to look beyond the school day to your personal life. Of course, you may be in a school or center that believes so firmly in the importance of child study that your schedule provides time for keeping and studying children's records and for parent conferences and interviews. Even with such an arrangement, you are likely to find yourself so involved that you try out more techniques than you had intended. You may start with one child, or one situation, and find yourself expanding your study to others. Or, despite our conviction that child study eventually "pays off," you may summarize a tremendous amount of evidence, and test and reject dozens of hunches, before the amount of effort you invest becomes obviously profitable.

If you are a beginning teacher, it often is especially hard to be realistic about how much you can do. Perhaps as a student you made an intensive study of a single child or of some aspect of a group's behavior. Now, in your own classroom, every child seems to need study; but you are also assuming for the first time complete responsibility for all of the other tasks of teaching. Until you are comfortable managing those, you can hardly expect to be able to "know" your children as adequately as you can after you have gained more experience.

Child Study Takes Time

It may take years before you become adept and comfortable with many ways of studying children.[6] Many people, often those who are most skilled, never become completely sure of themselves. When you consider the complexity of human beings, their behaving, their thinking, their feeling, perhaps this is only to be expected. Consequently, child study is a never-ending process.

Child Study Doesn't Work Miracles

Have you ever worked with a group of youngsters and thought, "I wish I knew them better, understood them better. Then maybe I could help them"? It isn't the knowing and understanding that does the trick, that gets them on the road to increasing maturity. It's what you do with your knowledge, with your understanding, that counts. Unfortunately, too, for some children no amount of insight, no amount of teaching skill, will be sufficient. Some children need help in addition to what they get in school or center.

The school's job, and the teacher's, has to do with children's learning and thinking. But learning and thinking do not occur without emotion. Emotion, which underlies and influences the other aspects of the personality, may facilitate learning and thinking, or it may hamper and disrupt. Some knowledge of the emotional life of each child is essential if the teacher is to direct learning wisely.

We stress the need for caution, for not tackling every problem that comes to light, because in the first efforts of child study, after the initial insecurity passes, solutions to problems often seem deceptively simple. The more experience teachers have with child study, however, the less inclined they are to subscribe to the easy answer.

Child Study Touches Deep Feelings

In the process of growing up most of us learn to handle our emotions and desires in ways that are more or less acceptable to other people. Once we wanted and needed comfort for each cut and bruise; we are now reasonably stalwart. Earlier we cried at the first pangs of hunger. Now we can wait. We wept when we were left alone. Now we seek companionship and affection, but we can tolerate solitude. We once demanded all the toys. Now we can share. Then we hit, or bit, or scratched, or spat. Now we talk things over. But our childish wishes and desires, our fears and rages, did not vanish into thin air. As we grew and learned, we became better able to cope with them. We learned to control some because doing so brought us the affection and appreciation we so enjoyed. We feared the consequences of others. For some of the primitive wishes and desires, we found substitute satisfactions. We do not remember how we learned or what was learned through pleasure and what through pain and anxiety. But even as mature adults, we occasionally catch glimpses of the feelings of the child we were. We are ill and want to be babied. Someone criticizes us, or we think that someone has gotten the better of us, and rage rolls up in overwhelming waves. Perhaps we indulge ourselves, and the guilt we suffer is like that we once experienced.

The children we teach are still in the process of learning to manage and direct their feelings. In the intimacy of the family, as they grow from completely dependent babyhood into childhood and adolescence, they acquire their characteristic ways of behaving, of thinking, and of feeling. Each develops a picture of the kind of person she or he is, and would like to be.

In school and in their play, as they get to know other children and other adults, this basic early learning is added to and modified. Nevertheless, it continues to influence them, just as ours influences us, for as long as they live. We do not remember much of this early learning. But it has a great deal to do with our feeling comfortable and at ease in some situations and anxious and uncomfortable in others.

If we are to work effectively with children, if we are to understand them adequately and use our understanding to promote their learning and well-being, we need to understand the importance to the children and to us of the unconscious aspects of experience. We think it is impossible to study children without sometimes uncovering evidence of motivation of which a child is not aware. As teachers, however, it is not our job to deal directly with these unconscious factors. Rather, we have the responsibility of helping youngsters cope as adequately as they can with the problems of which they have a conscious awareness.

We shall come back to this point from time to time, but a few examples may be in order here. Take the sad-eyed quiet boy whose history of pillar-to-post existence, often bereft of his own mother, suggests a deep yearning for love and affection. A wise teacher surely would be sensitive to this but would also recognize the improbability that a teacher's affection alone could adequately fill the lack the child probably felt. A teacher can give kindness, warmth, appreciation, and interest. A lonely youngster needs these. They help to take some of the edge off bitterness toward people. But lonely children also need a relationship that is much more intense and much more dependable than a relationship with the teacher can be.

For another example, consider the girl who in various ways reveals deep feelings of hostility and anger. Perhaps as the teacher gets to know her, the probable sources of the resentment will become apparent. The teacher can use this knowledge constructively in various ways. For example, if it appears that the child is having a struggle to maintain her position in the family in relation to a seemingly more favored sister, the teacher will try to help the child build up her own strengths and avoid placing her in too many situations in which comparisons are inevitable. But it is not the teacher's job to deal with the child's feelings more directly. Although the teacher lacks the training of a therapist, there are many ways to show the child—through discussion that deals with people generally but not with individuals she knows, through stories and plays, through acceptance of the mean feelings of other children—that anger and resentment are feelings everyone shares. The teacher can show her through the kind of activities offered her and through the way angry episodes are handled that some ways of handling one's feelings are better than others.

Here the need for a cultural perspective becomes imperative. The teacher's sensitivity to the customary modes of expression of the different ethnic and cultural groups represented in the classroom can prevent misjudgments about the meaning of children's behavior, When the teacher knows how the children customarily are taught to express affection and respect, when and how they are encouraged to be assertive, the kinds of experiences that are expected to bring them joy or sorrow, and the ways they may express such feelings, she or he is better qualified to distinguish psychological problems from cultural difference. (It is important that the understanding of cultural differences be based on the realities experienced by the children in her or his classroom, not on stereotyped notions.)

We have said that child study techniques should never disturb the child. And we have suggested that teachers should not use any techniques that explore areas they are unwilling to face in themselves. But even granting such precautions, teachers may find that they are unprepared for the intensity of feelings, the extent of hurt and heartache, they may encounter among some of their youngsters. Child study may touch the feelings of the teacher as well. We think teachers have a right to some sensitive areas. Child study, because it is not limited to children's behavior and thinking but includes their feelings as well, may highlight these sensitive areas. One teacher may become aware that the expression of angry feelings frightens her. Another may find that clinging, dependent demands for affection are irritating to him. His neighbor may become aware of a preference for brighter children. A fourth may discover that her reasons for choosing a particular kind of discipline have more to do with her own feelings and needs than with its effects on the children.

To really get to the cause of some of these sensitive areas demands a degree of self-understanding and insight that is seldom arrived at outside of psychotherapy. From their own individual self-study, teachers can recognize points where they are particularly vulnerable, and avoid unwittingly creating problems for themselves and the children. But they also need the help of other people.

Consultants Can Help

The teacher's study of children is facilitated by consultants who can talk about problems and bring to the situation at hand their experience and the experience of others working in the field. They can offer suggestions based on their specialized study. Finally, they have the advantage of a more detached and perhaps more objective point of view. Consultants do *not* have first-hand information or the sense of the day-to-day persistency of classroom problems that a teacher has in a particular classroom. These factors make a difference not only in the way the problem is approached but also in the nature of the problem itself. Consultants do not have "answers" any more than the teachers working with a particular class have them. Behavior is too complex for immediate, ready-made answers. At best, what we accept as solutions come in the form of "good tries," guesses, hypotheses that we find through the efforts of interested persons and the test of experience.

Teachers Need Help

There are many occasions when teachers need assistance, whether it is to get perspective on their own views, or to secure professional help for children who are presenting problems too severe for them to handle. In some schools, a psychologist, a psychiatric caseworker, or a psychiatrist is a member of the staff. Where such specialists are not on hand, the teacher may need to seek them elsewhere. In communities where skilled psychological help is not readily available, individuals such as principals, ministers, physicians, or others who are wise in human affairs may be called on. Every community has some resources.

Although individual teachers often attempt, sometimes quite successfully, to study children independently, child study may be most effective when it is undertaken cooperatively. A team of teachers or a whole staff may be involved. They work together in formulating and testing hunches, compare insights and learn not only from their study of the child but from one another. The focus of such cooperative child study is, of course, the identification of the most effective ways of working with a particular child or group of children.

Administrators Can Share

Considered in the context of "child study as a cooperative matter," administrators have their role to play. They may give support and encouragement, provide time and facilities, and help in interpreting and applying findings. By working with teachers, administrators dispel those insecurities that teachers feel when they don't know how administrators stand. Administrators who identify themselves with such programs profit also. They learn to see the teachers' need for time and materials; as a result, administrators may plan organizational work to facilitate good teaching.

Privacy Must Be Protected

When child study becomes a cooperative venture involving a number of individuals, one hazard needs to be recognized and dealt with directly. When teachers, as they come to know a child, run across values, feelings, and ways of doing things that a family regards as its own business, they are obligated to protect the family's privacy and maintain confidentiality. If there is evidence of child abuse, however, the evidence must be shared with the principal or center director so that referral to protective services can be made.

The teachers who are directly involved with a particular child may keep and share with each other, and with the principal or center director, records relating to the child's behavior and functioning. Such records may not be shared with other teachers or with specialists not attached to the school or center, unless explicit permission to do so has been given by the parents. Information about the child must be available to the parents if it is placed in the child's cumulative record.[7]

Since teachers must be prepared to share the results of child study with the parents, teachers need to collect evidence about the child that is both suitable and adequate,[8] and consider the views of the parents as well as their own views in studying the evidence they gather. Both precautions seem likely to enhance the quality of their child study.

SUMMARY

We have asked you to share our thoughts about what involvement in child study can mean to the children and to the teacher. We emphasize:

1. Teachers who want to teach effectively can use some of the methods of scientific research to find answers to many of their problems and questions.

2. Evaluation of the effectiveness of any aspect of the education of children demands the collection of evidence about how children behave and think and feel.

3. Child study is not new. This manual offers no panaceas, only ways of improving what teachers are already doing.

4. Child study can benefit children. But since it deals with feelings as well as children's behavior and thinking, it demands artistry and sensitivity on the part of the teacher.

5. Child study can benefit teachers. If it is to be really effective, it demands time and devotion, and sometimes courage. In such study, the teacher needs assistance and consultation as well as administrative support.

NOTES

1. The reader will note that we generally use the term "handicapped" rather than "disabled" or "exceptional." Handicapped is the term used in Public Law 94-142 mandating "education for all the handicapped children" and to "the maximum extent appropriate," "with children who are not handicapped," or what has come to be known as "mainstreaming." "Handicapped" also appears to be the term most commonly used by early childhood teachers.

   In many respects the term "disabled," referring to a person who has an objectively defined impairment of structure or function, is preferable to "handicapped." Whether or not an impairment is a handicap depends on its personal and social consequences. For example, a disabled individual who is confined to a wheelchair is severely handicapped in a school and community where everyone is expected to be able to negotiate curbs and climb stairs. When ramps and elevators are easily accessible the person can function much more independently and is less handicapped.

   Another term that is often used is "exceptional." This refers to any individual for whom the usual educational program is not entirely appropriate. This term can refer to gifted children, children who have been abused by their parents or guardians, and children from cultural minorities, as well as to those who are physically or mentally disabled.

2. Ann Cook and Herb Mack, "The Teacher as Researcher," *Elementary Teacher*, 55, (March/April 1976), pp. 47-51.

3. Virginia Klaus et al., "Teachers-As-Researchers, A Cooperative Study of Dominion Behavior in Young Children." Submitted to *Young Children*.

4. Preschool Parent/Staff Development Project, Berkeley Unified School District and Instructional Laboratories, School of Education, University of California, 1974-76. The project involved both school and university staff.
5. Amity P. Buxton, "Journals—Further Dimensions of Assessing Language Development," Presentation at conference of National Council of Teachers of English, Chicago, November 22, 1976.
6. For example, it takes a long time to master Piaget's clinical method of questioning children. In one of his earliest books he wrote, "At least a year of daily practice is necessary before passing beyond the inevitable fumbling stage of the beginner. It is so hard not to talk too much when questioning a child, especially for a pedagogue! It is so hard not to be suggestive." Jean Piaget, *The Child's Conception of the World* (London: Routledge & Kegan Paul, 1951), pp. 8-9.
7. Teachers should become familiar with the requirements of the Family Educational Rights and Privacy Act of 1974. This law is intended to protect families from institutional invasion of personal privacy and to insure parental involvement in decisions about children's education.
8. The nature of such evidence is discussed in chapter 2.

SUGGESTED READING

For reading and reference in the area of child development, the following are suggested.

Elkind, D. *Child Development and Education: A Piagetian Perspective.* New York: Oxford University Press, 1976. Elkind, a well-known developmental psychologist, was for several years directly involved in the teaching and administration of a small school. In this book he deals extensively with understanding and planning for children of different ages. The book also includes a chapter on developmental assessment.

Highberger, R., and Schramm C. *Child Development for Day Care Workers.* Boston: Houghton Mifflin, 1976. This book provides basic information about child development in the infancy and preschool period. Many of the illustrations are drawn from day-care settings.

Mussen, P.H.; Conger, J.J.; and Kagan, J. *Child Development and Personality.* New York: Harper & Row, 1979. The fifth edition of a classic text provides a chronological approach to the study of development including sections on the preschool years and middle childhood (the elementary school years). This approach is supplemented by special chapters on language, cognitive development, and intelligence.

Samuels, S.C. *Enhancing Self-Concept in Early Childhood: Theory and Practice.*

New York: Human Sciences Press, 1977. This book deals only with the development of self-concept, but it includes a comprehensive review of the related literature and a very practical application section related to the study of children.

Stone, L.J., and Church, J. *Childhood and Adolescence: A Psychology of the Growing Person.* New York: Random House, 1979. This informative, well-written book traces development from conception through adolescence. One chapter deals with toddlers, two with preschools, and two with school-aged children. Some attention is given to schools and centers and the ways they may affect children. The book is rich with illustrations drawn from teachers' and parents' observations.

Some books that focus specifically on child study are:

Marshall, H.H. *Positive Discipline and Classroom Interaction: A Part of the Teaching-Learning Process.* Springfield, Ill.: Charles C. Thomas, 1972. This useful book discusses the factors involved in maintaining effective discipline. It sees child study as a vital requirement to meet the needs of individual children and find solutions to a variety of classroom problems.

Murphy, L.B., and collaborators. *The Widening World of Childhood.* New York: Basic Books, 1973. This reprint of a classic study of young children shows how observations collected over time illuminate the individuality of children and reveal their typical ways of coping.

Rothney, J.W.M. *Methods of Studying the Individual Child: The Psychological Case Study.* Waltham, Mass.: Blaisdell, 1968. An introduction to the case study as a means of understanding the development of the individual. It includes material on interviewing, behavioral description, and the preparation of a written report.

Rowen, B. *The Children We See: An Observational Approach to Child Study.* New York: Holt, Rinehart & Winston, 1973. This book is intended as an introduction to child study. It includes discussion of several observational methods and how they may be used at various levels of development from infancy through school age. It also presents case studies of children with developmental problems.

For assistance in taking one's own biases into consideration when studying children:

Croft, D.J. *Be Honest With Yourself: A Self-Evaluation Handbook for Early Childhood Teachers.* Belmont, Calif: Wadsworth, 1976. This workbook is intended for the person who is learning to teach, but the questions it raises are also applicable to more experienced teachers.

Jersild, A.T. *When Teachers Face Themselves.* New York: Teachers College Press, 1955. This classic presents a discussion of the responses of over 1,000 teachers to questions about their concerns. It provides evidence that the psychological and

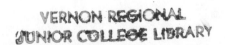

philosophical problems teachers encounter when they study children are problems shared with all other teachers. It also suggests that resolute facing of these problems related to one's teaching role usually leads to deeper satisfaction in teaching.

The following provide useful background for teachers concerned about children's problem behavior as well as those involved in mainstreaming.

Rutter, M. *Helping Troubled Children.* New York: Plenum Press, 1976. The author is an English psychiatrist who writes with great clarity about the common emotional and behavioral problems in childhood. The book is comprehensive and will be helpful in developing knowledge about problem behavior that is to be expected within normal development, minor disorders that can be readily helped, and major deviations that require special interventions.

For information regarding action research:

Cook, M. "Where the Action Research Is." *Times Educational Supplement,* 11 July 1975, 3136:17. This article reports on an action research project in England. The forty teachers involved were interested in getting an objective view of their own teaching in order to isolate the difficulties inherent in the "discovery" method.

Isaac, S. and Michael, W. *Handbook in Research and Evaluation.* San Diego: EDITS Publishers, 1976. This handbook includes do's and don't's for many kinds of research. Some sections are devoted to action research.

Rainey, B. "Action Research: A Valuable Professional Activity for the Teacher," *Clearinghouse,* 47, Fall, 1973, pp. 371-375. This article describes the kinds of action research undertaken by classroom teachers and presents procedures for it.

2 OBSERVATION: THE BASIC WAY TO STUDY CHILDREN

To observe is to take notice, to pay attention to what children do and what they say. Young children confront teachers with a barrage of behavior. How can they possibly pay attention to all of it? In the first five minutes in a preschool center, even before all the children have arrived, Jennifer is crying, Mark has started to paint without putting on an apron, Lynne is pulling blocks off the shelf, Tony is trying to tell the teacher about the new puppies at his house, while a noisy dispute between Julia and Geoffrey is about to involve blows.

Even in a classroom for older children where more time is spent in sedentary activities, an assortment of behavior merits the teacher's attention. Julio takes up his reading books and seems lost to any distraction. Cathie's attention is riveted on some small pieces of paper, and she is painstakingly drawing tiny figures around their borders. Dolores is straining over her book, changing the position of her head as though to see better. Daphne and Carmencita, who should know that this is a time for assigned work, linger in the science center.

The children's movements, their gestures, their changing facial expressions, their comments—all their responses offer some clues about what they are learning, what they have learned, what they feel, and what they think. Observation, together with knowledge of child development, can provide teachers with hunches as to how learning may be facilitated and what kinds of learning may be most important for a particular child at a particular time.

But teachers are not machines. They cannot take in everything that happens to each child during every moment of the day. They are more concerned with certain aspects of the child's development and learning than with other aspects. Or, for various reasons, they are more concerned

21

at times with some children than with others. So they focus their observations in certain situations or on certain children. Their concerns influence when they observe, whom they observe, and what they observe. To put it another way, the kind of evidence they seek in observation varies with the problem for which they seek solution.

Working with children, teachers develop mental composite pictures of each child. These global impressions guide teachers in many situations. They draw on these composite pictures when they make a comment like, "That's typical of Hermine," or "I really wouldn't have expected Deirdre to do that"; when they are planning class activities; and often when they talk to parents. Teachers also call on the pictures in their minds when they respond to certain evaluation or research instruments that require rating children on certain dimensions of behavior. For example, teachers may be asked to indicate whether each child "always," "sometimes," or "never" "puts on a coat alone," or "speaks in sentences," or "looks at the page from top to bottom."

The more carefully teachers observe children, the more accurate their impressions are. Because children in the early childhood period are developing rather rapidly and are learning a great deal, the teacher's picture of each child should change over time. From time to time, the teacher makes very specific observations to see where a child stands. Can Denise, who is five years old, tie her shoes? Does David, a six-year-old child, understand what a word means? Such observations contribute important information to the teacher's changing picture of the child. Moreover such observations need always to be tied into the teacher's picture of the child as a developing and whole person.

In this book we shall return many times to the importance of relating specific behaviors to the ongoing development of the child. Our conviction that the child is more than the sum of his or her behaviors at any one time permeates our approach to child study.

This contrasts with approaches where the major emphasis is identifying behaviors in order to prescribe teaching to modify those behaviors. In one such behavioral approach teachers are expected to identify behavioral characteristics related to 50 behavioral strands. Among these strands are eating, toileting, dressing, self-identification, language development, impulse control, attention span, practical math and reading. For each strand, the teacher is given an average of 36 possibilities for describing the child's behavior. The self-identification strand, for example, has 50 possibilities. These range from "responds to name when called," "points to own mouth, eyes," "points to own nose, feet," and "identifies self by first name" to "tells own sex," "tells own age," "tells parents' occupations," and on to behaviors well beyond the early childhood period such as "discusses own strengths and weaknesses" and "discusses own hierarchy of values."[1]

Teachers report that the procedure has made them more aware of some of the finer details of children's behavior. But they also note that the time spent in such fine-grained assessment precludes more global observations of children in a variety of situations; they feel such observations are essential to know children as individuals and monitor their development.

If education consisted of nothing more than the acquisition of behaviors or facts to be reproduced on demand, and if all children learned in the same ways, the observation we emphasize would be unnecessary. Teachers would present the material to be learned in the same way to all children and would evaluate learning by the simple procedure of checking responses right or wrong.

Merely to "know" certain facts, however, is insufficient. When are they relevant, and how does one apply them? Even young children are expected to begin to "think for themselves." Further, education is concerned with attitudes as well as with knowledge. To understand attitudes, you need to know much more about a child than the child's grasp of factual information.

The more psychologists study the ways children learn, the more individual differences are revealed in the acquisition of both knowledge and attitudes. In learning to read, for example, one child remembers how whole words look, another how their sounds go together. Still another retains most vividly the words that he or she has copied. Only by careful observation can the teacher pick up these subtle differences.

There are differences not only in the ways children approach learning but also in what they have already learned. Children who enter kindergarten knowing how to recognize their own names and the names of their favorite storybook characters provide a striking contrast with those who have had no experience with books. Despite differences in background, however, some children enter school with an apparent thirst for knowledge. They lap up whatever new information and new ideas come their way. They seem to learn almost in spite of the teacher. Other children have had early experiences that set up blocks to certain kinds of learning or to learning under certain conditions.

Differences extend to many areas. One youngster can deal with almost any idea verbally. Another is more motor-minded; she learns little unless she can be active. One child finds numbers of any kind consistently confusing, while another seems poorly oriented to space and has difficulty with any learning involving a sense of direction. One child learns readily when given step-by-step instructions, but another seems to need to try out things independently before conforming to the instructions. One child will stop when his work is compared with that of another child, while another will push on to increased activity when she becomes aware of another child's work.

Teachers can better adapt their provisions for each child when they are alert to subtle as well as obvious differences in the ways children learn. With this knowledge of differences, teachers can individualize instruction not only by pacing it to the child's rate of learning but also by varying it according to each youngster's preferred learning style.

WAYS OF OBSERVING

To become aware of the many ways young children differ in their approaches to learning, to be better able to teach them, teachers can use different kinds of observation, One kind is the casual, incidental observation that everyone uses in everyday life. For example, three individuals are witnesses to an accident. Each has a somewhat different version of what happened. To some extent, this difference occurs because all were intent on something else. None came to the scene prepared to observe an accident occur. Similarly, teachers acquire a considerable amount of knowledge of the children in their classes from observations with no special preparation.

The knowledge that comes from casual, incidental observation is likely to be incomplete. It needs to be amplified by more systemaic, deliberate observation. For example, Mrs. Chang's casual observation may lead her to believe that Alfonso is always teasing Roger. When she watches the two together for longer intervals, however, she notes that it is Roger, not Alfonso, who instigates the teasing.

Observation such as that done by Alfonso and Roger's teacher may be recorded or not. Teachers who work alone seldom have time to write a complete record of a child's behavior, although they may be able to jot down a brief anecdote. When the teacher has aides, or volunteers, they may assist with both observing and recording. Then the child's behavior may be viewed in a variety of contexts. For example, in one cooperative nursery school, each child, in turn, is observed during most of a morning. One parent observes and records for fifteen minutes, then turns the observation over to another parent for another fifteen minutes, and so on. Having a more complete picture of a child's activities over a day, or perhaps from one week to another, provides teachers an opportunity to better understand individual children and their ways of coping.

Deliberate observations such as those just described are planned to occur at particular times, as "whenever Alfonso and Roger are together" or during particular activities, such as "block-building," "at the science center," or "during the independent reading period." In these observations, no constraints are placed on the child other than those that are customary in the particular activity observed. Such observation is often referred to as "naturalistic."

Observation also is used when the child has a specific task, such as an individual test or interview. (Testing is discussed in chapter 8, and interviewing in chapter 4.) Here the situation limits what is likely to be observed, but the observation is deliberate and focused.

USES OF OBSERVATION

However observation is done, it can serve a variety of purposes in the early childhood classroom. Perhaps the most common use for observation is the study of individuals and their progress.

Getting to Know Individual Children

From the first day teachers meet a group of children, they gather information about the individuals in it and modify their approaches to each child in the light of the pictures they are forming. For the children, a new teacher and often a new school or center setting represent an important transition in their lives. The way each child copes with the changes provides some clues to the expectations each has for self and for adults. It also may provide some beginning indication of the child's sources of security and satisfaction, and perhaps of apprehensiveness.

As children and teachers become accustomed to one another, observation provides teachers with more clues to children's functioning. Teachers note the kinds of skills the children have in physical, social, and intellectual areas. Equally important, teachers begin to accrue information about the children's interests. Teachers begin to formulate hunches about the variety of experiences they should provide to match current learning styles and promote development.

An example provided by a teacher involved in mainstreaming illustrates the importance of observation in planning to meet children's needs. The teacher's class of eleven two-year-olds included five who were handicapped. When a sixth child with a disability was to be added, this teacher hoped for a mild problem. Andrew, the three-year-old child accepted for the vacancy, engaged only in limited and repetitious activity, "shuffled aimlessly, made only a few grunting and cooing noises and cried endlessly" during his first days. The teacher found it necessary to hold him reassuringly and to remove from his reach items the other children had already learned to manipulate, which seemed beyond him.

On the basis of this initial observation the teachers decided that the first goal for Andrew would be to order his day so that he would begin to feel a sense of security and familiarity in the new situation. They saw to it that Andrew followed the same morning routine as did the other children. Within a week, observation indicated that he was beginning to anticipate the next steps in the routine. At the same time, it was noticed that he was beginning to observe the activities of the teachers, sitting and staring at them as they moved about the classroom working with the other children. "One day," the teacher reports, "as I was working with him, he looked up and smiled, pointed toward his work and cooed. I smiled too and nodded." The teacher saw this as an incident of mutual acceptance. It was also indicative of the realization of the first goal the teachers had set for their work with Andrew.

As children grow and as they experience a particular educational program, social and motor skills increase and become more differentiated. Intellectual understanding and competence also advance. Observation is essential in determining progress and in modifying the curriculum to insure that learning occurs.

The teachers of one four-year-old group were involved in continuous assessment through observation. At staff meetings, they pooled their observations and made plans for particular children. Some examples from their meetings indicate how the teachers combined observation and continuous assessment.

One child, Jamie, had been observed by all staff members to be very resistant to adult suggestion. One teacher, however, had noted that when the adult proposed a suggestion in the form of a choice between two acceptable behaviors, Jamie readily complied. The teachers decided to allow Jamie more opportunities for choice.

In looking at the different children, the staff of this group considered six aspects of the children's functioning. In addition to the child's relationships with adults, they looked at relationships with other children, intellectual capacities, models of learning and skills, handling of emotions, self-acceptance, and the regulation of physical functions such as eating, sleeping, and energy output.[2] This framework prevented them from overlooking any important aspects of the child's development.

In reviewing one youngster, Sumner, all were impressed with his accomplished social interaction, the scope and depth of his intellectual life, and the variety of his activities with large motor equipment. They were surprised when they realized that he never painted and indeed was seldom engaged in any endeavor that required small muscle coordination. Further examination revealed that this was an area in which Sumner was not making good progress and where special help was in order.

Observation of another child, Margaret, revealed considerable conservatism. Margaret liked to do, and did well, those things that she had become accustomed to early in the preschool curriculum, but she did not spontaneously try anything new. One of the teachers observed, however, that given teacher direction, Margaret would tackle something she had not previously tried. It seemed important to widen Margaret's range of activities and interests through increased teacher intervention.

The teacher who understands the important role of interests in the child's development of knowledge notices the things children do and say that indicate intellectual involvement or potential interest. For example, one teacher observed a child studying the imprints of her feet in the snow. This led into opportunities for that child, and others, to study tire tracks in snow and in mud, and later, the tracks of animals and birds in their neighborhood.[3] Of course young children are interested in many things, and building a curriculum around interests involves more than observation on the part of the teacher. In addition to being keen observers, teachers must have a sense of the possibilities for extending a particular interest. They must also weigh the possibilities in one interest against those in another. Not all interests are equally productive or feasible in the education of young children.

Studying Groups

One factor in a teacher's decision about the encouragement of a particular interest is the understanding of how pursuit of that interest might affect or be affected by the particular group of children in his or her class. Teachers, as they get to know individual children, are also getting to know them as a group. As all experienced teachers know, groups—like individuals—have identities of their own. The group is more than the sum of the individuals in it. The teacher's observation focuses not only on individuals, but from time to time, on the group as a whole, and on the various subgroups that arise. (Chapter 5 deals with ways of studying children in their groups.)

Studying Progress

Observation is the basic tool teachers of young children use to appraise the progress of the individuals and the group. Observations made at one time are compared with those made later, and the development and learning that have occurred are inferred.

Teachers carry many such comparisons in their heads. One comments that Laverne was afraid to climb on the jungle gym when she came to preschool in September. Now in January she climbs skillfully to the top. A second grade teacher notes in March that the class no longer needs to be reminded of each step in the classroom routine.

Informal appraisal based on recollected observations often is inaccurate. It is hard to remember how a child performed six months ago unless the observation has been recorded in some way. A brief anecdote, possibly in the teacher's own shorthand, or a check on a list of possible behaviors, is essential if progress is to be appraised accurately.

In appraising children's progress, it is also important to keep in mind the nature of development in the early years. It does not move ahead in regular increments in all areas. Rather, for one period progress may be concentrated in one area, perhaps motor development; or during a period of continued emotional stress, progress in all areas may be slowed down. Again, progress in one area eventually has an impact in other areas, as when a child's ability to climb as well as other children do leads to an improvement in social involvement.

How progress in the acquisition of academic skills may affect behavior in other areas is shown in the case of James, a child who was spending a second year in kindergarten. During lesson time he would hang his head, or hide it in his arms, or blurt out an inappropriate answer, or act "silly" and do something disruptive. Arrangements were made for him to get special help from the teacher in the math and reading resource room. As he developed skills (playing twenty questions with attribute blocks of different shapes, sizes, colors, and thicknesses), and in recognizing letter sounds, his behavior in the regular classroom also changed. He raised his hand, usually giving the correct response when called on, and appeared alert and well motivated.

Observation is an essential tool for appraising the child's progress in any area of development. The interrelatedness of one area to another, however, suggests the importance of observation that takes into consideration what may be happening in all areas.

Observation is basic to the appraisal of group as well as individual progress. In the activities provided, observation provides information about the involvement of the group as a whole, and of its subgroups, and is an essential part of the process of documenting the intellectual content of those activities as they change over time.

Figure 2.1 shows the plan for beginning-of-the-year activities made for a mixed group of six-, seven-, and eight-year-olds. The teacher's observations, joined with those of co-teachers, assistants, or volunteers, will provide information on the learning that actually emerged, the relationships the children discovered or were assisted to understand, and the directions of the activities.

Figure 2.2, although derived from a different classroom from that depicted in figure 2.1, shows an observation record form that could be modified to fit any classroom. The observer has made a record of the children's activities during a single morning, and the time involved in each. Focusing on a smaller subgroup of the class, an observer could note the nature and level of the children's intellectual involvement in the various activities observed.

Figure 2.3 shows a record form that can be used at a single point in time to record children's activities. The teacher has made a map of her room and has noted where the children are. Such records, particularly when they are made on different days, enable the teacher to study the "drawing power" of various activities and which children choose to work together; these records may also suggest the need for changes in room arrangements.

Appraising Teaching Techniques

The focus in observation shifts somewhat when it is used to appraise teaching techniques. In such instances, the observer is interested in the interaction between what the teacher does and how the child responds. Or perhaps the observer will focus on the responses of a group of children. Teachers may serve as their own observers or ask aides or volunteers to assist. With information about the effectiveness of a particular technique, they may try a different procedure, again noting its effects.

One teacher had been working with a group of first-grade children who were making slow progress in reading. In keeping with the school's curriculum, she had been using a phonics approach, carefully introducing one sound at a time in an animated way and using attention getters like rhyming words and tongue twisters. After several weeks in which she became increasingly discouraged, she decided to try a different approach, utilizing whole words in the context of sentences on big posters. Her observer, noting the increased animation and interest of the children, was

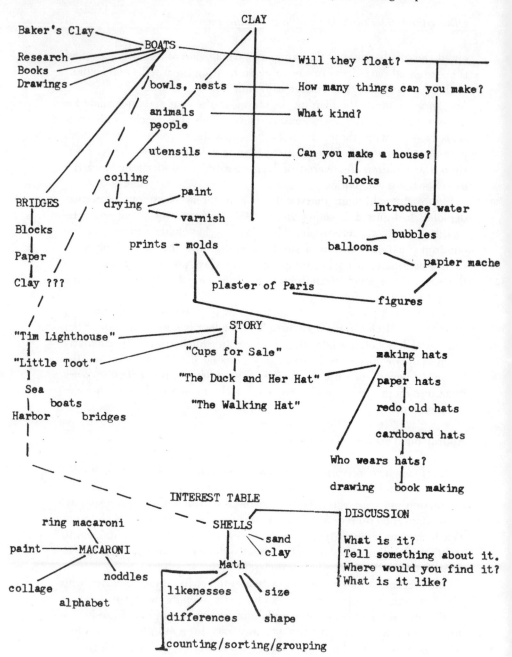

FIGURE 2.1. CURRICULAR DIAGRAM OF BEGINNING OF THE YEAR ACTIVITIES FOR A CLASS OF SIX- TO EIGHT-YEAR-OLDS

The teacher has recorded the materials made available to the children, together with the ideas that can be pursued. The lines suggest the connections that can be made among the various activities.

Reprinted, by permission, from Brenda S. Engel, A Handbook on Documentation (Grand Forks, N.D.: University of North Dakota, 1975), p. 64.

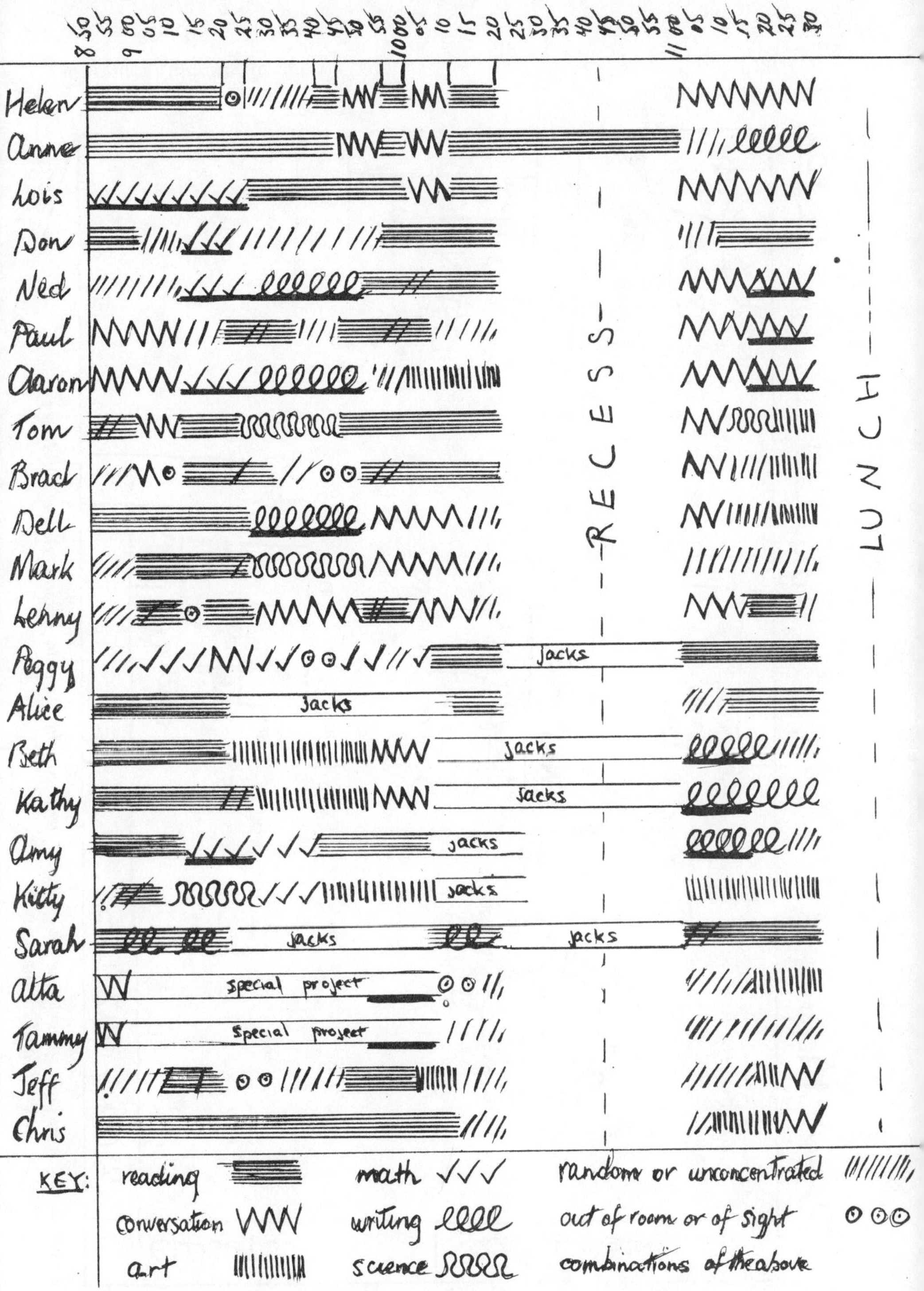

FIGURE 2.2. TIME-ACTIVITY CHART

The observer has recorded the activities of individual children over a period of two and a half hours. The key can be modified to suit other purposes.

Reprinted, by permission, from Engel, A Handbook on Documentation, p. 47.

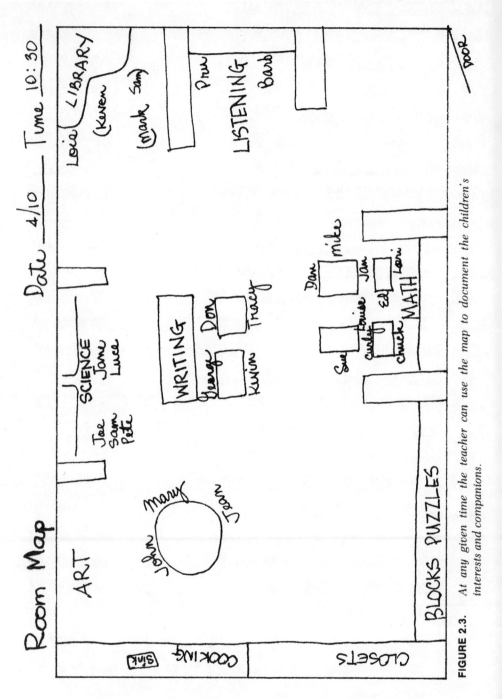

FIGURE 2.3.   *At any given time the teacher can use the map to document the children's interests and companions.*

also impressed with the changes in the teacher's pacing of the lesson and also in her speaking style. Her voice was softer, pauses after questions longer, and positive remarks to individuals more extended. Without the observer's comments, the teacher might not have realized that changes in her method and style made her teaching more effective.

Since teachers always deal with a group as well as with individuals, they have to study the effects of their procedures on both. Sometimes what can be accomplished with the individual does not work in the group situation. Sometimes, too, the effects of a particular technique do not show up immediately, although over a longer period it may have considerable impact. For example, one teacher at a school that lacked any resources for dealing with a very disturbed child found it necessary to protect herself and the group by avoiding issues with him wherever possible. She demanded a minimum of conformity, and so far as her observations revealed, the only effect of this was a year of relative peace for herself and the other children. He did not appear to participate in any of the learning activities of the class. Some time afterward, however, when psychological help became available for him, he was found to have excellent reading ability. He explained to the psychologist that he had learned to read in the classroom of the teacher who was sure she had taught him nothing.

This example is not meant to imply that such "last-resort" policies as this teacher had to use are always appropriate. It does point up the very subtle complexities of the teacher's job and the difficulties inherent in appraising techniques.

Such complexities include the influence that the teachers' concerns and anxieties have on the children. The importance of this influence is reflected in the concluding comment from a professional diary kept by a teacher during her first teaching experience. The focus of her diary had been on discipline problems. She wrote, "The stress (in her college preparation) on trying to understand your own self, your own feelings, helped me to recognize my own prejudices, biases, fears, anxieties or insecurity in various instances and such a beginning helped me to decide on the proper line of action. It helped me to get a better understanding of the students."

When the focus of teachers' observations is on the effectiveness of their own teaching techniques, they look for clues that indicate whether children are learning as anticipated. Recognizing their own biases, they try not to overlook the clues that suggest inadequate learning or learning of a different sort from what was expected. Not infrequently, teachers surmise that factors other than their teaching may be affecting results.

When such factors are identified, the problem requiring a solution is clarified.

Identifying Problems

The teacher often confronts situations that do not go well: instances where, at the preschool level, the children at a particular time of day, go berserk; or in an older group, too many children are inattentive. Observation can help in the identification of such problems. For example, what were the children doing just before they lost control or became inattentive? What precipitates the change in their behavior? Obviously problems such as these may arise out of circumstances that are beyond the immediate classroom, and teachers have to draw on their knowledge of child development in developing hunches about possible solutions. Factors might include hunger from an inadequate breakfast, or fatigue associated with too little sleep, or too much stress. But school or center schedules that provide a poor balance between vigorous and quiet activity lso may be factors. Or the curriculum may be inappropriate to the developmental level and interests of the children. Usually problems, even when the related factors are identified, are complex.

Sometimes, of course, they are relatively simple. Adequate observation provides a safeguard against oversimplification. At the same time it may help the teacher to avoid overlooking simple solutions when they exist.

Recent emphasis on cognitive development in early childhood education sometimes has led teachers to pay too little attention to other aspects of development. The more teachers observe and listen, the more they know about the youngsters, the better equipped they are to appraise the children's development, and to plan more effectively for their learning. Teachers can evaluate more fully what and how the children have learned, and which ways of teaching them are most appropriate.

Observation can help teachers clarify problems and see and test out possible solutions. But, though observation has many uses, it also has certain limitations.

LIMITATIONS OF OBSERVATION

As we implied in the introduction to this chapter, many of the limitations of observation relate to human limitations. Teachers are more than recording devices. They do not merely record observational data as it comes to them. Rather, each one accepts some of it, rejects some, transforms it, fits it to what is already known. Time and energy are limited. Teachers cannot possibly use all of the data available to them. Even if they were more perfect recording instruments, and indefatigable, their conclusions still would be tentative. Development never stands still. Even while we study children, they grow and learn. They change, often imperceptibly, from day to day and week to week.

No two people looking at a child see precisely the same thing. Watching a kindergarten youngster hammering a nail into a board, one observer notices her coordination. Another focuses on her facial expression. Still another hears strain in her voice as she asks for help. Experienced observers pay attention to all these details. Yet even they may make different inferences about the meaning of the behavior. One regards the child's efforts as effective and well directed. Another sees them as overexertion. But, the longer these observers watch, the more evidence they have, the more likely they are to see the situation similarly.

Learning to take in all the details of behavior, learning to separate the subjective aspects of an observation from the objective, and learning to rely on accumulated evidence rather than making snap judgments are essential steps in becoming a good observer. But the personal element in observation can never be eliminated completely. No matter how much experience in observation teachers have, they are bound to feel more sympathetic toward some children than others, to find certain kinds of behavior more disturbing or more satisfying, to be more involved with some youngsters and less with others. Such biases grow out of their own personal experiences and have to do in part with the kinds of children they once were or would have liked to be.

Halos, Horns, and the Average

Along with personal predilections, the teacher who relies on observation has to cope with another human tendency likely to distort what is seen and heard. This is the inclination to generalize and to simplify. When teachers usually see a child in a favorable light, they tend to expect the same response in other situations. Thus a teacher may have a spontaneously warm feeling about a well-dressed, polite youngster observed only at those moments when behavior is exemplary. In a sense, the "halo" ascribed to the child obscures the teacher's vision when the child is engaged in something less creditable. Unwittingly, too, the teacher under these circumstances may "make allowances" for behavior that does not fit the usual picture. Similarly certain youngsters acquire "horns." The teacher expects to find them engaged in some mischief or other, or not accomplishing their work as they should. Not very surprisingly, such expectations often are fulfilled. Systematizing observation so that each child has as much of a chance as another to be seen in a favorable light provides some correction to this tendency.

Perhaps in reaction to their own recognition of this tendency to generalize about individual children's behavior, teachers tend to lump a great deal of behavior together as "average" or "typical." It is true that in any group of twenty youngsters of approximately the same age the behavior of the majority is likely to be similar in many aspects. In a group of kindergarten children engaged in rhythms, or second-grade youngsters taking turns in reading orally, those who are markedly inept and those who are highly skilled are readily identified. It is not as easy to discriminate among the performances of those in the middle. Only with considerable practice over an extended period of time can one learn to perceive the finer distinctions in behavior.

Tentativeness

Possibly the greatest danger in any deliberate plan of studying children is that one may arrive at conclusions too soon. Perhaps the best guarantee against this is to consider all findings tentative. They provide clues as to how children are doing. Just as development never stands still, so the study of children never is really complete.

IMPROVING OBSERVATION

Teachers observe children continually. When they set about to improve their ways of observing they do not begin a new activity, rather they pay more attention to what and how they observe, and they try to keep some kind of record of their observations.

The necessity for appraising their own observations sometimes makes teachers feel self-conscious, and for a time they may feel that they do not do as well as when they looked at children more casually. They feel confused and inept, very much as swimmers may feel when learning a new stroke, or a golfer when trying to correct an improper stance.

In the pages that follow we shall point out the characteristics of a keen observation and a complete record, and indicate possible errors.

Three Aspects of Observation: Description, Feelings, Inferences

When we observe, we see how children look and what they do. We hear what they say. These we can describe. At the same time, particularly when we are a participant observer, as the teacher usually is, we respond to what we see and hear. We feel pleasure at the youngster's appearance or accomplishments, or annoyance at inattention, or sympathy when he or she is rebuffed, and so on. This aspect of observation—our own feelings and emotions—is one that we often try to ignore. Perhaps we have been told that observation should be "objective," and so we rule out what we know to be subjective. In point of fact, however, our emotional responses color what we see and hear, and we cannot eliminate their effect.

Coming to terms with feelings is especially important for the teacher who works with handicapped children. Only careful, detailed observation can provide the teacher with the knowledge of the child's capabilities and possibilities for learning that is essential for effective teaching. In order to see the child clearly, however, the teacher must first recognize whatever feelings of pity, anxiety, or frustration the child's handicaps arouse.

The final step in observation is inference. From what we see and hear, and in part from what we ourselves feel and know from past experiences, we infer what the child's behavior means.

In the following example, the observer, a student teacher, has tried to sort out the describable behavior of the child, her own feelings about it, and the inferences she made.

> Michael is four years old. He is small in stature. He has thinnish brown hair. Michael usually walks with a bounce, head down, hands in his pockets, and feet shuffling. He usually appears sullen. He talks in a loud voice and has a raucous laugh. His clothes are shabby. Michael is the younger of two children. He has been in this group of twenty-five four-year-olds for more than a year.

Child's Behavior

> A group of six children were playing with dough. Michael had two cookie cutters and a rolling pin. Howard wanted one of the cookie cutters. He asked Michael for one of them. Michael said, "No, this is mine. I had them first." Howard said that he would give it back to him when he finished playing with it. Michael clutched the two cookie cutters close to him and then quickly grabbed the rolling pin and held it nearer to him. Howard grabbed at one of the cookie cutters and Michael held them still closer to him. His expression became more sullen. He clenched his mouth more tightly. Another child put a cookie cutter down on the table and Michael grabbed it and held on to it. Michael kept his face down. He moved his chair slowly from the table. Howard tried again to take it from him and Michael threw the cookie cutters and rolling pin on the floor. He hit Howard and kicked the chair. He looked penetratingly at the teacher and said to her that he was never coming to this school again and he didn't care if he didn't play with the dough. When the

teacher did not reply to this statement, he walked away from the table sulking. He kept his hands in his pockets and held his head erect.

Feelings and Reactions to the Incident

I was annoyed with Michael's refusal to cooperate with Howard regarding the cookie cutters. He and the other children were told that they were to share all of the materials which were placed in the center of the table for that purpose. Despite my annoyance, I also feel sympathy for this child because of the pathetic qualities in his behavior and his general appearance. The futility of the situation as expressed in his statement that he would not return to this school depressed me. I feel inadequate because I realized that my interference at this point would not help the child.

Inferences

I know that Michael comes from a broken home and from very miserable circumstances. There is some evidence of parental rejection. Under the circumstances with the accompanying insecurity it appears that he has not at present the ability to share or cooperate with other people. At home he needs to hold on to whatever he has or can get. His philosophy would appear to be that everything which he takes is his. Does the nonchalance he expresses regarding the dough-play and school really indicate his extreme need for assurance? His fierce and penetrating gaze at the teacher accompanying his threat to leave school forever might very well indicate his attempt to convey to the teacher his desire for her to care about him and what he does.

The record was made by a student teacher who was not participating in the activity of the group at that time. Obviously the busy teacher will be unable to analyze observations so intensively. Indeed, even experienced nonparticipant observers who have no responsibility for the children often find it difficult to separate the behavior of the child, their emotional responses to it, and their inferences about it.

When teachers work with youngsters, they interpret the meaning of their behavior as it occurs and formulate their expectations for them accordingly. But when they study children, trying to get to know and understand them better, they need to discriminate between the actual behavior of the child and the emotional and intellectual elements that go into what is usually labelled "interpretation." This helps them to see behavior more clearly, and to use it more effectively as evidence to substantiate or refute whatever hypotheses they may have about the child. This, of course, does not mean that in the day-to-day work of the classroom they no longer interpret and act accordingly. It is rather that they become more skilled in both seeing behavior completely and interpreting it correctly.

In the following statement the teacher has seen Jane's behavior in considerable detail and has described it without mixing in her interpretations.

> Jane came soberly and slowly into the room today. She went directly to the puzzle table and effectively and methodically worked through the three that were laid out. When she had finished, she sat quietly, looking down with little expression. She played with the buttons on her jacket. This went on for five minutes. Then, still soberly, she went to an empty easel and began to paint.

Note that the teacher here has included more than the gross details of Jane's behavior. She has indicated that Jane came into the room, worked with the puzzles, sat quietly and moved to the easel. But she has also included some important finer details, particularly that she sat looking down and playing with her buttons. She also has given some indication of the quality of Jane's behavior through her use of the words "soberly and slowly" and "with little expression."

Contrast that statement with: Jane is a shy, reticent, unsocial child who does not make friends easily and is usually passive.

The words "shy," "reticent," "unsocial" are all evaluative terms that need to be supported by evidence. In addition, the statement contains several generalizations that may or may not be true, such as "does not make friends easily," and "is usually passive." Such a statement is a conclusive one that only could be made after considerable study of Jane, not only in school but outside of school as well. Even if the statement were basically true, it would not convey much of Jane as an individual. Every experienced teacher probably can think of a dozen youngsters who would fit the description equally well.

To see how youngsters differ from one another, to discern their individual characteristics—these are the goals of the keen observer.

Noticing Details

Anyone can observe that a child walks into a room or out of it, raises his hand or drums on his desk, answers questions or remains silent. But keen observers go beyond this. They study facial expression, note the steady and the shifting look, the tightly or loosely held jaw and lips, the grimaces and the smiles. They hear not only words, but tones, pitch, strain, hesitation, and pauses. They note body posture, slumping shoulders, and puppet-on-a-string gestures, as contrasted with flowing, graceful movements, and accurate, efficient coordination. They see all these details in relation to the settings where the behavior takes place.The clenched hands and intent frown seen in the reading period are different from the freedom and *joie-de-vivre* of the playground. These finer details, this attention to its quality, provide clues to the meaning of the behavior.

Keeping a Record

Because it is easy to forget what one has observed, and because the usual purpose of observation is to understand the child changing and developing, the teacher needs to make some kind of notation of the observations.

The most usual record is the *anecdote*, a narrative account of a situation. It describes one incident as seen by the observer. If it includes the observer's feelings or inferences, these are clearly marked off from the rest of the statement. Such an account may include all the fine details, all the nuances of behavior. When one is learning to observe, or when one is trying to improve observational skills, it may be a useful exercise to try from time to time to record an incident in such complete fashion. For the teacher's practical purposes, however, it should be terse, and may well be in telegraphic style. No more should be recorded than the teacher needs to bring it back to memory in its most significant detail.

Here, for example, is an anecdote as might be recorded immediately or even during an art period: "Clarence 3/18. With Thomas at clay jar. Getting very dirty. Painted third little dog, brown and white."

The teacher who observed Clarence actually expanded it as follows (note how she has used parentheses to separate her interpretations, and her tentative hypotheses, from the behavior description):

> (Clarence, who has been "watching" people do things and retiring to a corner to read during periods which gave him a chance to work with other children, has begun to show some interest in working with others.) Clarence and Thomas were both working at the clay jar, and Clarence was really getting dirty during our art period today. He has made three little dogs which are graduated in size and which he has painted brown and white. (I think he likes Thomas, and this association is helping him get into the swing of group activities.)

A good way to test whether or not one's anecdotal records are sufficiently complete is to read through those that one has made to see if each brings back a vivid picture of what happened. Even better, teachers in a classroom may exchange anecdotes with one another and question each other about details that are unclear. The other person's indication of further information needed to understand the incident exactly as it occurred should suggest details that are important to notice and record. If the opportunity arises, colleagues also can aid one another in improving both observational and recording techniques by writing anecdotes describing incidents they observe at the same time. In such records, one expects to find considerable agreement about the behavior described, even though the reactions of the observers may be different.

Individual Child Study

Following are excerpts from records of the oral reading of Maria, a child in a K-2 class. The teacher asked parents to volunteer to listen to the children's reading and to leave a brief note in the record when they did so. Two different parents made recordings about Maria's reading.

9/16/76 *Frederick* Completed the book. An excellent reader. We talked about the role of artists and poets. Do they work? Do they contribute? H.G.

9/21/76 *Furious Flycycle* pp. 66-68. Maria told me a bit about what had gone on in the book. She is a very fluent reader. The only word she really had trouble with was "through." H.G.

10/15/76 p. 72. Reads well. We discussed the story. She told me about Melvin, what kind of character he is. She could tell me about the story but needed help looking at the story critically. She was more interested in what the class was doing. Maybe she should go outside to read. M.S.

10/19/76 Maria is an excellent reader. She could tell me about the story. Seems to enjoy this more than any previous reading we have done. H.G.

10/26/76 Maria can even read difficult words whose meaning she does not know. She does not seem to remember what went before; her favorite answer: "I don't know." She does not seem very interested in the book. H.G.

11/5/76 Maria finished *Furious Flycycle*. She told me about Melvin's adventures and retold the story. Before I can get into the critical end of things I may have to do some reading of their books. M.S.

11/8/76 Began *Harriet the Spy*. H.G.

11/18/76 *Harriet* to end of chapter 8. Maria is beginning to learn to read aloud, lower voice at end of sentence, etc. H.G.

These excerpts suggest that the parents brought somewhat different interests and expectations to the reading situation. Note, though, the picture of Maria, the level of her reading competence, and the fluctuations in her interests that begin to emerge from the notes.

Intensive study of an individual child is frequently recommended as a way to improve both one's observation and one's understanding. By taking particular note of one or two individuals, observing their behavior in many situations, and relating such information to what is available from other sources, the teacher gains insight that can be applied in dealings with other children. Obviously, the child studied is not to be openly singled out in any way. Care must be taken that the child's privacy is thoroughly protected. Any notes that are made should remain in the teacher's possession and be shared only with the parents or with other professionals that the parents have agreed shall study the child.

To highlight individual differences, we think much is to be gained if the teacher will study two youngsters at the same time. Even if the information is not as detailed as it is for one child, the advantage in other respects is considerable. Study may reveal that seemingly identical behaviors of the two children are precipitated by different circumstances, or that they cope with similar situations in different ways. Such comparisons aid the teacher in developing a more reflective and objective stance.

For most effective use, a child study needs to be organized according to some framework. It need not be written, but the observations do need to be pulled together in some meaningful way. One possibility is to consider the various aspects of development—physical and motor, cognitive, social and emotional, in turn, then consider their possible interrelationships.

A more dynamic approach is to consider development more from the viewpoint of the child. The ways children see themselves often differ from the ways adults see them. What are the areas of living the child seems to find satisfying, as contrasted to the areas of difficulty?

Even if one does not attempt to infer the child's viewpoint, the balancing of the child's competencies against the problems often provides a helpful picture for those responsible for guidance. Too often a child's difficulties, or those aspects of development that the adult sees as problems, loom so large that many strengths are overlooked.

For the child study to be complete, and for the teacher to make still more use of it, the child's behavior outside of the school or center can be included. Information for this comes from the parents. (Contacts with parents are discussed in Chapter 7.)

Teachers who are beginning such child studies often ask how to select the children. Actually, they can learn from studying any child. Some have found it satisfactory to pick one youngster they found particularly interesting or likeable, and another child they viewed with less enthusiasm. In any event it seems important to pick at least one on the basis of warm and positive feelings. The second can be like the first, or different.

Having decided which children are to be studied, the teacher next faces the question of when observations are to be made, how many are necessary, and other questions. These are general questions that apply not only to the use of observation for individual child study but also to the use of observation in appraising various kinds of school activities. They relate to how observation is to be organized.

Organizing Observation

Teachers cannot observe everything. Even if they could, recording what they had seen would be an impossible chore. So the first step in organizing observation is to decide the purpose it is to serve. Observation can be used to provide evidence for any number of purposes, but its focus will depend on the precise nature of the purpose. For example, to appraise progress in oral reading, the observations obviously would be made during the oral reading period. On the other hand, if the teacher were interested in identifying the sources of difficulties in reading comprehension, the observations would need to go beyond the reading period. It might be profitable to listen to children's conversations about their activities outside of school in order to get some picture of the background of experience they bring to their reading. The purpose of the observation suggests the nature of the observations to be made. Of course, as study progresses, other kinds of observations may also become relevant. In any event, the basic problem is to observe the children in appropriate situations and to get adequate samples of their behavior.

Securing Appropriate and Adequate Evidence

A question that can be used to check the adequacy and appropriateness of evidence secured from observation is: "How many of the situations in which significant behavior may have occurred are actually represented?" Thus a teacher studying an individual child might run through the various periods of the day to see whether some attention had been paid to the behavior in each. This would not mean a record for each period each day, but rather that no period had been overlooked completely. Further observation would focus on the situations not yet observed.

Another way of getting a more adequate sample of behavior is to focus on a particular child throughout a given period of time, trying to record all that he or she does. The data about Michael earlier in this chapter is an example of this kind of observation.

When observation is set up in such a way that a particular child may happen to be observed more consistently in one kind of situation than in another, a biased picture is bound to result. Unless there is some reason for limiting the observation to a single activity (as when the purpose of observation relates only to that activity) a youngster ought to have as good a chance to be noticed in one period of the day as another. Children who hate math should be observed not only there but also in the reading or social studies they like. Similarly, they ought to be seen in their helpful, happy moods at least as often as in their unhappy or ornery moments.

Teachers who use observation as a source of information for evaluating progress and reporting to parents on all the children in their class sometimes find it helpful to set up some schemes for scheduling observation. Each week they plan to be particularly alert to four or five selected children. Other teachers find that by reviewing their records from time to time, they become aware of children who are being missed, or who are receiving more than their share of attention.

Review of the records sometimes suggests the possibility of setting up situations especially for observation. For example, a kindergarten teacher whose anecdotal records on a particular child indicate that he seems rather inept in motor areas might set up a game involving skipping, jumping, and other activities to compare his performance with that of his peers. Or, thinking that a particular child might benefit from knowing another one better, a teacher might assign them to a common task, taking special note of the results.

Sometimes situations arise that are particularly appropriate for observation. The teacher interested in how various children affect one another, and who has noted that one youngster seems to have an unusually stimulating effect while another seems disruptive, will not miss taking notes on the group when such children are absent. Similarly, what happens when these children return will be observed. Again, in the study of individual children, behavior following an absence is often revealing.

There is a caution to consider. The more adequate the recorded samples of behavior, the more useful observation will be. But the machinery for getting and recording adequate and appropriate samples should not be so elaborate that it is burdensome. Good teachers, we repeat, always have used observation effectively. Simple recording procedures can enhance teachers' effectiveness, but too much concern about what and how they record may interfere with their teaching. Sometimes shortcut observation procedures are as effective as more detailed records.

Shortcuts

Although detailed anecdotal records provide much information that cannot be made available in any other way, there are many occasions when less information is needed. This is particularly true when the focus of concern is not so much the individual child as the whole group. When trying to pick out children in need of special help, or to distinguish children whose performance in a particular area is outstanding, it is not necessary to have as much detailed information as is necessary for studying an individual child. In such situations checklists and rating scales serve the purpose of helping the teacher to organize observation quickly and efficiently. Basically, both these devices are dependent on observation. In a sense they ask the teacher to summarize observations and make a judgment about the typical or usual performance of each child.

In a checklist, the teacher works from a list of activities or characteristics and records a check to indicate the presence or absence of whatever is being observed. A rating scale is similar except that the characteristics or activities are so arranged that the observer records a rating based on some objective scale of values. A rating may be numerical or quantitative or descriptive.

Commercial checklists and rating scales are available in abundance. Some of them are useful when they fit the goals of the program in which they are being used. Teachers also may construct their own.

The teacher-constructed checklist shown in figure 2.4 was designed to remind the teachers and various assistants and volunteers in kindergarten and first grade classrooms to look for behavior of significance in math and reading and to make brief recordings about it.

Figure 2.5 shows a rating scale designed to assess young children's use of language. Spaces are provided for making four entries a year for each of the goals. Note that the chart shows "how much," that is, quantity, rather than "how well" or quality.

The difficulties in constructing rating scales lie in the danger of including items that are clear only to the person who makes the scale and in the tendency to provide so many items that too fine a distinction is demanded. In using such a scale, the observer needs to be alert to personal bias, to a tendency toward rating most children at a particular point on the scale (usually in the middle), and to an inclination to rate a youngster similarly on different scales.

Various shortcut procedures may save the teacher time in organizing and recording information about the children. But they do not eliminate

Areas in which you have observed the child having experiences, problems,
    or success.

Mathematics	Reading
Experiences with discontinuous materials (beans, rice, etc.)	Asks to be read to
Experiences with continuous materials (water, sand)	Dictates words (Organic Reading)
	Dictates sentences
Shapes	Dictates stories
	Matches letters
Space(above, below, beside, behind, next to)	Matches words
Size (small, large, larger, smaller)	Identifies initial words
Matching (size, shape, sets)	Recognizes initial letters
Measuring (teaspoon, tablespoon, cup, ½ cup)	Recognizes words
Using number words	Looks up words in own dictionary
Recognizing number symbols	Looks up words in children dictionary
Reproducing number symbols	Can phonetically sound out words
Number or size relations (taller, shorter, wider, length, width)	Looks for words in stories that are read.
Sorting and categorizing	Can read on own
Sets, recognition and reproduction	Overwrites
1-1 Correspondence	Underwrites
Ordering, seriation	Can write alone
Pictorial representation	
Ordinals	
Cardinals	

FIGURE 2.4. TEACHERS' CHECKLIST FOR MATH AND READING EXPERIENCES

This list helps teachers or other observers to focus on behaviors that are significant in the development of understanding in mathematics and reading.

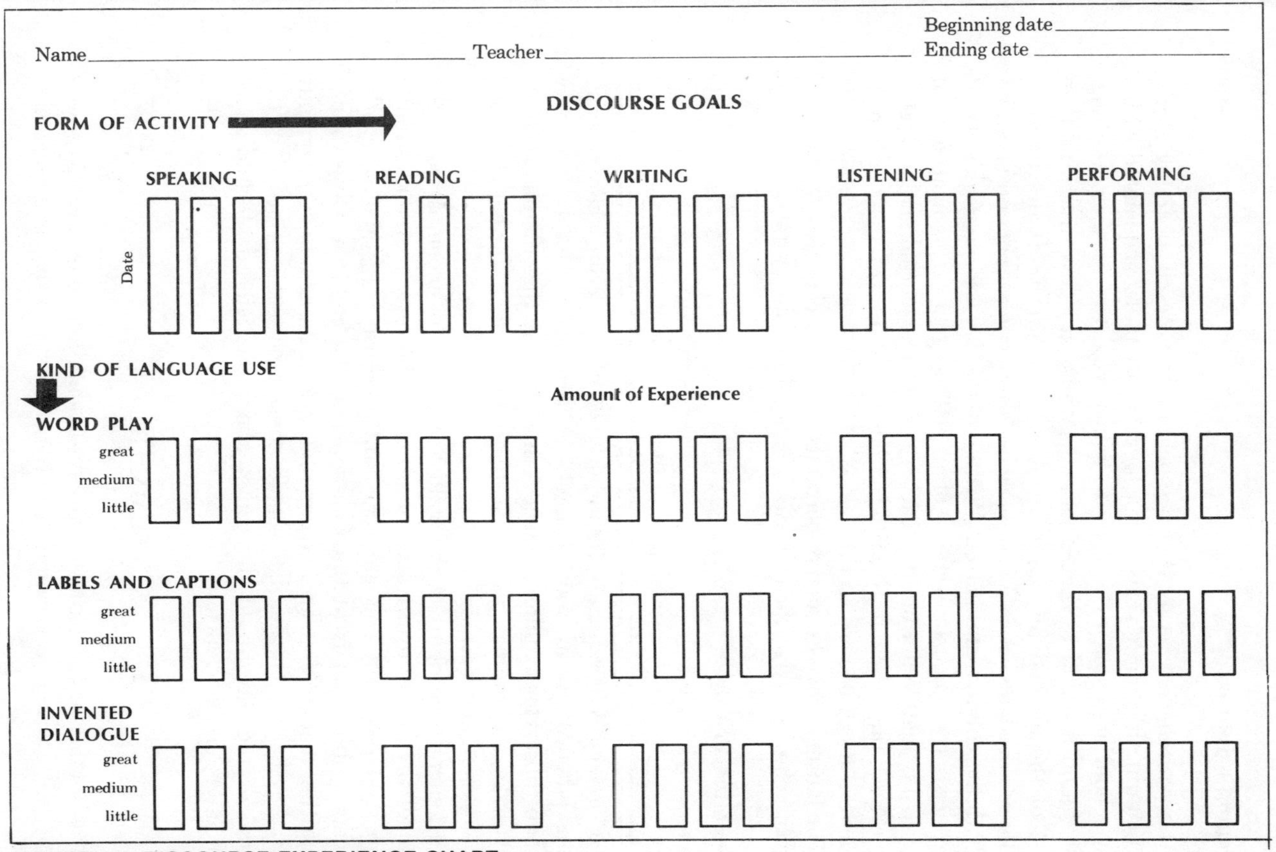

Name _____   Teacher _____   Beginning date _____
                                                              Ending date _____

DISCOURSE GOALS

FORM OF ACTIVITY ➡

| Date | SPEAKING | READING | WRITING | LISTENING | PERFORMING |

Amount of Experience

KIND OF LANGUAGE USE ➡

WORD PLAY
great
medium
little

LABELS AND CAPTIONS
great
medium
little

INVENTED DIALOGUE
great
medium
little

FIGURE 2.5 DISCOURSE EXPERIENCE CHART

The boxes provide space for four entries for each of the goals. The teacher writes in the date, then indicates by shading in the appropriate box the amount of experience the child has had with reference to a particular goal.

James Moffett and Betty Jane Wagner, *Student-centered Language Arts and Reading, K-13: A Handbook for Teachers,* second edition (Boston, Houghton Mifflin, 1976), Fig. 21.5, p. 426.

the need for observation. And their usefulness is entirely dependent on the quality of the observation.

Keeping a Journal

Many teachers, whether they are beginning to teach, or trying a new curriculum after many years of teaching, or becoming acquainted with a new school or center, or wishing to gain perspective on their teaching, have found it useful to keep a journal. A journal is less structured than most of the methods of recording observation previously described. It includes anecdotes as well as the teacher's reflection on her observations of both the children and herself. Written at the day's or the week's end, it provides not so much an overview of all that has gone on, as an account of what really mattered, from the teacher's view. The journal may be highly subjective, but when it is written from the stance of the participant observer,[4] it can be very useful.

The journal provides good opportunity for the teacher to note questions and hunches as well as the evidence gleaned from observations.

Protecting Privacy

Just as the teacher, keeping a journal of teaching experience, usually prefers not to share mistakes, poor judgments, or "failures," children too need privacy. We reiterate the importance of protecting children from being labelled in any way. Though teachers cannot teach effectively without observing children, teachers must be sure that the observations they make, and the records they keep, are used only to further children's development and learning.

In general, the rights of the child to privacy are encompassed in the right of the family to privacy. Occasionally, however, parents suffering from their own problems are neglectful or abusive. In these cases, the teacher's obligation is to the well-being of the children. Observations indicating that children are in danger because of the actions of the parents must be shared. The teacher should consult with the principal of the school or the director of the center about the referral of children to protective service agencies.

SUMMARY

Observation is the basic way to study children. We have suggested many ways to use observation. All of them are uses that many teachers already have discovered. We have described the limitations of observation. Thoughtful, sensitive teachers already are aware of these limitations. We have described some of the ways teachers have found to improve their observations, some of the means they have found to organize their observations, and finally, some of the shortcuts that are available.

Most of all, we have wanted to convey the satisfaction that keen and sensitive observation can add to teaching. As one teacher put it, "The more carefully you observe, the more you see to be done." To this we would add, "The more carefully you observe, the more sure you are about what to do and the more effective you become."

NOTES

1. "Behavioral Characteristics Progression," 1972, Developed through ESEA Title VI, B Funding, Project Number 44-00000-00000-925, charts from Santa Cruz County Office of Education, Santa Cruz, Calif.
2. Details to consider in each category were outlined by Rebekah Shuey. A similar but more comprehensive outline for written summaries on children, including a number of questions for teachers to consider is found in S. Provence, A. Naylor, and J. Patterson, *The Challenge of Daycare* (New Haven: Yale University Press, 1977), pp. 251-270. The book also provides an example of a teacher observation report on pp. 271-286.
3. The example is taken from Anne M. Bussis and others, *Beyond Surface Curriculum: An Interview Study of Teachers' Understanding* (Boulder, Colorado: Westview Press, 1976). This book reports on the ways teachers experienced the open education programs in which they taught. It does not deal with observation per se, but the teachers' comments do reveal the ways they used the information they gained from studying their children.
4. For suggestions on the role of the participant observer, and the keeping of notes related to one's observation, see John Lofland, *Analyzing Social Settings: A Guide to Qualitative Observation and Analyses* (Belmont, Calif.: Wadsworth, 1971).Chapter 5 is on participant observation and includes a number of suggestions for observing and for making field notes, or a journal.

SUGGESTED READING

Boehm, A.E., and Weinberg, R.A. *The Classroom Observer: A Guide for Developing Observation Skills.* New York: Teachers College Press, 1977. This book is highly recommended for both the beginning and the experienced teacher.

It provides a series of graduated tasks that help the teacher check on and improve observation skills. Corrective feedback is provided at each level. The book also shows how teachers can develop observational strategies appropriate to their specific needs. A chapter on the use of media for observation and an excellent, detailed bibliography are included.

Cohen, Dorothy, and Stern, Virginia. *Observing and Recording the Behavior of Young Children*, 2d rev. ed. New York: Teachers College Press, 1978. Written particularly for teachers in preschool, kindergarten, and the early elementary grades, this book offers specific help on details to look for in observation, and on how to record, summarize, and interpret. It includes many examples of records, and an up-to-date list of suggestions for further reading.

Lindberg, L., and Swedlow, R. *Early Childhood Education: A Guide for Observation and Participation*. Boston: Allyn & Bacon, 1976. This book focuses on activities and behavior of three-, four-, and five-year old children. Worksheets call attention to the various aspects of the curriculum and provide guides for both observing and reflecting on what has been observed.

Wright, H.F. *Recording and Analyzing Child Behavior: With Ecological Data from an American Town*. New York: Harper & Row, 1967. This book presents the method of the specimen record for describing naturally occurring situations and the behavior of individuals. It draws on an earlier study, *Midwest and Its Children*. The records included were made in home, school, and other community centers, and relate to both normal and handicapped children. Although the book is intended primarily for researchers, the "how to do it" instructions provided also will be useful to teachers.

3 STUDY THE WAYS CHILDREN THINK

In the two decades since the first edition of this book was published, researchers have given much attention to the ways young children think. Teachers have become more aware of their role in facilitating cognitive development. Publishers and manufacturers have produced a multitude of materials, toys, and games to assist teachers in this role.

The usefulness of the materials and equipment available depends heavily on the teachers' ability to appraise their appropriateness for the individuals in their groups. On the one hand, teachers consider how the children are likely to use the materials and the equipment and the thought processes they may engender. On the other hand, they observe how the children do use them and document the progress the children make.

Keeping "tuned in" to the thinking of the children is complicated, not only because of the number of children and their diversity, but also because the teacher serves as a stimulus to thinking. What the teacher says or does in response to a child's comment or action can further or deter the child's thinking.

Worry about this responsibility could immobilize teachers. How can they attend to all that is going on? Obviously, they cannot, but they can become increasingly sensitive to the marks of confusion or insight, effective problem solving, changing organization, and creativity on the part of the children.

METHODS OF STUDYING CHILDREN'S THINKING

Good teachers always have been concerned that young children become increasingly competent in their thinking. Teachers noted children's errors or misjudgments, often with amusement, and tried to correct them by supplying the information they seemed to need. Sometimes they noted that the children did not always make use of the new or correct information. Then the teachers may have concluded that the children were not "ready" for it.

The research and theory of the last two decades throw some light on "readiness" and offer teachers greater possibilities for precision in describing the children's thinking. Teachers are better able to tell whether the child could grasp the information if it were presented differently, or whether the concepts truly are beyond the child's level of thinking.

The methods that teachers today can use to appraise young children's thinking are basically similar to those that good teachers always have used. What informs those methods and differentiates them from methods relying largely on intuition is the teacher's knowledge of cognitive theory. In this chapter we outline briefly some elements of one theory that we regard as particularly useful to the teacher of young children. First, however, we turn to the basic methods available for studying thinking.

Study What Children Do As Well As What They Say

The younger the child, the more closely thinking is tied to actions. For example, the young child's definitions often reflect this association, "A hole is to dig," "Orange—you eat it." Young children are quick to pick up and repeat the words they hear, but they do not always comprehend what they say. Accordingly, the teacher observes what the child does as well as listens to what he or she says.

The girl playing in the water and persistently pushing all the floating objects to the bottom apprises the teacher of the level of her thinking about the phenomena of floating and sinking. A boy, playing the role of working mother, waves good-bye to the baby he has just left at "the day-care center," and pedals off to the side of the playground to "work"; there, he sits idly on the tricycle, suggesting to the teacher the paucity of his associations to the world of work.

Early childhood teachers concerned with children's thinking are alert to the verbal facade that may conceal uncertain or erroneous knowledge. They avoid verbal definitions for phenomena that are too complex for children to understand. For example, in one first grade classroom, the children observed a demonstration in which a jar was placed over a lighted candle. The teacher explained, "Fire needs air, or oxygen, to burn." The children learned to give the teacher's explanation, but confusion was evident when one youngster pointed to some moisture in the jar saying, "See the oxygen."

At the early childhood level, educators place a premium on language, especially on speaking, or the production of language. A person who worked with three-year-olds described one girl as being so quiet that she must "have cotton between her ears." This typical assessment was revised, however, after the child took an intelligence test. She not only performed better than her peers, she also spoke a good deal while she was taking it.

The quality of children's thinking, even after they master language, may not always be reflected in what they say in everyday situations in school or center. Quiet children, because of their personalities or because they are of a culture that does not encourage talkativeness, may be busy solving problems silently.

Children's use of language to demonstrate what they know nonetheless is an important part of their schooling. Young children cannot readily talk about their thought processes, but when they use words in particular ways, as the child used *oxygen* in the example cited, they indicate whether or not they understand new vocabulary or new concepts.

Learning words, however, is not the only factor in the development of thinking. The child begins to construct the foundations of intelligence well before he or she uses language; doing precedes verbalizing.

We view language as one major activity that children engage in and use in conjunction with other kinds of activity, as they develop intellectually. Language by itself does not lead to the understanding of concepts, and linguistic facility does not necessarily reflect superior intelligence. Language and thought are interdependent, not identical.

Consider the Context of What Children Say and Do

Young children frequently behave in ways that are appropriate in one situation but not another. Teachers often cite the testing situation, for example, as one that may elicit responses specific to that context. A four-year-old boy may perform well on an intelligence test item requiring him to listen and to follow directions, such as: "Put the pencil on the table, and then open the door." But his parents might find him forgetful at home when he is not challenged by a test.

Another example shows that context affects children's thinking as well as their behavior. A teacher took her kindergarten class to visit a farm. They were surprised to find that milk comes from cows. The next year, when the teacher had the same children in first grade she asked them to tell her how we get the milk we drink. They responded, "From the store," showing that they recalled their learning from the familiar context better than from the context they knew less well.

The teacher is an important part of the context for learning. Some of the responses the children make are rewarded and others are not. Children often come to pay more attention to the teacher's signals of approval or disapproval than they do to other elements in the learning context. Thus a child struggling with a math problem may focus on the teacher's face more than on the figures in the book.

Sometimes the classroom or school context is so restrictive that it inhibits the child's thinking. The senior author recalls interviewing four-year-olds in a school that placed a heavy premium on following teacher direction. The curriculum was dominated by readiness workbooks. In individual interviews, a box that was taped shut and contained several smaller objects was placed in front of each of the children. The interviewer asked them if they could find out what it might contain before it was opened. Hands neatly folded, each child guessed wildly. Only when specifically encouraged to hold the box, shake it, listen to the sounds, did any child explore the box. It is difficult to believe that the children would have responded so passively in a nonschool context such as a home or playground.

Change the Environment or Ask Appropriate Questions to Clarify or Promote Thought

To be sure that children are expressing what they really know, the teacher may need to modify the context by changing the materials that are available. Or a well-phrased question may be in order.

A teacher watching a child pushing all the "floaters" to the bottom of the water table might provide the child with a transparent tube that could be closed so that it would float, or opened and filled with objects of different density, so that it might float *or* sink. In so doing, the teacher challenges and extends the child's beginning, unverbalized conceptualization of the relation between water and the properties of objects.[1] Such an intervention on the part of the teacher need not be accompanied by verbalization. Nevertheless, it serves as an opportunity to verify or discard whatever conclusions have been arrived at through the earlier manipulations.

Questions also can stimulate thinking, provided they are phrased so that the way is left open for the child to express what *he* or *she* thinks. Too often, teachers pose questions that give the child the option for only one kind of answer. Compare, for example, "Did the little girl (in the story) feel hungry?" with, "How do you think the little girl felt?" or "What can you tell me about the little girl now?" (Chapter 4 contains specific suggestions for asking questions.)

Study and Document the Changes in Children's Thinking

The years from two to eight bring enormous changes in the ways children think. Not only does thinking become more organized and logical from the adult view, but the content of the concepts also changes.

Change is revealed by the ways children act on objects as well as by what they say. For example, preschool children actively investigate the properties of objects, and the relationships between their own behavior and the activity of the objects. One two-year-old announced, "Water doesn't stay in this sieve," revealing something of his notions of the properties of water and containers. The four-year-olds cited earlier were focused on the floating properties of objects and their own abilities to modify those properties. Older children may be seen to separate "floaters" from "sinkers." They begin to develop more systematic approaches, generalizing perhaps that light objects float, heavy ones sink, and small objects float, big ones sink. Such classifications may or may not lead to correct predictions, but they do reveal increasingly orderly thinking.

Good teachers of young children are aware of those instances where children have reasoned insightfully or solved a problem particularly well, as well as instances of confusion and ineptness. Teachers carry in their heads a lot of information about each child's progress. If they are to demonstrate that a child is developing increasing competence during a period of time, however, some kind of record is essential. They may make brief jottings of incidents, as they occur. They may want to present each child with the same, or essentially similar, tasks at the beginning, middle, and end of the year to see how thinking changes. They may keep examples of children's dictation, and later their writing. Or they may sketch or photograph block-building and other constructions. Samples of the children's paintings and drawings kept over a period of months or years offer clear evidence of the changing view and organization of the world. The paintings shown in figures 3.1 to 3.4 were selected from a series made by a four-year-old during the first two months of preschool. Note the features of the paintings that seem to be characteristic of the child and are repeated in various ways. Note also the changes over time.

Fig. 1

Fig. 2

Fig. 3

Fig. 4

FIGURES 3.1-3.4 SELECTIONS FROM A SERIES OF PAINT-INGS BY A FOUR-YEAR-OLD GIRL

Figures 3.1 and 3.2 were made on October 10 and 20, Figures 3.3 and 3.4 on November 7 and 28. In the mean-time the child also made many other paintings showing similar attention to and absorption in form.

AN EXPLANATORY THEORY OF CHILDREN'S THINKING

To show that development has occurred, teachers need a framework to help them understand the child's thinking. Most useful for that purpose, we believe, is the theory of Jean Piaget. Many teachers of young children already have found it helpful. Some, however, have heard or read about it and have decided that it is too complex to be grasped easily. We agree that Piaget's writing is difficult, and that his ideas must be wrestled with if they are to be comprehended. We believe, however, that teachers who apply Piaget's theory to the development of their own understanding will find the experience worth the effort they put into it.

Essentially Piaget's theory says that present knowledge in the various disciplines has evolved over time. The basic concepts in mathematics and the physical and social sciences have been constructed over generations. Each succeeding generation uses the basic concepts of the preceding generations, combining and altering them so that new concepts emerge. We might think that whatever concepts constitute the current knowledge in any discipline could be communicated directly and immediately to any adult who wanted to acquire them. Piaget thinks it's not that simple. Rather, each adult, in the process of development from infancy to adulthood, constructs individually the same concepts that were constructed by the early mathematicians and scientists. Before beginning to comprehend modern mathematics and science, individuals have to give attention to the order and relations in their own early concrete experiences and be able to hold on to those aspects that remain unaltered when objects are transformed in some way.

An example is provided by the adult's comprehension of the principles of physics relating to the floating and sinking of objects. Such comprehension can be traced to the time when the child first began to take note of the properties of objects, comparing their sizes or other properties and later their weights. The adult understanding also builds on the child's eventual ability to recognize that a change in an object's shape does not alter its weight or its volume. These elementary experiences provide mental structures that enable the child to think about the density of objects and to compare their weight with the weight of equivalent volumes of water. The latter abilities are not achieved until the beginning of adolescence. So, Piaget thinks, the child during development retraces the intellectual steps taken by the Greek mathematician Archimedes in arriving at the principle of floating bodies. Piaget's theory provides a description of the processes of development that are involved as the person moves toward adult comprehension in mathematics and science.

Adults do not grasp a new set of ideas, like Piaget's theory, all at once. We learn new terms slowly, and invest them with meanings from prior experience that may or may not be the meanings Piaget intended. Thus, each of us, in a sense, constructs our own Piagetian theory.

As we introspect about the process, we also can gain insight into the child's developing thought. The child deals with different content but the process basically is similar.

As the child abstracts meaning from concrete experience, readers of Piaget's theory find that they understand the theory best when they observe for themselves the thinking that Piaget describes. They can pay attention to the protocols of Piaget's interviews with children, or better, replicate the interviews. (Such interviewing also provides an opportunity to test one's ability to ask appropriate questions.)

Another, and perhaps more fundamental, way to come to grips with the theory is to begin with infants. In *The Construction of Reality in the Child,* Piaget offers the grand design of his theory and illustrates it with the behavior of his own three children. The observant teacher can understand the rudiments of Piaget's theory by watching the ways infants at different ages respond to the "experiments" Piaget presents, or by watching the behavior of an individual infant over the period of several months.

Observation of the ways sensorimotor schemes develop and are elaborated provides good background for understanding the evolution of concrete and formal operations. Initially, for example, the baby uses similar movements to grasp both a rattle and soft toy. Gradually the baby's actions are differentiated. One set is used for the rattle, another for the soft toy. Although the baby does not yet have words, the concepts "shakable" and "cuddly" are beginning to form. For Piaget, thought evolves from such patterns-of-action, or sensorimotor schemes. An *operation* is Piaget's term for the mental actions involved in logical thought.

Logical thought, the ability to reason consistently, requires the ability to classify and compare objects and data and involves such operations as addition, subtraction, multiplication, division, and recognition of the relations "more than" and "less than." Piaget stresses that operations are internalized actions that are reversible. (One can think about adding two sets of objects together, and mentally return them to their original state.) During the period of years covered by this book and until the beginning of adolescence, operations are referred to as "concrete." They always relate to actual things or experiences.

In contrast, "formal" operations—achieved in adolescence—are applied to possibilities as well as actualities. For example, one of the problems Piaget has posed to youngsters involves four unidentified liquids. The task is to find out what combinations of liquids will turn yellow when a particular chemical is added. Concrete thinkers mess about, using unsystematic trial and error methods. Formal thinkers mentally map out the possibilities, systematically trying each of the four liquids in turn, then the possible combinations in turn.

The Stages of Children's Thinking

According to Piaget, the thinking of the adult evolves from several stages that begin with infancy: each of these stages is qualitatively different from the other. A central feature of the differences in stages is the nature of the actions that link the individual with his world. As Piaget puts it, "To know an object is to act on it."

The Sensorimotor Period.   For the newborn infant, his or her body, his or her actions and the world are continuous. Gradually, as actions bring him or her into contact with a variety of objects, the patterns of these actions are modified. The infant accommodates or modifies the early grasping pattern, for example, to round objects, square objects, and to those of varying sizes. These new patterns are in turn assimilated into the developing repertory of action patterns. Eventually toward the second half of the second year, when this repertory is applied to an increasing variety of objects, the objects themselves take on permanence for the infant. No longer does out of sight mean out of mind.

Paralleling the discovery of object permanence is the beginning of representation. The child, at first by imitative actions, later by words as well, indicates an awareness of absent objects and events and can recapture them mentally. For example, the toddler who has observed with interest the rhythmically beating wings of a butterfly may return to the place where the butterfly was poised when it is no longer present, and indicate by imitation of the rhythmic movement the memory of the moment.

The Preoperational Period.   The onset of representation marks the beginning of the preoperational period. The preoperational period extends roughly to the age of seven or eight. Thus it encompasses the period of early childhood education as defined in this book.

Children reflecting on their own actions with concrete objects come to understand the relationships among those actions. Confronted, for example, with an array of pebbles, differing in size, color, and shape, children eventually know not only that they can be sorted, separated, and combined in a variety of ways, but also that the relationships among them are reversible. The white pebbles and the black ones are part of the whole array. The black ones can be taken away from the array and also be returned to it. The black ones can be sorted according to whether they are big or little and then recombined. The number of black pebbles can greatly exceed the number of white pebbles, but there is no question that there are more pebbles than either black pebbles or white pebbles. The understanding of these relationships and the consequent ability to think in a way that begins to approximate adult logic marks the end of the preoperational period.

The early half of the preoperational period, encompassing roughly the years from two to five, has received less study than the latter half, extending to about age eight. The work that has been done, however, shows that one accomplishment of the earlier period, corresponding to the earlier achievement of object permanence, is the recognition of "qualitative identity." The child comes to know that the material properties of an object remain the same even though its shape may change. For example, wire is still wire when it is bent or cut.

Another achievement of the earlier period is "functional dependency," the beginning understanding of the connections between specified goals and the actions necessary to achieve them. The child understands that the harder he or she pushes a truck, the farther it goes. Or if one rolls a ball of clay, it becomes longer; it also becomes thinner.

Clearly, play and exploration during the preoperational period offer the child many opportunities for the discovery of the qualities of objects and also the relationships among his or her actions on the objects. Play also provides opportunities for the child to extend the ability to represent experience and to deal with symbols. In play, objects or a gesture can stand for another object or an event. Piaget has not dealt with the relationships, if any, between dealing with the symbols created by the child's imagination, and the arbitrary symbols (*signs* in Piaget's terms) involved in learning to read. Nevertheless, it seems likely that the child with a rich background of experience with play symbols is better equipped for beginning reading than the child with more limited experience.

Another characteristic of the preoperational period is the tendency of children to see things more from their own individual points of view than from those of other persons. Each is centered on his or her own perspective. Only gradually, through the give and take of their play, do they become more flexible and able to assume different points of view.

Some lessening of egocentric tendencies characterizes the latter part of the preoperational period. The child becomes able to concentrate on an assigned task and can carry through several steps without going off on a tangent.

The research of Piaget and his collaborators has shown how children from about the age of five begin to organize their knowledge of their world in increasingly orderly and systematic fashion. Studies of children's conceptions of physical causality, number, time, space, chance, the logical relations involved in classifying and ordering, and investigations of moral judgment, mental imagery, and memory, provide a myriad of windows from which teachers can view the changing thinking of children in this period.

The Period of Concrete Operations.   The emergence of true operations around the age of seven or eight is marked by the ability to conserve number and to understand class-inclusion and seriation relationships. Conservation and the experiments used to demonstrate its existence have become well known to most teachers in the last decade.

The child's ability to conserve, that is, to recognize the equivalence of two sets of objects when visual one-to-one correspondence is transformed, constitutes a benchmark for the emergence of thought that is reversible and systematic. This is not to say that the logic involved will immediately penetrate all areas of the child's thinking. A child is likely, for example, to be able to conserve a given amount of clay, and the number of a set of objects, but not to conserve the weight of the clay. On the other hand, once a number, say eight, for example, is really grasped, the child will never be misled into thinking that four plus three could be eight, or that eight doughnuts might be fewer than eight rubber tires.

Two illustrations show how the ability to conserve evolves and how children may resist instruction about it. Charlene, a four-year-old in preschool, expected that things that look big must be big. She demonstrated this belief when a researcher showed her two clay balls identical in size. When the researcher rolled one of the balls into a long sausage, Charlene said there was more clay in the sausage than in the ball. The researcher then showed her that the sausage could be rolled into a ball again. Or it could be flattened into a pancake, or broken into small pieces and still returned to its original state. He emphasized that "the way the clay looks doesn't matter." Charlene went from the session with the researcher to have a snack of juice and crackers. She broke her cracker into small bits and said to her neighbor, "I have more cracker than you do!"

Bob, an eight-year-old, provides another example. Bob reported to a visitor in his home that he had been interviewed by another adult friend who had shown him some matches "in a straight line and zigzag." He said, "She asked me on which of those paths a person would walk further. That was easy. It's harder to walk around those corners."

The visitor, who knew the Piaget experiment on the conservation of length, repeated it with Bob. She placed

five matches as in *a* ▬ ▬ ▬ ▬ ▬

and another as in *b* ＞＜＞＜＞

and verified that the previous interviewer had done likewise. She then said, "You told her a person walking along here [b] would walk further than on the other path. You said this path [b] is longer than this [a]?"

Bob agreed. The visitor pressed harder, "The last time I showed a boy this problem he said there were five matches there and five matches here, so the paths were the same length."

"He forgot about the corners," said Bob. At least for the moment, his cognitive structures were impervious to instruction.

The construction and application of logic goes on throughout the period of concrete operations and may proceed more rapidly in some areas of the children's experience than others. The appearance in a particular area, such as number, however, provides the teacher with clues for expectations in other areas.

The term *concrete* refers to the child making mental references to prior concrete experience. It does not mean that all of the curriculum should consist of direct manipulation of objects. Clearly, however, the child who is first entering the period of concrete operations will need more support from such manipulation than may be required by the older child.

The Period of Formal Operations. When the child can reason without concrete references, considering systematically all the possible relations that might obtain in a particular problem, the period of formal operations has been reached. Such transition does not usually occur before the age of twelve, and a surprising number of adults seem not to have reached it, or seldom seem to handle problems in a formal way.

The major significance of the stages outlined by Piaget for teachers of young children lies in the sense of sequence or direction they provide. Piaget's reports of the experiments he has conducted indicate stages and substages in the development of the children's conceptions of various aspects of their world. The teacher who observes a child functioning in a particular way can draw on knowledge of the next step in the sequence to provide further experience for the child.

A word of caution is in order here. We do not think that the early childhood curriculum should be made up of tasks derived from Piaget's experiments. Nor do we think that teachers should constantly use Piaget's tasks to assess children's development. Rather, teachers should be alert to the possibilities for the children's thinking in all of the ongoing curriculum activities.

Kinds of Knowledge

The early childhood curriculum encompasses a variety of activities drawing on, or intending to develop, different kinds of knowledge. Not all knowledge is understood or communicated in the same way. Effective instruction, undergirded by observation and understanding of the ways children think, depends on the teacher's awareness of the distinctions that can be made among different kinds of knowledge.

Logico-mathematical or Operational Knowledge.   Piaget's major concerns, and the bulk of his experiments, have to do with the construction of what he terms logico-mathematical or operational knowledge. The development of this kind of knowledge enables the child to classify objects and events on the basis of their similarities and to relate or order them on the dimensions or properties in which they differ. In so doing, children become able to deal efficiently with transformation. They eventually can think of all the blocks in the room as a totality, and as subsets made up of rectangles, triangles, and half-circles. They can compare the rectangles that are numerous with the circles that are not and recognize that the total of blocks is greater than the rectangles. If the rectangles are of differing lengths, they can conceive of the relationships between the quadruples, the doubles, and the units, without putting them into actual juxtaposition.

The ability to organize one's thoughts in a systematic and logical way is an obvious prerequisite for dealing with mathematics and science. A little reflection indicates that it is also relevant to both beginning and later reading, to understanding social studies and to understanding as well as performing in music, art, and dance. Some of these areas of the curriculum also call on ways of thinking and knowing that have been largely neglected by Piaget.

The source of logico-mathematical knowledge, according to Piaget, is the child's actions. Information about the relationships among the objects and the ways they may be ordered is abstracted from what is done to them. Similarly, it is reflection on his or her own actions that assures the

•

child the number of objects in a given set does not change when the objects are rearranged.

Significantly, for the teacher of young children, activity alone is insufficient for the construction of operative thinking. There has to be, rather, an intellectual engagement on the part of the child. The teacher, by providing new material, or by asking a judicious question, may promote the child's reflection on this action that is essential to logico-mathematical knowledge.

Careful observation is necessary if the teacher is to intervene appropriately. As an example, consider Jill, a preschooler, with a formboard puzzle. Her initial manipulations of the puzzle's pieces seem random and uncoordinated. Later, as she becomes absorbed in figuring out how the pieces should go (a kind of spatial reasoning) her attention and movement become clearly focused. Once she has mastered the puzzle's solution, and she returns to it later, her approach—though effective—reflects less absorption and may even be characterized as slapdash or playful. She no longer has to analyze the relationships among the pieces. In Piaget's terms, in these playful episodes, Jill practices the actions that were needed for the puzzle's solution and thus assimilates them into her increasing repertory of actions available for dealing with puzzles. Jill's teacher will not want to circumvent such play, but as it is repeated, will take it as evidence of Jill's readiness for a more challenging puzzle.

In considering the challenge that a particular puzzle may offer, or indeed in looking at any activity, the teacher needs to consider the kind of knowledge to be derived from it. In the case of a puzzle, when children must reflect on the actions that lead to the correct completion, the beginnings of logico-mathematical thought are involved. Children must pay attention to both successful and unsuccessful maneuvers and note the relationships among them. Some puzzles do not call for such reflection and so contribute more to physical knowledge than to logico-mathematical knowledge.

Physical Knowledge. Physical knowledge differs from logico-mathematical knowledge in that its source, instead of being the thinking individual, is the external world. In the case of the puzzle, physical knowledge of the shapes of the pieces, their color, their hardness, the sound they make when dropped is derived directly from the objects. Other examples of physical knowledge are the malleability of clay, the lack of permeability of metal, the readiness of liquid to flow, the bounce of a rubber ball. Much of the experience of young children can be seen as gaining physical knowledge of the world around them and knowledge of the physical properties of their own bodies.

Of course, since the child can reflect on actions that relate to physical knowledge, noting for example, that cardboard puzzles can be bent but wooden ones cannot, the distinctions Piaget makes do not always seem clear-cut.

Figurative Knowledge. Just as Piaget differentiates between logico-mathematical knowledge and physical knowledge, he also distinguishes between operative knowledge and what he terms *figurative* knowledge. This distinction seems to us to be particularly useful in planning early childhood curriculum and in assessing children's thinking. Figurative knowledge focuses on static configurations of acts or events that are external to the child. No transformations are involved. Charlene in the conservation experiment described earlier provides an example. She focused on the immediate configuration and was misled by the appearance of the clay in the elongated ball. Her knowledge was figurative, not yet operative.

Our suspicion is that many early childhood classrooms promote figurative more than operative knowledge. They offer the children learning tasks that provide many clues to the expected response. The children only have to imitate the response the teacher has given for that particular set of clues in order to be correct.

In some instances the equipment available to the children may also call largely on figurative knowledge. One such example would be the Montessori cylinders, designed to assist the child in learning to make fine size and weight discriminations. All the clues are in the apparatus: the cylinders will fit properly only in the holes that correspond in size. The child does not have to deal with transformation.

An example from a first grade teacher illustrates the limitations in figurative knowledge. In using a particular workbook, she found that many children had difficulty at the same place. They had been successfully completing exercises that required them to write in the sums for rows and columns in a series of diagrams. The trouble came when the format changed, and the children were required to fill in the appropriate figures for the rows and columns, given the sums. Until they encountered this transformation, the children could rely more on memory than on reflection.

Our criticism of instructional methods that promote only figurative knowledge does not imply that these methods should never be used. It is rather that methods relying on figurative knowledge are not appropriate when the children's source of information should be objects themselves, as in the case of physical knowledge, or the children's reflections on their own actions, as in the case of logico-mathematical knowledge.

Obviously much that children do need to know can be effectively acquired by associating static pictures, symbols, or words with specific responses. Such methods are appropriate to the learning of knowledge that is social.

Social Knowledge. Social knowledge has its source in other people. It is knowledge that varies with culture and community. One acquires such knowledge by being told rather than by acting on the environment or reflecting on those actions.

Examples of social knowledge are the names for things, social customs, and rules for behavior, Social knowledge can be thought of as what the child would need to be told, or shown how to do, if he or she were transported to a strange culture. Included would be such customs as shaking hands, using a knife and fork or chopsticks; and saying good-bye, *adios, au revoir,* or *ciao* at the end of a conversation or visit.

Since children appear to learn a great deal simply by being told, it may seem that all knowledge can be acquired in the same way as social knowledge. Piaget's research and the observations of teachers, however, confirm that young children must experience the world directly, and reflect on that experience before they can understand many concepts.

An example of the slow process involved in understanding the rules of a game comes from a first grade teacher. She reports on joining a first grade kickball team to make the number of its players equal to another first grade team. She was the pitcher. When a boy kicked, she caught the ball and put him out before he reached base. One boy, Kevin—tall, athletic, and an apparent leader—told her she couldn't do so. She asked when she could put out the player. Kevin said, "When I say so." Kevin was, according to Piaget, in the first stage of the practice of rules, when the child does not know the rules or how to apply them but is convinced that he does. The teacher then called for "time out" to discuss the rules with the other team members. None could present a statement that made sense to the teacher, although all acted as though they knew the game. Finally, however, they agreed that Kevin could say when the pitcher could put someone out. It appeared that they regarded Kevin as an authority and were content to go by his rules.

Clearly, all these children would need to be nudged many times by the different opinions of adults and older children and to reflect on their own behavior before they would be able to grasp the logic of the game.

Social knowledge of this sort can be differentiated from moral knowledge or judgment. The latter involves reasoning about what is right or wrong, in the ethical sense. It is concerned with the obligations one has to other people. According to Piaget's view, and to the works of others who have elaborated on his ideas, the moral development of children is furthered when they are helped to reflect on their behavior. Merely telling them what to do, or rewarding some behaviors and not others, is less effective than helping children to construct their own judgments. Such help must take into account the level of judgment children already have attained.

Other Kinds of Knowledge.   Piaget's work has dealt less extensively with social knowledge than with logico-mathematical and physical knowledge. He also has given relatively little attention to personal, self, or existential knowledge, and aesthetics.

Piaget has described the child's discovery of self, the differentiation of self from other objects. He has shown how the processes of decentering involved in social collaboration enable the child to think from the perspective of another. Eventually, in the period of formal operations, the individual becomes able to reflect on his or her own thought, consciously conceptualizing personal mental processes. Adolescents tend to think a lot about their own ideas, the ways they think about the world, and how their own ways differ from those of their friends and their parents. Piaget focuses on these cognitive aspects of the developing self, but he has been less concerned with the affective or feeling aspects, although he acknowledges their importance. The teacher of young children must turn to other theorists for help in understanding certain individual and personal aspects of the child's development and learning.

One author, David Elkind, highlights the importance of what he terms "connotative learning" in young children.[2] Connotative learning refers to children's attempts to make sense out of their world by relating their concepts to verbal symbols. It is a process of matching the words they know to the words they hear. Later on the process extends to words they see. For example, one three-year-old, when her teacher began a discussion of the circus, spoke about the "circle cookies" the class had made. Even though young children are not consciously aware of their own thought processes, it was as though she were saying, "I know what circle means. Is circus like that?"

The process of establishing meanings is very evident in children's play, and in the representations they make in painting, drawing, and movement. Thus, provisions made in the curriculum for play and aesthetic development provide opportunity for children to clarify and extend their thinking.

The child's products in art, music, and oral and written expression, and sometimes the movements in dances also reveal the level of logico-mathematical thinking. The increasing complexity of children's drawings, for example, reflects the changing organization of their concepts. Artistic production, however, also is laden with feeling and personal meaning. It is valued in terms of the aptness and uniqueness of its expression.

Motivation and Interest

According to Piaget's theory, the desire to know is built in from infancy. Just as healthy infants apply a growing repertory of actions to more and more of the objects in the surrounding environment, so older children test out ideas about their world. In the process, the infants' patterns of action are modified and combined; they become more and more effective. Older children's ideas also are modified and combined; they understand more and more about the people and things in their environment.

The twin processes of accommodation (shaping action and thought to the demands of the environment) and assimilation (incorporating the new actions and thoughts into one's repertory) are subsumed in the process that Piaget calls equilibration, or self-regulation.

Piaget's theory applies to children in general. He does not deal with the differences among children, although he is clearly aware that a variety of factors, such as prolonged illness, physical or emotional neglect or trauma, may impede the normal processes of development.

Aside from these unusual circumstances, three factors contribute to the equilibration process: maturation, encounters with the physical environment, and social interaction with adults and peers.

Maturation, as Piaget has said, opens up possibilities, but it is never sufficient in itself to actualize those possibilities. Active encounters with the physical environment provide direct information about the properties of objects. Each child's reflection on his or her own actions is the source of logico-mathematical constructions. Adult instruction is filtered through the child's existing cognitive structures. The child believes what those structures can assimilate.

Two examples cited earlier in this chapter illustrate these points. Charlene was so intent on the appearance of things that she did not respond to conservation instruction. Similarly, Bob believed so firmly in the difficulty of walking around corners that he denied the equality of length of five matches and five matches.

We have sometimes referred to the equilibration, or self-regulation, process as "do it yourself" from the viewpoint of the child. The child is in charge of the construction of new cognitive structures. This means that the process is not directly available to the teacher's observation. The interest the child manifests can guide the teacher in providing activities that are intellectually challenging.

There is no way the teacher can accurately predict how much manipulative activity, or direct instruction, or nudging by peers will be required before a child will reorganize a particular set of cognitive structures. The challenge, and it is a major one, for teachers is to apprise themselves of · the nature of each child's interests.

This is a tricky business because children often manifest interests that are transitory or that have little potential for extended pursuits. Furthermore, some teachers, caught up in the idea that early childhood is a period of intensive learning and discovery, seem to confuse intellectual interest and satisfaction with fun and excitement. They become caught in a trap where every day, or at least every week, they must provide some novel activity that will stimulate the class to a frenzy of ideas, questions, laughter, and gleeful reports to parents. We take a more sober view of interest, at least of interest that is educationally productive. Interest that can be prolonged and built on is manifested not just in initial curiosity but in continuing absorption, and the pursuit of many possibilities.

The materials and equipment that long have been regarded as basic to the early childhood curriculum—clay, paint, sand, water, blocks, props for dramatic play—all have potential for capturing children's interest and hence for promoting intellectual development. All can be used in increasingly complex ways, requiring more and more complex thought on the part of the children. To help the children derive the maximum benefits from the use of these and other materials, the teacher needs to know both the likely sequence of possibilities for the use of the materials and the variety of ways that they may be used at each level. One second-grade youngster revealed his understanding of the sequence in water play when he commented, "Yesterday we just poured. Today we measured." Water play, at the second-grade level, could also lead into other science and social studies areas. The single question, "Where does the water we use in school come from?" might lead in a number of productive directions.

APPLYING PIAGET'S THEORY

A number of years ago, when Piaget's theory was first becoming popular in this country, someone wrote that the teacher who read Piaget from then on would always see children differently. Such a teacher would have insight into the ways the child's thinking differs from that of the adult. This insight into the nature of the child's thought seems to us essential for applying Piaget's theory in the classroom.

How is such insight to be gained? We doubt that reading this chapter will be sufficient, although we hope it may help. Reading from Piaget's voluminous works, or from those who have explicated them, also will help. The observation and interviewing of children are most important, however. Watching and working with the infant are desirable, but talking with children of different ages and conducting "experiments" with them, as Piaget has done, are essential. Only by contrasting the way children of different ages—say four, six, eight, and ten—respond to the same task can the teacher gain a sense of the way thought develops.

Through interviewing children, teachers also may gain skill in clinical interviewing techniques. One way to proceed, after familiarizing oneself with a particular experiment, is to tape-record one's interview of a child doing the experiment. Afterward, compare the questions that were asked with the questions that Piaget and his collaborators asked in their clinical interviews. Such a procedure sometimes reveals that the teacher's questions implied expected answers rather than offered the child opportunities to express his or her own thoughts.

The impulse to teach is strong, even when the goal is not instruction but diagnosis and assessment. One kindergarten teacher expressed this impulse when she said plaintively after her first round of Piagetian interviews, "It's so hard for me to find out what they don't know."

In some of Piaget's early work, in which he questioned children about their ideas and beliefs without presenting them with concrete tasks, Piaget found that children often were inclined to give the answer they thought he wanted. One thing Piaget did to improve his questioning was to listen to the questions the children themselves asked. That way he could ask questions that were appropriate to their level of wondering about various aspects of their world.

Later on, Piaget began to develop concrete representations of the phenomena he wanted to discuss with the children. Then his questions could refer to what the children thought about what they saw or could do. There was less likelihood that they would indulge in fantasy.

In questioning children about the floating and sinking of objects, for example, Piaget not only asked, "Why do big boats stay on the water?" or "A big boat is heavier than a stone, yet it doesn't sink. Why does a boat not sink?" He also presented the children with an array of objects including matches, corks, an eraser, a key, a needle, and a heavy wooden ball. These could be immersed in a container of water. He also provided two cylinders of the same size, one filled with a cylinder of wood, the other with water. These cylinders could be opened and closed. They provided means for the child to compare the weight of wood to the weight of an equal volume of water. In another experiment to find out about children's understanding of spatial relationships Piaget showed them a transparent jar partially filled with liquid. He asked the children to represent from memory the level of the liquid as it was when the jar was oriented in a particular direction. The pictures drawn by the younger children usually showed the liquid parallel to the inclination of the jar. They drew this way even though they had seen that the liquid always assumes a level position, parallel to the floor.

Techniques in Interviews

Several of the techniques used by those who have been trained in Piagetian interviewing also are useful for teachers who want to find out what children are thinking.

One such technique is pacing the interview so that the child has time to think. The pace is slower than teachers typically use when instructing children.[3]

Another technique is reflection. The interviewer repeats what the child has said. Sometimes it is used when the interviewer does not understand what the child means or wants to be sure that the child's statement was correctly heard. At other times it serves to assure the child that the interviewer is listening and involved in the child's thinking. A noncommittal "mmmhm" serves a similar function.

A third technique is countersuggestion. This technique assumes a good grasp on the part of the interviewer of the possible explorations of the phenomenon under consideration. It is used to probe the strength of an assertion the child has made and the child's possible willingness to abandon it for another. The countersuggestion may take such forms as, "Another child I talked with said . . . ," or "Some people say that." In each case the child is expected to reflect on the countersuggestion.

The following report from a teacher who worked with five- to eight-year-olds shows some of the ways teachers can assess children's thinking in the course of their activities. The example comes from the children's involvement in the operation of a farm that was maintained in connection with the school.

Recently, I had been asked repeatedly by children about the heat resulting from the composting process. They had seen steam rising from the three tier wooden compost boxes and from piles of freshly cut tree leaves and bark brought to the Farm by the local tree trimming service. One day as we worked with our hands to transfer these trimmings from the pile to a cart that was going to take the trimmings to the goat's pen for bedding, the children noticed the steam. One child remarked, "There's steam. It's hot." I questioned him, "Why is it hot?" His response was, "There's a match in there. " I suggested that we look for the match. As we dug through the pile it got hotter and hotter but we, of course, didn't find the match. So, I remarked, "We didn't find a match so how come it's hot?" The children responded, "It burned." And they brought up handfuls of "burned" leaves that had turned from green to brown or gray in the composting process as proof. "See, there's burned stuff down here. See, there was a fire." Though we never found the fire, they were convinced it had occurred because of the "burned" leaves that they found and the heat that was in the pile. Some were afraid to touch the green composting leaves that were still hot for fear that they would get burned. In the cold, brown places, the children explained that the fire had long since gone out.

The same incident occurred a week later with the same group of children. The responses had not varied.

Other children responded to the same situations by saying that the sun made the heat. It was shady so I looked up at the sky questioning that I didn't see the sun. How could the sun make it hot? The response was, "It was shining yesterday." When I said that I didn't see it now though, the child repeated, "It was shining yesterday." The child didn't consider the time a factor.

One morning I observed steam rising from a wooden sandbox outside the Farm classroom window. I went with a group of seven eight-year-olds to investigate. We looked at it and touched it. A child declared that "There's no fire," discounting younger children's explanation that fire causes steam. "It's cold on the inside and hot on the outside," explained another child. Later in the day another seven-year-old explained, "The rain came, then the sun came and that made it hot" and thus steam.

Note how the teacher in this illustration seeks the children's understanding of the phenomenon in question. She follows the leads the children give her, suggesting, for example, that they look for the match, and turning their attention to the cloudy sky. Thus she gives them opportunities to verify or disprove their own beliefs. When they fail to discern any contradictions between their statements and the evidence she has suggested, she does not press further. She recognizes that more experience as well as more maturity will be necessary for more adequate understanding. She respects their ideas and does not try to change them with a verbal explanation.

Cautions in Adapting Piaget

In considering how teachers may adapt Piagetian interviews to class-room use, some cautions are important. Piaget's tasks were designed for the specific purposes of revealing how children construct knowledge. Interesting though they are, they are not intended to provide instruction. They may be used for assessment purposes (see chapter 8), provided their relationship to various curriculum activities is clearly understood. We should also note that Piaget's interviews generally were conducted with one child at a time, while much that the teacher does will involve several children, if not the whole group. When the teacher develops some skill in Piagetian interviewing and a corresponding grasp of the theory, the major benefits come from the way the teacher thinks about the children. Piagetian theory carries with it no prescriptions for the curriculum or for instruction, other than that the teacher be alert to the ways children think. Such alertness is not limited to noting a child's progress from one level of thought to another. It includes awareness of the depth and breadth of the children's ideas, and of the curiosity, inventiveness, and creativity that each child's thinking reveals.

SUMMARY

Studying the ways young children think in part is a matter of listening to what children say and paying attention to what they do. It is also a matter of respecting their thinking while providing them with activity and experiences to nurture and challenge it.

The theory of Piaget provides a framework for the study of young children's thinking, suggesting to the teacher the likely sequences of development. At the same time, the distinctions Piaget makes between logico-mathematical and physical and social knowledge help the teacher to plan activities that will enable the children to develop and learn appropriately in all three areas.

The methods of the clinical interview, although not directly applicable to the classroom setting, offer the teacher a number of techniques that can be used there. In mastering both the theory and the method, the teacher is faced with the necessity of accommodating customary ways of thinking about children and talking with them to Piagetian ways. The tendency to assimilate the Piagetian ideas into the old ways will be strong and must be resisted. In the process, however, the teacher stands to gain a new, more realistic, and more satisfying intellectual appraisal of the thinking of the children for whom he or she is responsible.

NOTES

1. For an excellent description of how changing the environment can promote children's thinking, see Frances Hawkins' report of her work with deaf children, *The Logic of Action: Young Children at Work*. (New York: Pantheon, 1974).
2. David Elkind, *Child Development and Education: A Piagetian Perspective*. (New York: Oxford University Press, 1976).
3. The value of "wait-time" in questioning young children in science is discussed in Mary Budd Rowe, "Science, Silence, and Sanctions," *Science and Children* 6, no. 6 (March, 1969), pp. 11-13.

SUGGESTED READING

Almy, M.; with Chittenden, E.; and Miller P. *Young Children's Thinking: Studies of Some Aspects of Piagetian Theory*. New York: Teachers College Press, 1966. This is a report of early studies substantiating Piaget's theory. It includes a chapter that many students have found a useful introduction to the theory.

Brearley, M., and Hitchfield, E. *Guide to Reading Piaget*. New York: Schocken, 1969. These authors believe with us that the best way to understand Piaget's theory is to conduct the "experiments." Their little book describes a number of the experiments in sufficient detail for replication and gives sample protocols.

Forman, G.E. and Kuschner, D.S. *The Child's Construction of Knowledge: Piaget for Teaching Children*. Monterey, Calif.: Brooks-Cole, 1977. This book, about children ages two to five, interweaves theories of knowledge, development, learning, and teaching. It is rich with examples drawn from the authors' School for Constructive Play, and includes a clear exposition of Piaget's theory.

Furth, H. *Piaget for Teachers*. Englewood Cliffs, N.J.: Prentice-Hall, 1970. This book is not for the beginning student of Piaget. The teacher who has some familiarity with the theory, however, and wishes to dig deeply into the issues involved in application will find it useful.

Ginsburg, H., and Opper, S. *Piaget's Theory of Intellectual Development: An Introduction*. 2nd ed. Englewood Cliffs, N.J.: Prentice-Hall, 1979. Designed for undergraduate students, this book presents Piaget's theory clearly and accurately. It provides clear explanations of concepts that often are difficult to grasp.

Isaacs, S. *Intellectual Growth in Young Children*. New York: Schocken, 1966. This classic report covers three years of the early schooling of a bright group of English two- to eight-year-olds. The detailed observational records reveal the children in an environment that was clearly responsive to their interests.

Kamii, C., and De Vries, R. "Piaget for Early Education." In: *The Preschool in*

Action: Exploring Early Childhood Programs, edited by M.C. Day and A.K. Parker. Boston: Allyn & Bacon, 1977. Kamii and De Vries provide an excellent, lucid discussion of the major concepts in Piaget's theory. The remainder of the chapter deals with applications of the theory to the development of curriculum and with principles of teaching in both cognitive and socioemotional realms.

Schwebel, M., and Raph, J., eds. *Piaget in the Classroom.* New York: Basic Books, 1973. Although not limited to the early childhood period, this book is particularly rich in illustrative material for early childhood. Chapters by Sinclair and Duckworth illuminate theory, while those by Kamii and de Meuron cogently apply to classroom practice.

When teachers read any or all of the following books by Piaget, they are urged to concentrate on the protocols describing what the children did and said. Piaget's discussion often is extremely difficult. In part this is because he often makes several circles around the points he wishes to make, and weighs pros and cons at great length. Also his philosophical approach is foreign to our traditional American ways of thinking. Accordingly, one does well to skim the discussion, trying to get the major ideas rather than each of the finer points. Further clarification comes either from rereading or from reading another of his works. Remember that the process of understanding Piaget in many respects resembles the process whereby the young child comes to understand the world. The sample of Piaget's books we have included is limited to those that have been read with interest and profit by some early childhood teachers. Where possible, the edition we cite is in paperback.

Inhelder, B., and Piaget, J. *The Early Growth of Logic in the Child: Classification and Seriation.* New York: Norton, 1969. Beginning with children as young as two, this book traces the development of classification from the perceptually dominated sorting of the toddler to the class inclusion operation of the ten-year-old. It provides interesting light on the sorting and ordering activities of most early childhood curricula.

Piaget, J. *The Child's Conception of Number.* New York: Norton, 1965. In this book, first published in 1941, Piaget asks children to comment on the actions they have performed on various collections of objects, and traces the development of the concept of number.

Piaget, J. *The Child's Conception of the World.* 1929. Reprint. New York, Humanities, 1960. Originally published in 1926, this book belongs to the period when Piaget relied more on questions than on experiments. The first chapter deals with the clinical method of inquiry.

Piaget, J. *The Construction of Reality in the Child.* New York: Ballantine, 1975.

This book, first published in 1937, is based on Piaget's observations of his own three children when they were infants.

Piaget, J. *The Moral Judgment of the Child*. New York: Free Press, 1932. In this investigation, Piaget began with children's understanding of the rules of games, and moved on to their understanding of cooperation and justice.

Piaget, J. *Play, Dreams and Imitation in Childhood*. New York: Norton, 1962. Drawing mostly on observations of his own children, Piaget analyzes the sensorimotor play of infancy, the symbolic play typical of the preschooler, and games with rules.

Piaget, J., and Inhelder, B. *The Child's Conception of Space*. New York: Humanities, 1963. This book deals with elementary spatial relationships, linear and circular order, and the problems children encounter in knots; the book moves on to the coordination of perspectives and the development of spatial reference systems.

Piaget, J., and Inhelder, B. *The Psychology of the Child*. New York: Basic Books, 1969. The authors describe this as a synthesis or summing up of their work in child psychology and a useful introduction to other volumes.

4 ASK CHILDREN ABOUT THEMSELVES

To ask children questions long has been the teacher's prerogative. Indeed, teaching effectiveness often depends on the kinds of questions asked. Teachers may limit themselves mostly to questions that draw parroted responses from the children, revealing little understanding. In a second-grade classroom, for example, Mrs. Roser presents a lesson on magnets and asks, "What have we learned about magnets? What can we do with them?" One child responds, "They only stick to metal, like iron." The answer corresponds to what the teacher has just told the class and what she has written on the board. Yet, when she asks for further application of what she said, "Will this magnet pick up a piece of paper?" the same child says confidently, "Yes, because paper's lighter." To be more effective the teacher may follow this response with many kinds of questions. She is, as we pointed out in the previous chapter, a facilitator and stimulus for thinking. Through questioning she learns something not only about what the children have learned but also about the ways they think and feel.

In this chapter we are concerned with the use of fairly straightforward questions to gain better understanding of children and their ways of learning. We discuss the informal conversations teachers have with children and the opportunities for asking them about themselves that occur so frequently in the course of each school day. We also look at more formal ways of getting information from children, including interviews and "logs."

Offhand it may seem that asking children about themselves is the easiest and most reliable way of finding out more about them. Often it is, but there are limitations. Sometimes children do not understand the questions in the same way as the teacher does. Their answers, then, do not mean what the teacher thinks they mean. Sometimes children fake their answers. They may want to please the teacher or to protect themselves from revealing their true state or feelings. The information the teacher gains from questions, like that from other ways of studying children, seldom provides definitive answers. Rather, it offers clues to support or negate whatever hunches the teacher may develop from previous information.

What the teacher can learn from asking children about themselves depends to a great extent on the kind of relationship he or she has with them. If the children tend to feel they can trust the teacher, if most of what is done makes sense to them, they are likely to participate freely and cooperatively in the reporting asked of them. If the teacher's questions continually poke and pry, the children will develop appropriate defenses against them. What they say or write in response to questions then will have little significance. The sensitive, intuitive teacher does not ask children to reveal aspects of themselves that they may feel are inappropriate for the teacher to know. Self-reporting is incorporated into the ongoing life of the center or classroom in such a way that the children regard it as a natural and expected part of the day. Probably the major part of it goes on informally.

KINDS OF QUESTIONS

There are many ways, direct and indirect, to ask children about themselves. We suggest that when using direct questions, teachers consider not only the question but also the context in which they ask it. This context includes the activity that brought the question and what teachers do to lend support, both intellectual and emotional, to the child's answer. Teachers impart information at the same time that they demonstrate interest in the child as a unique person. Questions, then, are not asked for their own sake but to promote learning, thinking, and the expression of feelings.

The kind of question teachers formulate depends largely on the topic or activity at hand. In their planning, teachers know it is essential to have an activity, whether it is informal or formal, that is worth asking about. They are purposeful in finding out what is on the child's mind. Regardless of the nature of the activity, teachers' questions often determine whether the child's experience will be constricted or will lead to new interests and discoveries.

Questions that constrict thinking are often "test" questions with one

FIGURE 4.1.

The question, "What can you be when you grow up?" stimulated this drawing, along with the descriptive statements, written down by the teacher.

correct answer. Children responding to such questions probably are aware that the teacher knows the answer and that their task is to say the right word or words: this answer may reflect little of the child's thinking or ways of thinking.

Teachers recognize that lessons like the following may capture the attention of young children at times but are unlikely to promote thinking or extended interest:

> *Miss Henry:* What did we call this? *(She points to a picture of a ball.)*
> *Claudia:* A ball.
> *Miss Henry:* We called it a ball. Whose ball is it?
> *Claudia:* Dan's.
> *Miss Henry:* What else can you tell me about it? What color is it?
> *Claudia:* Red.

Miss Henry's questions require this preschool child to use her memory, or recall information that the child may have known before the lesson began, and to translate pictorial information into words. Each question has one correct answer. The question, "What else can you tell me about it?" is "open-ended," but it is immediately followed by another that requires a single correct answer.

In contrast, this kindergarten teacher stimulates a greater variety of responses after making popcorn with the children:

Miss Bell: If you didn't watch me, how did you know we were popping corn?
  Carol: I heard it.
  Kevin: You could hear it.
    Bob: When the popcorn comes out of that shell, it hits up on the lid [of the pan] and falls back down. That's how come you hear it pop.
Miss Bell: What's happened to the part that pops? What happens to the kernel?
  Kevin: Miss Bell, the corn just turned inside out.
  Carol: Mine looks like Mickey Mouse.
    Bob: It looks like the kernel blew apart.

Here, the children have drawn on their memories, described sensory experiences, interpreted what they saw by making relationships, and in one case, a child analyzed the movement of corn kernels inside the pan.

The second teacher's choice of activity led children to make their own observations and lent itself to the formulation of questions that promoted thinking. Miss Bell hears, responds to, and assesses children's descriptions and interpretations because she has asked appropriate questions. This way of studying children may be facilitated by the use of audiotapes, since many schools now have tape recorders. Teachers can check on the kinds of questions they ask by recording a lesson and listening to it afterwards.

There are a number of published systems for categorizing teachers' questions.[1] Most of them differentiate among questions that require a "low-level" and a "high-level" of thinking. When teachers ask low-level questions, they require children to recall or recognize something, for example, the name of a familiar object or the repetition of a word or phrase. In using high-level questions, teachers expect children to do additional thinking, perhaps to explain why they gave a particular answer, to observe differences, or to solve a problem. Teachers also may ask about children's values, whether they feel good or bad about something, or how they judge the actions of a storybook character.

Tutorial Techniques

Some children are eager to answer all questions a teacher may pose, whether they are "test" questions or questions with answers unknown to the teacher. These children appear to reflect on their actions even without the stimulus of the teacher's question. They freely raise their own questions and, in a sense, "take charge" of some of their learning.

Other children, who for various reasons show less enthusiasm for learning in a center or school, are in greater need of support from teachers. Recognizing this need, Blank has formulated what she terms a "dialogue approach" to developing children's thinking.[2] The dialogue occurs between one adult and one child and depends heavily on the teacher's ability to ask appropriate questions, interpret the child's response—or lack of response—and to follow up with further questioning.

Although the tutorial is often impractical for teachers who must deal with many children at once, its principles apply to many questioning sequences, whether they occur between teacher and child or in a large group.

The child who has not had many experiences at home or elsewhere that encourage him or her to be a curious or active learner, or who is anxious or withdrawn, may do well with a tutorial. The adult provides intellectual support by focusing the child's attention, asking questions, specifying instructions, and so on. The teacher also supports the child emotionally. What the child gains in increased self-confidence and willingness to trust teachers is clearly of equal value to any measurable cognitive gains.

Another benefit of a tutorial approach is the specificity that results with the teacher's and child's contributions to a lesson. Lessons may be tape-recorded, and questions later may be analyzed. Close analysis of tutors' questions probably will show that purposeful questions can be both low-level and high-level, as the following examples from Blank demonstrate:

Dialogue	*Interpretation*
Teacher—Did you ever see this book?	The teacher and child had read this book together about a month previously.
Child—One time.	
Teacher—That's right. We read this together a long time ago. Sometimes I like to go over things we did a long time ago. We call this book *Are You My Mother?* Do you remember the name of the person who writes a book?	
Child—Uh, uh (shakes head).	

Teacher—Do you think he's called a doctor?

Only a single clearly incorrect alternative is offered. Multiple alternatives are avoided (is it a doctor or an author?) because the teacher knows of this child's tendency to unthinkingly select any options when several are offered. In addition, doctor is used rather than pilot since all the children in the school were well acquainted with doctors through their medical checkups. The teacher could not be sure that the child had a comparable knowledge of pilots.

Child—No, he checks people?

This spontaneous elaboration is a marked sign of progress in this child. Nevertheless, even when she was correct she was so unsure of herself that she phrased many statements as questions.[3]

The teacher's knowledge of this child's style of responding justified her use of questions with a single answer. In contrast, another teacher, in an equally directive fashion, offers a different child greater opportunities to extend her thinking.

Teacher	*Child*
Do you remember what I asked you to do with the paper and sponge?	Uh-huh. Wet them.
Fine. Then do that.	(Wets toweling and sponge) They are full of water.
Do you need all that water?	(Shakes head to indicate "no.")
What could you do to get rid of the water that you don't need?	(Squeezes water from both sponge and paper.)
What did you do?	The water comes out.
That's fine, Julie. You really didn't need all that water (they return to the table). Now, I'd like you to draw something for me on the blackboard.	
What color would you like to use?	What color?
Green is fine. Draw some green lines for me.	Green (and selects green crayon).
	I'll make some big ones (she proceeds to draw).
Okay. We can work with big ones. Oh! Those are very big lines. What will happen if you wipe the sponge on those lines?	I don't know.

Think about it, Julie. If you put this
sponge over your lines and wipe them,
what will happen?   (Moves sponge over drawing.)
(Holds sponge down to prevent child
from lifting it.) If I lift up the sponge,
what color is going to be on the sponge?   White.
Why white?   Green.
Tell me why you said green. Why do
you think it will be green?   'Cause I wipe it off.
What did you wipe off?   The green color.
Let's see if you're right. (Lifts sponge)
Green! You're right. Very good.[4]

The teacher asks Julie to recall information ("Do you remember what I
asked you to do with the paper and sponge?"); make predictions ("What
will happen if you wipe the sponge on those lines?"); and describe a
phenomenon ("What's happening to the lines, Julie?").

Such carefully structured questioning, of course, is not appropriate at
all times nor is it appropriate for all children, but we believe Blank's point
is well made: children do not necessarily learn because adults provide
opportunities for them to use and explore materials. The children
themselves must engage in thinking about what they do. For most
children, the teacher's intervention by means of thoughtful questions—
whether narrow or broad in focus, numerous or few—is essential to
learning.

Following Through

Whether a sequence of questions is precisely planned for a tutorial or
grows out of an unplanned encounter between teachers and children,
teachers who follow a child's response with additional questions enable
the child to pursue a line of thought.[5] We suggest these general ways to
find out more about the child's thinking:

1. Ask for elaboration: "What else can you see in the terrarium? You've
   never seen an animal like that before. Why don't you tell us how it
   looks?"
2. Ask for children's opinions: "What can we do to keep the terrarium
   clean? How will we decide who'll do that?"
3. Encourage other responses that will relate to what another child has
   already said: "David thinks this stick is longer than the one in the
   terrarium. What can we do to find out if it is, Tracy?"

4. Ask for an analysis: "The milk in this jar does look different today from the way it looked yesterday. What things did we do to it that might've made it look this way?"
5. Ask for an interpretation: "That's right, the captain got mad. Why do you think the captain in this story got mad at Sam? Why did Sam stay on the ship even after the captain got mad?"

Each way of building on children's responses carries with it potential hazards. Questions for elaboration may be asked for the sake of asking questions. Children may not add new information on their own because they have stated all that occurs to them: to add more would be to look for minutiae. Soliciting a child's opinions and views about other children's responses may encourage children to give their own responses simply to be "different." Or, on the other hand, it provides an opportunity for children to echo each other, as often happens in groups of preschoolers.

Questions intended to foster analytic thinking need to be realistic. Children should have enough prior information to perform the analysis and enough prior experience to understand reasons underlying a character's behavior. Questions dealing with interpretation should push the child to make inferences and not to repeat what has been explicitly presented.

Teachers' questions are among their most powerful means to find out about children's thoughts and feelings. Questions should, therefore, be posed judiciously; they should be both purposeful and substantive. A question based on recalling simple information may be useful for one child, while for another the same question is superfluous.

Questions for Teachers

Teachers may want to ask *themselves* these questions when planning for and reflecting upon what they have asked their children: Do I know the purpose of the questions I ask? Are my questions appropriate for the differing cognitive abilities and emotional states of individual children? Do I speak and behave in a way that encourages children to say what is on their minds? Or do I suggest by my facial expression and in other ways that I want a specific response or that I prefer some kinds of responses to others?

The questions teachers pose to children during lessons are one important source of information. Next, we look at other sources teachers can use to discover more about the children they teach.

INFORMAL SELF-REPORTS

Each school day presents the teacher with dozens, or possibly hundreds, of opportunities to ask children about their views, their thoughts, their feelings, events in their lives. Some of these opportunities come as children arrive at a center, on the playground, or during class discussions when work is being planned or evaluated. Teachers who make the most of these opportunities obtain added knowledge of what goes on in the mind of the child. This is directly helpful in planning fruitful learning activities. Teachers are not so intent on the material they have to present to the children that they cannot *listen* to reactions to it. Indeed, in obtaining self-reports from children, the question asked—important though it is— often is less crucial than the teacher's comprehension of the answer the child gives.

Working with children involves so much telling, so much talking to children, that teachers sometimes minimize or overlook the listening aspects of the task. Or they may listen selectively, so that with very young children teachers mainly attend to those who are most able verbally. In the primary grades, unless they hear the "correct" answer, they may pay little attention to what the child does say. Conversely, when they hear the expected response they may not consider its significance for the child. Teachers who are good listeners are in tune not only with the child's words but with emotions and feelings.

GROUP DISCUSSION

On many occasions, as the teacher works with a class, the youngsters reveal what they know, what interests them, and what they value. When working with young children, group discussions are most effective when groups are of the appropriate size. The primary grade teacher, under some circumstances, may be comfortable talking about a group activity with twenty-four children, but the nursery school teacher may want to talk to no more than one third of that number at one time.

One of the teacher's general goals in group discussions is to encourage children to listen to one another. To demonstrate in an enjoyable way the consequences of not listening, one teacher of a combined first and second grade played the old game "gossip," which involves a circle of children. One child whispers a message to the next child, and that child in turn tells the next child. Generally, the child who hears the message last hears something very different from the original utterance. In this group's case, the original message, "The Pilgrims and the Indians had dinner to-gether," became "Billy went through the river."

The teacher followed the game with a discussion about why the last message was not like the first. Children's first responses reflected their knowledge of social rules and what they thought the teacher *wanted* to hear. They said, "We didn't listen enough," and, "We shouldn't laugh." To indicate that she was concerned with the children's understanding of the process of communication, the teacher then asked, "What could we do so that the message stays the same when it goes around the circle?" Several children repeated answers like, "Listen better," and, "Be qui-eter," until one second grader suggested that they divide the class into two small groups. By pursuing her original question in a variety of ways, the teacher directed the children toward solving a problem. The teacher clarified what seemed like a question about appropriate classroom behav-ior so that it could be understood as a problem related to how people communicate in groups.

Planning for Group Activities

In order that children have opportunities to reveal what they know and what interests them, teachers engage them in planning their own activi-ties. At the beginning of the school day, the teacher of preschoolers may want to organize a short walk around the neighborhood. Questions to the children may be limited to such things as "Who wants to go for a walk with me?" If more than a small number want to go, she may ask how they can fairly choose five or six children. A day-care teacher, who has a station wagon at his or her disposal, may casually ask the group who would like to go to the supermarket to buy supplies for a cooking project. They may then have a brief discussion about ingredients to purchase.

In the primary grades, teachers may want to engage children in the details of planning. A group of second graders who live in a rural area, after studying the animals in their terrarium, may arrange a trip to a nearby farm. The teacher may ask such things as, "How can we find out if we can visit the farm next week?" "What animals do you think we'll see there?" or "What kinds of things do you want to see at Mrs. Kole's farm?" These questions tell the teacher something about what they know, what they have learned recently, and what they imagine a farm to be. Similar questions may be asked before a trip to a museum.

The next set of questions may have to do with the organization of the trip itself. Children will respond to, "How are we going to get to the farm?" or, "Whose mother or father would want to visit the farm with us?'' A question like "What shall we take with us?'' will encourage children to think of the concrete needs they'll have in the course of a day away from home, center, or school. Some children might say "lunch,'' "something to drink,'' while others will suggest a snakebite kit if they have camped or hiked in the past.

Planning for Learning

An appraisal of where children are in their experience is essential in planning for new learning, whether it is for a social activity or something academic. A preschool teacher who would like to begin an informal unit on growing plants may simply bring a seedling to school one day and take careful note of children's reactions. The teacher may keep a large piece of paper and marker next to it and write down what children say when he or she asks such things as, "How do we plant gardens?'' or "Do you know how you could grow one of these?'' or "Who has plants at home?'' The teacher may find, depending on where he or she is teaching, that many children have never handled a seed or soil before. On the basis of informal questioning, he or she may decide to provide potting soil and seeds so that the children will be able to observe the growth of different kinds of plants even if they cannot grasp the reasons for growth.

The primary grade teacher who wants to expose children to the process of growth may use the same technique of bringing in a seedling to the classroom but extend the unit considerably so that children begin to understand the complex interaction between the seed, the soil, sunlight, and other elements. The teacher's questions will encourage children to observe details, record what they see in drawing or in writing, and discuss causes and effects. Part of the planning for the sequence of activities and care of the plants may be done jointly by the teacher and children. When children make suggestions, they reveal what knowledge they already have as well as what values they hold about sharing or distributing responsibilities.

Teaching Academic Skills

As we pointed out in chapter 3, the foundation for learning academic skills is laid long before a child attends a center, kindergarten, or first grade. Children's experiences with people and things from the day of their birth later enable them to learn material that adults break down into subject areas, such as math, reading, and social studies. The concept of "plural," necessary in the understanding of both speech and print, for example, begins to develop when the child recognizes more than one person or wants two or more crackers.

Classroom teachers often assume that most children have had certain experiences that lead to a basic understanding of the concept of number and what a word is. That is, they assume that a child has a basic understanding of symbols and how they work.

From this perspective, the child's early play is a contribution to later ability to deal with symbols, such as words in print. Two-year-old Jay, who has been in the kitchen watching a parent prepare pie crust with a rolling pin, goes to his room and returns with a toy log. He has seen how the rolling pin and log are similar and has the notion that *one can stand for the other*. Similarly, Anne, who is three, decides that a large, discarded carton next to the playground of her day-care center will serve well as a house for herself and her friend.

The child's early conversations with parents and other adults also strengthen the basis for academics. For example, the following dialogue between an adult and a three-year-old shows how some questions quite casually and naturally lay the groundwork for later, more formal contacts with academic material:

> *Mrs. Brown:* Want to hear a story, Tim?
> *Tim:* Where my book is?
> *Mrs. Brown.* Do you know where you left it? It's over there on the shelf. Go get it.
> *Tim:* You read it, right?
> *Mrs. Brown:* OK, this is a story about a monkey. What's this a picture of, Tim? Know what this is?
> *Tim:* The monkey's house. He's sleeping.

The adult asks questions that encourage the child to translate the picture into words, yet there is no effort made to have the child actually read the letters or words.

In the realm of mathematics, children develop a concept of number without direct instruction. A four-year-old may spontaneously match colored chips and Popsicle sticks to make "lollipops" and demonstrate an understanding of one-to-one correspondence.

In the classroom, individual reporting in small or large groups frequently is used in the direct teaching of academic skills. In math, the teacher gives the children a problem to be solved. For a group of four seven-year-olds, he or she indicates who should do the recording of information and states that each child should be able to solve the problem in a different way. Thus the teacher learns about the kinds of mathematical thinking the children can do, and can plan for the subsequent experiences they need to move toward more mature thinking.

A first-grade teacher may appraise children's understanding of number by using small cubes or blocks. The child who does not know that the person with four blocks has more blocks than the person with two is most likely not ready to work problems with paper and pencil in a setting that provides no objects to support the child's thinking.

A second-grade class learning about metric measurement may also benefit from working directly with wooden rods of different lengths. The teacher may have a general question in mind, "How can we represent one meter?" The children's handling of the materials helps them discover the relationships among different units of measurement so that they will understand metric equivalencies and not simply be able to recite them.

On the other hand, Doug, a child in the second grade who does not even glance at the chips the teacher has distributed to answer the subtraction problems put before him, already is able to manipulate numbers "in his head." He may benefit from questions that lead him to see how addition is related to subtraction, or he may be ready to move on to the basis of division.

Additionally, in the primary grades children report on their academic progress whenever they read. They demonstrate their own strategies to arrive at the pronunciation or the meaning of a new word, or they show their understanding of a sentence by paraphrasing it. From these informal reports, the teacher can derive considerable information about the children who need help in recognizing new words, or those who need help comprehending what is read to them or what they themselves read. The teacher's questions, as in other content area lessons, vary; the questions test the recall of facts as well as prompt the expression of feelings.

In any situation in which children are asked to report on their own ways of thinking or feeling, the question of the effects of sharing with the group may arise. To what extent does hearing the other children's solutions to problems help or hinder the individuals in the group? Particularly in the academic areas, unless the teacher is clear about which of the procedures suggested leads to *correct* answers and why, some children may be misled or confused. Sometimes children respond much more to the personality of a classmate than to the content of his or her report. Whether they accept or reject the classmate's ideas may depend less on the validity of thinking than on their feelings about the individual.

Identifying Interests and Feelings

Many teachers use class discussion to provide children with opportunities to identify their own interests and feelings. Such discussions frequently relate to children's out-of-school activities. From these discussions, the teacher may deduce a good bit about the content and quality of the children's experiences. One kindergarten teacher, for example, noted that all of her children made frequent references to programs they had seen on television. Some of them, however, talked repeatedly about the same programs, while others seemed to cover a considerably wider range. Certain children appeared confused about what they had seen. Some reported a series of blood-and-thunder incidents that seemed to have little connection except in the children's own fantasy. In contrast, others reported in a surprisingly factual way. They knew what they had seen and on what program it had appeared.

Unless the teacher is alert to ways of using information gained from such sharing periods, they often deteriorate into aimless and repetitive recitals of what children have done or seen. Some children may use the situation for personal aggrandizement, developing elaborate and occasionally fictitious tales of their own or their family's exploits, while others with more restricted opportunities or less vivid imaginations sit idly.

The question the teacher poses, of course, often determines how meaningful the discussion will be. If he or she asks a large group, "What are you going to do on Thanksgiving Day?" children most likely will echo each other because their activities will, in fact, be similar. Or, if one child is doing something exotic, other children will be doing even more exotic things. A four-year-old at "circle time" announced that he and his family were going on a plane trip to Hawaii, which led other children to say, "We are, too," and, "Yeah, at Christmas, we're going to Hawaii."

By contrast, the same circle of nineteen four-year-olds became engrossed in hearing about Jean's upcoming stay in the hospital. Jean was to have her tonsils removed. She already had visited the hospital and had a suitcase packed for her visit. Because of the children's evident interest in this experience, the next day the teacher read a story about a young child's visit to the hospital. After the story was read, one child asked Jean if she were scared, and others wanted to know if her mother or father would be going with her. The teacher remarked that many children go to the hospital for a short while and asked who else had been in one. She guided the discussion so that the children's interests were pursued while their feelings about illness were expressed and fears about hospitals allayed.

Feelings, acknowledged or not, surround everything the child does. Some teachers find that they can use class discussion to help children identify or clarify their own feelings. As we already have indicated, deeply disturbed children have overwhelming feelings of anxiety and hostility that can only be openly admitted under the protection of therapy. At the same time, however, the reality of some emotional aspects of living can be faced directly with children on many occasions. In every class, the children experience varying degrees of elation and disappointment, warm affection and open conflict, confidence and timidity. At times it is best to live through these experiences without talking about them as when a child does not want to discuss negative feelings toward an older sibling. But sometimes teachers sense that it is well for children to talk over their feelings.

One of the difficulties in dealing directly with feelings is that the children may believe that only the expression of certain kinds of feeling is permissible. One teacher who was trying to help the members of her class think through some of the reasons for their group conflicts found that they all spoke in platitudes about "taking turns" and "being quiet when another kid talks." Not until they were sure of her sincerity and trustworthiness did their expressions seem to reflect real feelings. When the teacher's youngsters began to put their convictions about social living in such terms as "Don't punch a kid unless you gotta," she felt that she was beginning to get something genuine.

The teacher also needs to recognize that what is most troublesome to an adult does not necessarily bother the children in the same ways.

Children from three first-grade classes were shown a photograph of two older boys having a fight. In the picture, the boys had a good grip on each other, and one was pulling the hair of his opponent. After a discussion about what was happening in the picture, and what they thought might be the cause of the fight, the teacher asked, "Why do children of your age fight?" These were some of the responses:

> Sometimes we just don't like each other, and so we fight.
> We fight when someone else starts up. We like to fight. One hits the other.
> Somebody pushes you or takes a punch at you for no reason at all.
> We have an argument about the game to play.
> Sometimes it's just a "fooling fight."

The teacher felt that the children were indicating by their comments that they thought it all right to fight, and that it was something almost all children did. One child's answer, "Sometimes it's just 'fooling,' " was echoed by several others when they said they simply liked to fight.

Another strong motive was the defense of possessions. Typical comments were, "Sometimes someone takes our stuff. We fight to get it back," or "The one boy took the other boy's ball so he socked him, and then they were fighting." Other children referred to name-calling and to others' failure to "play fair," while some implied that "might makes right."

The technique of presenting the group with a picture, a film, or a story depicting a problem situation has frequently been used as a means to elicit children's discussion of feelings. It protects troubled children because ostensibly they talk about the character in the picture or the story, not about themselves. At the same time, it offers all the children in the group a chance to recognize the variety of emotional responses that may be attached to a single situation. It also provides an opportunity for children to begin to develop some understanding, however rudimentary, of the reasons people behave as they do. Teachers, too, gain insight into the motivations children attribute to themselves.

We caution, however, that different ethnic and cultural groups—and different families within these groups—may hold various attitudes toward the expression of feelings before a class or the teacher. A Mexican-American child, for example, might express himself or herself very differently from an Anglo-American or an Asian-American. Some families raise their children to be reserved about their feelings except with other family members and to guard the privacy of their emotional lives, while other families encourage a general openness and candor.

TEACHER-CHILD CONFERENCES

In centers and preschools, teachers often have opportunities to talk with children individually. Many of these talks, though brief, take on the character of an informal interview or conference and provide an excellent means for learning how a child thinks and feels. Teachers gather such information in numerous ways. They may talk with individuals as they walk to a park or playground; or opportunities may arise at the carpentry or art table.

Teachers in the primary grades who make relatively little use of group discussion to ask children about themselves use informal interviews with children to serve the same purpose. Others use them to supplement discussions. So much of classroom teaching involves dealing with groups that teachers often forget how many contacts they have with individual children during the course of the day. Teachers attentive to these contacts may record them in the form of anecdotes, even though the contacts are irregular.

The teacher's primary purpose in these conferences, regardless of the child's age, is to find out something from the child about himself or herself. This may be information about out-of-school experiences, why the child seems "out of sorts," the techniques used to solve a particular problem, the interpretation given to what is read, views and feelings about something that has happened at center or school, an evaluation of a piece of work, an estimate of what can be accomplished next, or an indication of some interest to be pursued further.

The minutes in a school day cannot be stretched indefinitely. There are limits to the amount of time a teacher, particularly with a large group, can find to give to such individual conferences. Yet many teachers do manage to learn much about their children's thinking and feeling in brief moments in which they concentrate on one child.

If the child is to feel comfortable and safe in these interviews, and his or her responses are to be truly representative, certain conditions should prevail. When conferences of this kind are customary procedures in which all children participate, they are unlikely to seem threatening. Some teachers routinely arrange for short talks with a certain number of individuals during particular periods of the day. For example, they move from one child's desk to another during work periods. A system of jotted notes on cards insures that all youngsters have their turn. Other teachers prefer to confer with children less often and to take more time for each interview. In either case, the children know that all children will be seen, and that no one of them is being singled out for special and perhaps unfavorable attention.

Routinely arranged interviews need not be perfunctory. Despite the complexities involved in *listening* carefully and attentively to one child without losing awareness of the rest of the group, many teachers have found that such conferences do eventually "pay off." Primary teachers who have individualized their teaching so that most of the children have their own work to do find it best to listen daily to children reading or to ask them how their portion of the class science project is progressing. The teachers have developed an effective way of keeping records to learn more about individual youngsters, help them learn more effectively, and, in turn, enable each child to work more independently.

Other kinds of interviews are not part of the daily routine but may be revealing about the child's academic performance and social behavior. Children who are bilingual when they come to a school or center make their own decisions about which language they speak with others who are bilingual. If teachers would like information about the children's attitudes toward the languages they speak, they may conduct informal interviews. The conversation that follows occurred between an adult and a kindergarten child, born in the United States, who spoke Spanish and English:

> *Miss Smith:* Do you know how come you speak Spanish some of the time and English some of the time?
>
> *Rafael:* Because some people don't know Spanish, and some people don't know English. And my mother doesn't want them to speak English.
>
> *Miss Smith:* How come she doesn't? Do you know?
>
> *Rafael:* 'Cuz, we ain't Americans.
>
> *Miss Smith:* Oh, you're not Americans. What are you?
>
> *Rafael:* A Mexican.
>
> *Miss Smith:* And what do they speak in Mexico?
>
> *Rafael:* In Spanish.[6]

This six-year-old was aware of his ability to speak two languages as well as of his ethnicity. A bilingual teacher interested in promoting the child's use of both languages receives support from the child himself—and his family.

On the other hand, there are children who see English, and not another language, as the language to be used in school. A different bilingual kindergartner had this exchange with his bilingual teacher at the art table:

> *Miss Gómez:* When you're at home, do you speak with your mother in English or in Spanish?
>
> *Miguel:* In Spanish.
>
> *Miss Gómez:* In Spanish?
>
> *Miguel:* Yeah.
>
> *Miss Gómez:* And when you were in your four-year-old school, did you speak in English or in Spanish, at school?
>
> *Miguel:* I speak in Spanish when I was in the four-class.
>
> *Miss Gómez:* Uh-huh. How come you don't speak in Spanish here?
>
> *Miguel:* We-ell—I don't want to.

Such interviews not only provide reports about the child's attitude toward his or her languages but also suggest what the teacher might consider in presenting lessons in one or the other language. The second child may appear uncooperative when a lesson is presented in Spanish; his behavior may be explained, however, by the feelings he has about a language he knows is not spoken by most people he encounters, rather than by a lack of ability.

Interviews often are more difficult when the teacher seeks the child's view and feeling on some incident that relates to a conflict with peers or the transgression of some rule. To give the child an opportunity to describe "what happened" as he or she saw it and to listen in such a way that the youngster reveals feelings freely is a real test of the teacher's ability to deal with self-reports. Sometimes such an interview of necessity must take place while the child still is upset, and it also may involve listening to several children at the same time. An anecdote from a teacher who was concerned about a small, volatile three-year-old in a day-care center shows what might be gained from such an interview.

Another argument centering around Jamie. Jamie was in tears again when I went up and asked him what was the matter. He shouted, "They won't let me have the truck!" I asked, "Do you know why they won't?" His answer, "I'm little and they won't let me have my turn, just 'cuz I'm little!" When I asked the two older children what the problem was they stated that Jamie didn't want a turn; he just came up and took Kris's truck.

In discussing this anecdote at the weekly staff meeting, Mr. McConnell revealed that he had thought other children took advantage of Jamie, but that perhaps he had been wrong. Jamie seemed to assert himself despite his size, according to the other children, by following his own rules. The teacher would be alert for other similar incidents in the future.

With somewhat older children, problems and conflicts may take on a different form. A second-grade teacher provided another example of an interview in which children seemed to feel free to express their feelings and concerns. The teacher received an important clue to understanding the child's situation.

Stormy, who I think is easygoing and not very conspicuous, was being told to stop bothering two or three other children. When I asked why there was so much noise, Neill volunteered that Stormy kept pushing their desks around with her foot so that they couldn't write. I asked Stormy if she had been doing that, and she said "Yeah," reluctantly. I later noticed that Stormy had stopped bothering the others but had also stopped doing any work. I asked her before lunch if she'd talk with me at my desk, and I asked if she might be feeling sick. She said she was fine. She was quiet for a while and then added that she didn't like to hear about Neill's father's birthday. I asked her why not, and she said that her father just moved out of the house.

Teachers can also have conferences with children, based on formal interview schedules. These can be adapted, depending on the age of the children and depending on the classroom situation. One such schedule has been used by researchers studying open classrooms, who wanted to learn about the children's perceptions of the classroom and of their relationships with peers and teachers. The following are examples of questions from the interview, made up of 34 items, called "And What Do You Think?"

Activities/Involvement
(The child's view of the activities in the room and the extent to which s/he engages in the activities are the focus here.)
—Tell me all the things that *you* (emphasis) can do in your classroom.
—Are there some things other kids do that you don't?
—What are the things that you have to do?
Peer Relations
(Inquiries into this area center around whether the child works with other children in a helpful or collaborative manner and whether the child sees this as beneficial.)
—Do you ever work or do things with other kids?
—Does it help you to work with others?
—Do you help other children do things in the classroom?
Classroom As a Whole
(Inquiries into this area encourage the child to express feelings about the classroom and to suggest changes.)
—What are the things you can't do in your classroom?
—Tell me something you can't do that you would like to do.
—Do you have a favorite place in your classroom? Where?[7]

As with other questioning techniques, teachers use instruments like this judiciously. Children will vary considerably in their willingness to respond to some items and will elaborate on responses only when they feel at ease with the teacher.

CASUAL CONVERSATIONS

When teachers sense that a child is troubled about something, they often do not wish to invade the child's privacy by direct questioning. They may get some clues from the usual conferences. In addition, important information may be derived from casual, unarranged conversations with the child. Teachers do not initiate such a conversation with the idea of asking the child about himself or herself. It may grow out of a simple request the teacher makes of the child. Often the child is the initiator. But if teachers listen attentively, they may learn as much as, or more than, they would in a planned interview.

A three-year-old, for example, became upset when one of her teachers asked if she'd like to help "clean up" the housekeeping corner. In the conversation that followed, the child, Carol, revealed that she "didn't like cleaning up anymore" because she had a new baby sister who never helped. The teacher was unsure that Carol actually had such responsibilities at home, but she knew that Carol was having difficulty adjusting to the new family member.

A five-year-old in a nursery school was a challenge to her teachers. Although she was clearly capable, it was difficult to engage her in the typical activities of the school. One of her teachers, Mrs. Goodwin, wrote:

> Kaye initially seemed like a quiet and cooperative child. She did not easily talk with other children, but she did nothing that would conflict with their activities, and was more than willing to do what teachers asked of her. One day I saw her near the water table and asked if she had ever used a funnel. She said, "No, but my mother has one." Then I asked her if she'd like to use the funnels we had, and she said very deliberately, "No, I don't think so. I think I'd rather talk with you."

This teacher realized that Kaye spoke easily with all the staff in a surprisingly adult way. "It certainly is!" was one of the expressions she used frequently. Mrs. Goodwin was not sure whether Kaye's verbal facility masked a lack of confidence in her ability to socialize with other children or in her motor abilities, but the staff later decided to make an effort to engage Kaye in group activities.

Mealtime in centers or schools is an excellent setting to hear child-initiated conversations. Although teachers are attending to the group in general, individual children often volunteer information that they would not mention in more formal contexts. A typical conversation in a center, involving six or seven children from three to six years of age, revolved around Thad, whose dog was lost. Eventually, the other children chose their own topics while the teacher asked Thad pertinent questions and consequently learned about his liking for and interest in animals.

Another teacher, who was curious about the interests of Alex, a second-grade child, gained important insight from his response to a remark she made to him.

> I noticed that whenever we had visitors in our classroom, Alex approached them and told them how many pages he'd done in his reading workbooks.

When we got several new trade books from the library, I asked him if he wanted to read one after finishing his worksheets. I said, "You might have read this book before, but if you haven't, maybe you'd like to look at it today." Alex said, "Oh, no. My dad keeps saying I should run around instead of reading so much."

The teacher realized that for Alex the practice exercises he completed did not constitute reading, but the workbook sheets still gave him a good deal of satisfaction. She wondered if she should have a talk with Alex's parents soon, and if it would be wise to provide occasional chances for children to "run around."

WRITTEN REPORTS

Asking children to tell about themselves in writing, as compared with asking them to tell about themselves orally, has both advantages and disadvantages. Even at the early childhood level, teachers may find that a few children appear to express themselves more freely on paper than in direct conversation. Other children find writing laborious and are hampered by limited spelling skills. What the children write becomes tedious for them without being informative for the teacher. Some writing, however, seems appropriate, at least for second graders. And teachers may want to help younger children tape-record or dictate their reports.

Logs

Some teachers have found that logs kept by the children provide another useful way of keeping in touch with the children's thinking and feeling. When children work at learning centers in small groups in social studies or science, the log provides the teacher with a continuing record of the accomplishments of each group. The log may consist primarily of lists of words or phrases that capture what children have observed. It also may be an oral record, dictated by children and audiotaped.

Teachers of preschoolers and kindergartners often keep "word banks," which consist of words the children ask teachers to write on individual cards; these word banks also can serve as a log of interests. The child whose bank contains "Motor Mouse" and "sports car" has interests different from the one who asks the teacher to write "wizard," "kingdom," and "magic." (A similar technique for assessing children's interests and progress in the primary grades is presented in chapter 8.) When children become readers and writers themselves, such collections of words not only reveal interests but also enhance their spelling vocabulary.

Logs in which children report on the day's happenings offer some clues to what matters to them. Compare the following two reports on the same Tuesday in a primary grade:

> *Susan:* We had our Halloween play. That was all that was important on Tuesday.
>
> *Larry:* Tuesday we had everything we should of, except in the afternoon we had the Halloween play.

Larry's inclusion of the "should of" suggests a somewhat different attitude from Susan's towards the importance of the play.

Even such slight differences in perception as these point up an interesting problem that arises whenever children attempt to evaluate their own work. Children who have had ostensibly identical experiences may emphasize different aspects in reporting on them. Some may report that they have learned something that corresponds with the teacher's expectations for their learning. Others do not mention this at all. We cannot tell whether this means that they did not learn as the teacher anticipated, or merely that that particular learning did not strike them as important.

Interest Questionnaires

Recognizing that children's happiness and success in school are related to their interests, teachers often seek suitable ways of studying interests. With younger children there are advantages in teacher-constructed devices, since these can be made to fit a particular school situation.

One instrument designed to discover children's attitudes and feelings, as well as to gain specific information about their interests, is the Interest Finder. Several questions relate to their likes and dislikes about both in-school and out-of-school activities. The responses not only indicate the children's interests but also provide some insight into their individuality.

The Interest Finder, with various modifications, has been used in all grades, from kindergarten through high school. Following are responses a seven-year-old made to items on the Interest Finder that are most relevant to her school experiences:

> *Name:* Nancy   *Age:* seven
> *Date:* April 30 *Teacher:* Miss Giardi

What I'd like to learn more about at school:
  birds
  plants
  flowers

What I don't care to study about:
  experimenting
  gardening, working with flowers

What I like best in our school:
  I like reading.
  I like art.

What I like least or dislike most at school:
  I like everything at school.

The most interesting thing I have done at our school during the past week or so:
  Dyeing eggs

One of the places I especially like to go in our city:
  I like to go uptown.

Why?
  I like to see all the things.[8]

A child's responses to the Interest Finder may be studied in several ways. The initial query the teacher should make is, "Did the child understand the questions?" In Nancy's case, the teacher must consider the possibility that Nancy's answer about what she "does not care about" is somehow influenced by the previous question. Perhaps she is still reporting on what she wishes to know more about. Or the first response may be faked to please the teacher, while the second represents the real feeling. Thus a second question the teacher needs to ask is, "Does the child appear to be answering according to some preconceived notion of what the teacher may expect?" Nancy's expansive liking for school may reflect her idea of what she ought to feel, or she may genuinely feel rather positive toward it.

The personal significance of the child's responses can be studied in relation to the teacher's knowledge about the child. Responses that are different from those of the other children in the group may indicate greater or lesser maturity, differences in background, or emotional concerns.

As with other available information, teachers can relate items on interest questionnaires to their knowledge of the children. Where there are discrepancies between what children say and what teachers have observed, as in indications of liked and disliked activities, teachers may wish to study the situations further to see whether the youngsters are asking for help or encouragement or whether questionnaire responses were only momentary whims. A question relating to "what I want to be" may throw some light on persons important to children and perhaps reveals something of how they see themselves. All such information is most useful for teachers when they look for patterns and realistically modify their curriculum in accordance with their findings.

Journals

Journals are another means for children to reveal their thoughts, feelings, and views of themselves. For young children, a journal is difficult to keep in the formal sense since they are generally unable to write with ease. Children can, however, be helped to tape-record, dictate to a teacher, or write short descriptions of what they have accomplished or what is currently on their minds. Such journals record past activities and also are a record of children's interests.

Many teachers combine information of this nature with drawing or painting. Journals differ from most expressive activities incorporating art and language not so much in content as in the teachers' use of them.

In one school for kindergarten through second grade, teachers valued highly the children's journals, consisting of drawings and writing. One teacher said of them:

> I tend to see the journals as a core to our whole teaching. The child has a picture or idea about something that interests him. . . . They tend to write out of their own experiences and don't use them in terms of an idea book, not at all out of their learning. The journals have become a very personal type of thing.[9]

In their analysis of the journals, teachers chose to study specific aspects, such as "organization," "language structure," and "themes." A theme was a "recurring subject or attitude or feeling or idea or value judgment."

For the teachers at this school one of the major purposes of the journals was to serve as a record of interests. Recurring themes, such as references to television characters or to animals, provided material for the development of curriculum related to expressed interests.

A kindergartner in this group dictated this for his journal, after drawing a picture, then copied the words himself:

> This is my Mom. She is coming back Friday. I am going home. I have a new baby brother.

This was written by a second grade illustrator-author:

Talking Book
The Talking Book a book that comes from another planet When you open
it up to read it it reads it for you.

Teachers reading these learn about important events in the kindergartner's life at the same time that they learn something of the child's
feelings. The second grader reveals an interest in a special kind of book,
which he imaginatively describes in riddle-like form.

When journals are accumulated over a three-year period, as these were,
they also provide a picture of the child as a developing person.

A preschool teacher collected similar "journals" from her children by
asking what they wanted to be. The dictated captions were brief, but they
indicated something, however transitory, of the children's interests and
views of themselves. Figures 4.2 and 4.3 show two such journals.

SUMMARY

A child's development and learning in center or school are, we know,
highly individual. No matter how supportive the child's peers and
teachers are, how exciting the environment or the material to be learned,
how capable and sensitive the teacher, no matter how quick or how dull
the child is, or whether he or she meets the expectations set, each child
learns selectively. Some of what is learned is meaningful and incorporated
in such a fashion that the child never forgets. Much is quickly sloughed
off. He or she learns more than what teachers make available or present
in lessons. The child's pleasure in accomplishment, the warm acceptance
of another child or the teacher, hateful feelings aroused by competition or
too harsh treatment, fears about his or her adequacy—all of these are
concomitant to intellectual achievements.

If teachers could know how a child perceives the activities in which he
or she participates or the learning expected in lessons and could understand what facilitates and what blocks it, their teaching would be more
effective. But the complexity of human development and learning and of
the human self are such that no teacher gets more than glimpses of the
inner self of children, from their self-reports or any other means.

We come again to the artistry of the teacher. He or she may use many
means of asking children about themselves and may heed what they tell
about themselves in group discussions, directed lessons, in interviews, in

FIGURE 4.2. JOURNALS *Shows how a boy in kindergarten revealed his interests through this drawing and through words, written down by his teacher.*

FIGURE 4.3. JOURNALS *Another kindergartener painted "WOW" and dictated, "The 'R' stands for Regina—the Movie Star!"*

journals. But whether or not this information makes any difference to the children's learning, whether it helps them to develop more fully, depends on the teacher's ability to relate what the children say about themselves to his or her other knowledge of them, not only based on listening to what they say about themselves, but on understanding what their behavior says about them. The teacher does not overlook the situations in which their behavior is best interpreted in relationship to the behavior of the group as a whole. We turn to such interpretations in our considerations of ways to study children in their groups.

NOTES

1. Norris M. Sanders, *Classroom Questions: What Kinds?* (New York: Harper & Row, 1966) is an example. See Suggested Reading following these notes.
2. Marion Blank, *Teaching Learning in the Preschool* (Columbus, Ohio: Charles E. Merrill, 1973).
3. Ibid., pp. 176-177.
4. Ibid., pp. 72-73.
5. For a useful paper on how teachers' questions and responses might affect the quality of children's thinking, see Selma Wassermann and Meguido Zola, "Promoting Thinking in Your Classroom," *Childhood Education* 54 (1977), pp. 24e-24k. It includes a "worksheet," which teachers may use to study their questions, responses, and the nature of the activity planned for children.
6. We present children's speech as spoken. Although some people may consider a nonstandard, colloquial form like "ain't" to be "incorrect," we view it as part of the dialect of many English speakers, young and old, from a variety of ethnic groups and geographic regions. The standard, or "correct," dialect of English is only one among many. Each has systematic variations, like "ain't" or "y'all," and speakers may use nonstandard dialect in some situations and standard dialect in others.
7. Clara A. Pederson, "'And What Do You Think?' Children's Interview," based on original interview by Nancy Miller, in *Evaluation and Record Keeping* (Grand Forks, N.D.: Center for Teaching and Learning, University of North Dakota, 1977). This interview schedule was originally used with third graders, but many items seem appropriate for first and second graders as well. The section entitled "Teacher Relations" is probably best used by adults other than the classroom teacher and sample questions are, therefore, not included.
8. Adapted from Arthur T. Jersild and Ruth J. Tasch, *Children's Interests and What They Suggest for Education* (New York: Bureau of Publications, Teachers College, Columbia University, 1949).
9. Amity P. Buxton, "Journals: Further Dimensions of Assessing Language

Development" (Paper presented at Annual Convention of National Council of Teachers of English, Chicago, 1976).

SUGGESTED READING

Blank, Marion. *Teaching Learning in the Preschool: A Dialogue Approach.* Columbus, Ohio: Charles E. Merrill Publishing Co., 1973. As the author herself points out, the program described in this book is based on assumptions still being tested about the nature of children's thinking and language. But the questioning strategies suggested are clearly presented and explained, and examples of dialogues between teacher and preschooler are plentiful. The book also is one of the few that highlights questioning strategies for young children.

Bloom, Benjamin S. et al. *Taxonomy of Educational Objectives: The Classification of Educational Goals.* Vols. I and II. New York: David McKay Company, 1956. This often cited work is the basis for many question-asking schemes. It outlines both cognitive and affective goals of education. The hierarchy of cognitive goals ranges from knowing specific facts to evaluating and making judgments.

Sanders, Norris M. *Classroom Questions: What Kinds?* New York: Harper & Row, 1966. This is one of many books based on Bloom's taxonomy of cognitive goals. The author discusses kinds of questions teachers can ask that are appropriate to different cognitive goals. Although the examples often refer to content beyond the early childhood level, the explanations and examples are clear, and review exercises are provided for the reader.

5 STUDY CHILDREN IN THEIR GROUPS

Teachers always have known that every group of children has its own distinctive qualities. Like individuals, each group or class is unique. One year a group of four-year-olds in day care may be "absolute terrors," and the next year children of the same age and same socio-economic background will be "quiet and sweet—different, less active." Or a first grade teacher might find last year's class much more eager to learn to read than this year's, which is less docile but more enthusiastic about such things as trips to museums.

To work effectively with a group, the teacher needs to know the children not only as individuals but also as group members. Certain children are readily accepted into any activity. Their roles vary. Sometimes they are leaders, sometimes followers. Other children appear more or less consistently in one kind of role—as "boss," or "peacemaker," or "idea man," or "evaluator," or "disrupter." Some youngsters are particularly apt to influence their peers, and others are markedly susceptible to influence. Some children usually are in the center of the group activity; others more often are on its fringes. Such patterns of interpersonal relationships may either hamper or facilitate whatever direction the teacher provides.

Knowledge of the group also enhances the teacher's understanding of individuals. How a child relates to other children and how they respond to him or her reflect previous experiences with people and reveal something about expectations for self and others. Some may enjoy playing alone much of the time while others have a greater emotional investment in the group. They are much more concerned with group acceptance than they are with meeting the teacher's expectations for their social or academic learning. Not until they have achieved a sense of belonging can they concentrate wholeheartedly on any other task. On the other hand, some youngsters withdraw from the group life of their peers and focus their energies on pleasing the teacher or other adults.

We appreciate the varied experiences children already have had when we recognize that they come from families that may differ in size, basic values, or economic and ethnic background. The way the child works or plays in groups is influenced by factors like these. The network of interpersonal relationships in a classroom or center, then, not only is highly complex, it also has different significance for each of the children. How is the teacher to deal with these complexities in a way that will be advantageous to both group and individual? How can patterns of relationship be identified? How are they to be interpreted and evaluated?

In this chapter we discuss some methods that researchers and teachers have used in studying children's social and intellectual development in groups. Because we know little about the social life of children, we also suggest some questions that might be raised when teachers arrange children in groups and interpret and evaluate the information they collect.

THE CHILD IN CONTEXT

We have become increasingly aware that each child functions in several interrelated contexts or settings, which make up the child's environment. The day-care center, preschool, or primary school is only one part of that environment. To study children in groups with understanding is to see them against the background of a variety of social contexts that encompass large institutions, such as the church to which their families may belong, as well as the small group with whom most children closely identify— their own families. (Figure 5.1 shows the possible contexts in which a child may spend segments of the day or week.)

What happens in any of these contexts may change so that behavior in the school or center will also be affected. Most likely, we will not know the details of children's activities outside of school or center. But bearing in mind that a child is at once a member of several groups—both large and small—helps us interpret what we observe with caution and, it is hoped, with greater insight.

If we have had the opportunity to visit children in their homes, we know that their behavior and the way they express thoughts and feelings vary from setting to setting. Mark, a six-year-old, is independent in his day-care center. He asks little of his teachers and is content to be with a

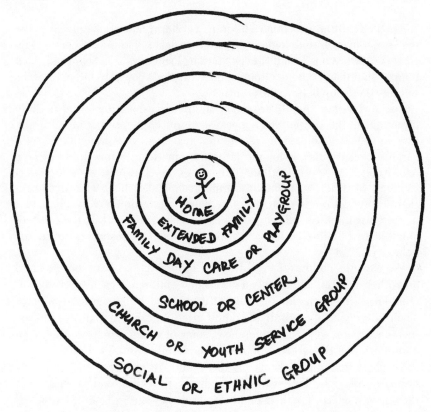

FIGURE 5.1. POSSIBLE CONTEXTS

A child may be a member of several groups simultaneously. What happens in one context may affect the child's behavior in the others.

handful of friends for long periods of time. He generally is able to negotiate for what he needs at the center, sometimes by arguing more successfully than his peers. At home, however, where he is the youngest of eight children, a visitor sees a different facet of the same boy. He is not always the autonomous Mark. Rather, he asks his parents to do many things for him and uses less mature speech than he does at the center. He occasionally lisps or speaks in a coy manner, especially when talking to his parents or grandmother.

Esperanza, a child who has just turned three, has come to this country from the Philippines. In her family day-care home, she seems to understand much of what goes on around her, but she says nothing to either her caretaker or to the five other children. Yet her mother tells the caretaker that Esperanza, an only child, talks a great deal at home in Tagalog. The caretaker or teacher who observes Mark or Esperanza in a peer group will temper judgments about either child with the knowledge that in other settings they may behave differently.

Acknowledging the diversity of children's experiences is especially important in the United States because of our large number of culturally diverse groups. We cannot assume that teachers of young children with various backgrounds, whether Hispanic-American, white middle-class, Afro-American, or other ethnicity, come to the classroom with an understanding of differences among ethnic groups. Teachers who are aware that differences might exist are more likely to interpret a child's behavior in groups cautiously and sympathetically. They are less likely to expect all children to be alike in their behavior and in their responses to others' behavior.

We view the child as one contributor to interactions between the child and other children and between adults and children. Teachers, as well as children, bring with them certain attitudes that influence their actions. Their judgments about individual and group behavior are always filtered by their expectations and preferences, some of which stem from their own membership in the larger contexts of community or ethnic group.

Teachers also have effects on the group by virtue of the role they ordinarily play. As the persons "in charge," they have said for years that they are "models" for their children—and they are right in many ways. Teachers not only teach content, they reflect attitudes toward people, toward what they teach, and toward the activity of learning in general. Teachers who spend time giving reasons for some of their choices of activities or who ask genuine, rather than "test," questions of pupils may find that their pupils will in turn seek to provide reasons for their own answers or behavior. Their exchanges with children in large groups or in one-to-one conversations, then, can affect what children know, and, in addition, the quality of their thinking and reasoning.[1]

In addition to children and teachers, we can consider the nonhuman elements of educational contexts, features like group size, the amount of space available, and number of hours spent in a single place or in a single activity. Such features may or may not change the behavior of children in large and small groups. Given the increasing numbers of preschool children in institutions like day care, however, we can begin to examine the possible effects of a child's participation in groups of forty or more children for many hours at a time. What happens to a child in such settings may be determined as much by the number of children enrolled as by the teacher's carefully made decisions about his or her program.

PURPOSES FOR STUDYING GROUPS

Our primary goal in studying children, either individually or in groups, is to help them develop more fully and learn more effectively. Especially at the early childhood level, it is difficult to separate development and learning into the traditional cognitive, social, and emotional domains. Practically speaking, however, there is commonly a shift in emphasis when a child enters the primary grades. In day care, nursery school, or preschool—and sometimes kindergarten—teachers often stress the importance of social and emotional development, while in the first and second grades, they are concerned with academics, the teaching of skills, and presentation of concepts. There are two main purposes for our study of children in groups, then: fostering social development and improving academic learning. Because every teacher must deal with conflicts among children and between herself or himself and children while working toward the two primary purposes, we will add a third purpose: improving classroom discipline.

Fostering Social Development

A young child's first experience with a group other than the immediate family is a landmark in the process of socialization. Therefore, one of the early childhood teacher's first concerns is incorporating the child into the group so that a balance results between each individual child's wishes and those of the rest of the group. Achieving the balance requires skill not only in dealing with many children at once but also in dealing with materials, materials that will interest children and so contribute to their adjustment to the group, as well as promote the development of thinking.

Children's ability to work and play productively and cooperatively with others is reflected in their ability to take others' points of view. As we said in chapter 3, until the stage of concrete operations, it is often difficult for children to consider anything from a viewpoint other than their own. To encourage children to consider others' needs and views as well as their own, teachers plan the curriculum to allow for the sharing of experiences and for contributing to common goals. Activities of this kind may range from building a "city" out of blocks at the preschool level to working on a social studies project on the community in the second grade. How children participate in such activities, with ease and enthusiasm or with reluctance, tells us something about them as social beings.

Improving Learning

The group setting facilitates certain kinds of learning, whether the group consists of two or thirty children. The preschool child may learn the rules of a simple game from another child at the same time that certain social rules are learned, such as, "Wait your turn when you play games." A group of three children may learn how to construct a wooden airplane by watching a four-year-old classmate hammer together two pieces of wood. Later, in math, understanding of basic processes develops as primary-grade children find a variety of ways to solve one problem. In science, children's skill in observation improves as they check one another. Working together, they are likely to formulate more reasonable hypotheses and collect more adequate evidence than they might working alone. A group of second graders learning about fish, for example, share a magnifying glass as they tell each other what they observe about the movement and body parts of the fish in their aquarium. Or the children might prepare a display of different kinds of insects and discuss which insects to include, as they learn about how the insects differ from each other, how they are alike, and so on. To further such group activities, the teacher needs a picture of which youngsters can work well together. In part, this is a matter of knowing the youngsters' abilities as individuals. But it also involves knowledge of the patterns of relationships within the group.

Improving Classroom Discipline

Teachers who know which groups of children can work effectively together have some important clues for maintaining a classroom atmosphere in which children find enjoyment and satisfaction. The teachers' knowledge of group structure, together with their understanding of individuals in the class, helps them to sense how much responsibility the group can take on and to what extent it must rely on adults for control. To some degree, teachers can measure their effectiveness by the changes they see in the behavior of the group. In an atmosphere in which youngsters feel trusted and safe, the usual direction of such shifts is toward more acceptance, more cooperation, and less antagonism. Sometimes, of course, the social pressures operating on children outside of school are so great as to make progress unusually difficult.

Many teachers and others associated with the schools believe that helping children to learn to get along well with one another is one of the school's prime responsibilities. They study their groups to see how well they are succeeding. Their observations of those individuals who form stable groups and those who seem never to associate with others provide some basic information for planning. Ways of recording the formation and accomplishments of groups, including simple sociograms, are discussed later in this chapter.

CHARACTERISTICS OF THE CLASSROOM GROUP

In many respects the group that the teacher confronts differs from any other group of similar size, but it also resembles all such groups in several important ways.

Like other groups, the class reflects the personalities of the individuals in it. Its members, with varying degrees of awareness, seek personal satisfaction and expression of it. Each in his or her own way contributes to it. Some individuals readily exert direct leadership. Others are strongly influential even when they do not take an obvious leadership role. Some individuals are unusually effective in communicating with other members. Some seem to intensify tension among the members, others to reduce it. The feelings of preference or indifference or antagonism that each person has toward the other members help to give the group its unique character. Thus a group in which there is a great deal of mutual attraction behaves differently from one in which the preferences center around two or three individuals.

Groups change. Individuals who did not know one another or were indifferent may come to like or dislike each other. Leadership and influence shift somewhat as circumstances vary.

Children's group relationships are even less stable than those of adults. Furthermore, the significance of the group changes as children grow older. In the earliest years, the family is the group that matters most to children. But after they go to center or school, they spend more and more of their playtime with particular groups of youngsters, usually those who live nearby. They learn to hold their own in this society of peers.

Beyond the preschool years, the classroom may serve as another setting for the activities of the peer group. Thus it may happen that youngsters who play together after school and on weekends find themselves in the same grade at school. A class of thirty youngsters may have in it four or five subgroups of children who are closely associated together outside of school. Just as likely is the possibility that it will have portions of several such friendship groups. Whatever the case may be, the members of the class who share group life apart from the school develop certain expectations about each other that importantly influence their behavior in the classroom group. Because of these outside associations, the picture of peer group life that the teacher gets from observations in the classroom necessarily is incomplete.

The fact that school attendance is compulsory adds still another dimension to the classroom group. It is unlike the neighborhood play group in which youngsters participate voluntarily, and where they usually must make their own way. Children may be no more acceptable to their peers in the school situation than they are on their own block, but the center or school atmosphere usually is less conducive to flagrant rejection.

The center or school group also differs from other children's groups in that adults play a special role. It is their responsibility not only to serve as leader but also to evaluate the adequacy of children's development and learning. Thus adults in a center or school are seen in a somewhat different light from adults who participate in children's groups in recreational or neighborhood settings. Confusion has sometimes arisen when teachers have seemed to emphasize one aspect of their role to the exclusion of others. One day-care center director, for example, thought it was of primary importance to keep her group of thirty-seven children on schedule. As a consequence, her colleagues felt that she restricted her role to disciplinarian and ignored opportunities to converse with youngsters. Clarity about the teachers' own functions in the group helps them establish and promote the kinds of group relationships that are most conducive to good learning.

We focus now on ways in which teachers might study particular functions and relationships.

FOSTERING SOCIAL DEVELOPMENT: YOUNG CHILDREN IN DAY CARE AND PRESCHOOLS

Like most teachers, the teacher in day-care centers and preschools often functions both as participant and observer. One teacher, Mrs. Tanaka, working with two- through five-year-olds in a center that had recently begun to mainstream disabled youngsters, sang short songs with her group of five children. She watched Brandon walk off and made a mental note of it but did not interrupt the ongoing group activity since an aide would tend to Brandon, who had Down's syndrome.

In another situation, the same teacher watched Brandon with two other children on the playground. The teacher quickly took notes on what Brandon said, whether or not the others understood him, and how long the three played together. In a week Mrs. Tanaka would observe Brandon again to see whether his play with other children would last for longer periods of time. At this point she felt encouraged that Brandon's activities in groups had been generally smooth for him and for the other children.

To document the way specified children behave in groups, teachers need time to record what they notice, even if their notes are brief. As we noted in chapter 2, relying on memory does not suffice; there are too many details to recall.

In addition to observing the social development of individual children, teachers in centers and preschools are concerned with particular kinds of behavior. Because of the size of some groups, especially in day care, teachers are quick to note aggressiveness and cooperation.

Although there is little research on the effects of day care on young children, some researchers have found that extended periods in day care are associated with more aggressive and less cooperative behaviors. More positively, some children appear to be aggressive initially but become socially well adjusted and more cooperative after a year or two at a center.

Staff members often casually mention the tenor of a group's behavior in the course of each day, but those who wish to document changes may keep anecdotal records, noting especially the behaviors of new children and making inferences about effects on other group members. Or teachers may write down observations, reactions, and possible reasons for changes in behavior in a log that includes a record of the number of times adults play "peacekeeping" roles. The responsibility for keeping such a record may be shared so that no one teacher need do it for long.

If arguments, crying, and aggressive behavior, such as hitting and kicking, are problems that predominate, teachers may use a more detailed technique and keep a tally of the number of incidents of such behaviors in a given period of time. They should note too which children are involved so that they can see later if specific children seem to be consistently troublesome. By using information of this kind teachers can go on to discuss possible solutions.

A less dramatic aspect of social development is the way in which children, aggressive or not, become part of the school or center group. Observant teachers not only make a child feel welcome at the beginning of the year, or whenever the child joins the group, they also make mental notes of how each child begins the day at school or center. Does he or she immediately select an activity, oblivious of the people present, or is a particular child or group sought out instead?

The fortunate teacher who works with other teachers or aides can take the time to observe and record the ways many children begin their day. The teacher without such help, on the other hand, can observe the first activities of only two or three children. The observations, written down later, help teachers build a picture not only of individual children as social beings but also of the groups they themselves form. Observation also yields clues about those children who are so withdrawn or shy that only the careful intervention of the teacher will draw them into any group situations.

The teacher's presence in a group activity may itself be a form of "intervention." He or she also is an element in the center or school setting. Not only do teachers observe children when possible and participate with them in a variety of activities, depending on where children choose to be, they also can *plan* to place themselves in specified locations.

If a teacher notices that there are seldom more than one or two children at the art table, he or she may choose to sit there to see if more children will then take advantage of the activity. Over the period of a week, the teacher may be found to be a clear influence on the formation of groups and perhaps on their sociability and talkativeness. In the area of motor development, four-year-old girls may participate in "catch" only when the teacher who suggests the activity is a woman. Teachers who view themselves as an effective part of their curriculum, and not primarily as impartial observers, may enable children to engage in a wide variety of activities while gaining opportunities to study what happens when they join children's groups.

Nonhuman Factors That Affect Groups

Whether a child fits easily or with difficulty into groups, the way the child thinks, feels, and behaves is affected not only by the teacher and the identities of companions but also by nonhuman, or environmental, factors that, in the context of the center or classroom, may encourage certain kinds of group experiences and hinder others. The way teachers organize those elements—such as activity, scheduling, and space—has a clear effect on how smoothly children work and play.

Teachers can vary and reorganize some of these elements as well as study their effects on children. They can rearrange their schedules, reduce the number of children at one table, and so on.

The effects of two major aspects of a program, nature of activity, and scheduling, were studied by Prescott and others in what they called "open" and "closed" structures in day-care centers.[2] They found that in closed centers, where adults exerted the most pressure on children and offered the least spontaneous activities, almost a quarter of each day was devoted to transitions from one activity to another. Teachers and children in open centers, because of the greater flexibility of scheduling, spent much less time in transitions.

With such findings in mind, teachers can consider how their own schedules lead to productive and peaceful periods of time or to less useful segments, characterized by routine movement from one area to another and frequent teacher reminders to the group about behavior. Open or closed organization can have different effects on children. Open organization may be associated with longer periods of cooperative behavior because children are free to select and pursue activities of interest to them. Closed structures, on the other hand, may promote less socializing among children and a greater incidence of teachers' instructions to children.

Other environmental elements that are known to make a difference are the kind and quantity of materials, the amount and use of space, and the number of children present. Teachers know that appropriate choice of materials is a crucial factor in adding to children's contentment in their groups. They also know that conflicts often arise over the issue of ownership. At one nursery school, teachers noticed that the source of many arguments was the limited number of tricycles they had available. After the tricycles were replaced by a larger number of teacher-made hobbyhorses, there were fewer arguments over ownership.

Teachers and researchers also have noted that certain kinds of equipment or facilities encourage groups of children to play cooperatively. Clearly the block area or housekeeping corner invites children to show how they can lead an activity, act as a follower, or disrupt whatever is occurring. The junior author recalls observing a group of children engaged in animated play while they were partially enclosed in a large wooden box with a movable top that parents and staff had recently made for their center. When the dramatic play ended, one child instructed the others in a cooperative effort to shift the top to a different position before leaving it for another activity.

Questions related to how children make use of new or old equipment and materials, and how their interactions proceed may be answered by using a simple chart. (See figure 5.2 for an example.) The kinds of information teachers may gather with such a chart include whether or not:

Date_____

Group_____

Time	Activity	Children's names	Peaceful yes	no	Alone	Pair	Gro
	Art						
	Blocks						
	Carpentry						
	Housekeeping						
	Sandbox						
	Other outdoor						
	Other indoor						

FIGURE 5.2. ACTIVITY CHART

Teachers can record which children engage in what activities as well as the nature of their interactions.

1. One activity is often "overloaded" because many more children prefer it to another; for example, more children may consistently choose the water table over the carpentry table;
2. Certain materials are in constant demand, such as dress-up clothes or Lego sets;
3. The activities teachers plan offer opportunities for children to be alone, be with a partner, or work or play in a group;
4. The children work or play smoothly and cooperatively; some activities may be commonly associated with arguments and dissatisfaction.
5. Children spend long or short periods of time in individual activities; teachers may want to see which children show sustained interest in what they do, and which activities promote such interest.

Charts like the one in figure 5.2 easily can be modified to include other features of importance in particular schools or centers. Those teachers who wish to know if cooperative behavior is enhanced when children select their own activities may add a column called "child-initiated" vs. "adult-initiated" to see if a pattern emerges.

Teachers can alternatively choose one factor at a time to study systematically as they develop hunches. They may think that the children's behavior in groups would be more cooperative if the number of children inside the center or school building were reduced during certain periods of time. After recording numbers of children and whether conflicts arise, teachers may corroborate their hypothesis. Or they may find that the number of conflicts does not change appreciably; the teachers will then seek other explanations.

Focused study of groups may yield surprises. Teachers who suspect the incidence of running indoors depends on the number of children present may eventually find that an increase in materials and apparatus available is related to less running. They may also discover that a different arrangement of furniture and equipment indoors inhibits such activity.[3]

Children's Developing Social Competence

In this chapter we have so far dealt largely with studying children's behavior with respect to elements of the environment, such as space, number of children, and teachers themselves. These factors affect the development of social competence, or the children's ability to secure what they want without conflict, use acceptable means to gain attention, speak appropriately in different situations, and so on.

As in other aspects of development, individual children will vary in their degrees of competence as participants and communicators in large and small groups. They also have their own thoughts and feelings about being members of groups. Earlier we said that children, whether in preschools or primary grades, have their own preferred roles. They may seek their peers' or adults' approval, be leaders or followers, or appear to be "loners."

For teachers documenting social development, we again emphasize the importance of observing and listening carefully. Teachers may find the anecdote, in which they separate their own reactions and inferences from the description of events, a useful way to follow development. They may supplement such information with more quickly recorded observations. The anecdote presents a more detailed account of the quality of children's behavior in groups and reveals which children dominate actions and conversations, which are ignored, and which "blend in" without calling much attention to themselves. A first grade teacher wrote:

> I joined Esther's group to hear Rob review his word file. Rodolfo and Tico were there too. Rob read through his A-words and B-words without stopping. Esther interrupted us at that point to tell me that Bibi needed me at the next table. (This is the kind of thing Esther often does when I am nearby but not listening to her.) I told Bibi I'd be with her in a minute and saw that Rodolfo was staring intently at Bibi. (I guess he had finished writing over an old story.) Tico, meanwhile, had started to read Rob's next set of words with Rob. They were making a game of seeing who could read the fastest.

Because teachers ultimately wish to use such information to promote development and learning, they may employ additional techniques that reveal how they themselves respond to children who are more socially competent and less so. It is likely that teachers react positively to a child whose behavior toward them is positive and whose contacts with them are frequent; that child is already "sociable." Yet some children who do not initiate conversations or in other ways gain the attention of teachers may be most in need of positive interactions with them.

To insure that children are treated fairly and given opportunities to demonstrate their competence, teachers may converse with a few children selected each day. (This is similar to teachers' attempts to ask individual children about themselves, described in chapter 4.) The goal is not that teachers force themselves on the child but that they provide the opportunity for him or her to socialize. The quality of these encounters may be noted in writing at the end of the day. For more detailed study, teachers may regularly tape-record their activities with small or large groups of children. Such recordings may reveal whether or not teachers do, in fact, respond more positively to children who readily demonstrate their sociability.

Regardless of how at ease individual children are with adults, teachers always have an incomplete view of the range of children's competence. Some children outshine their peers in the presence of adults, others are intimidated, while others simply choose to expend their energies only with peers. When this last kind of child feels it necessary, he or she may effortlessly communicate needs to the adult the child perceives to be the most helpful.

IMPROVING LEARNING:
THE CHILD IN THE PRIMARY SCHOOL

When the child moves from the preschool or kindergarten to the primary grades, he or she may be undergoing important developmental changes socially, intellectually, and emotionally. Changes occur not only within the child but also within the structure of most schools. The physical appearance of the setting may change as well as the teacher's expectations for the child's thinking, feeling, and behaving.

Techniques for studying children's choice of activities and their involvement in group tasks at the primary level are similar to those described earlier for centers and preschools. Ways of recording observations in primary classrooms were presented in chapter 2. Because there is a shift in emphasis at the first and second grades toward academics, teachers' concerns will also shift toward studying group progress in learning.

Grouping

At the preschool level when teachers think about groups, they may think first of the importance of children's first social experiences in groups. In contrast, in the primary grades the word *group* takes on an additional meaning. Teachers at this level are more apt to think of academic groups and ways of *grouping* first and second graders to make their learning more effective as well as more efficient.

Traditionally, the teacher at this level has been primarily interested in instructing the young child in the "basics"—reading, writing, and math. This emphasis on academic skills has persisted for many years despite recent interest in "open" education.

Certainly we need to teach academics. But when we look at children from a developmental perspective, we realize that we may need to revise our ways of looking at children and our ways of grouping them. Textbook series often make children appear to be step-by-step learners, who learn in predictable sequences in predictable periods of time.

Yet, teachers know that very few children are so docile and "on schedule." The unevenness of their development is a major reason for the most popular way to form groups: the use of test results, either standardized or teacher-made. On the basis of these results teachers often establish groups of "high achievers," "average achievers," and "low or slow achievers" in both reading and math. Although this homogeneous arrangement is prevalent, there are numerous alternatives to it. Teachers may combine children of differing levels of achievement or use other criteria for forming groups, such as friendship, interests, or age in multiage settings. Some teachers allow groups to form themselves.

To study children in groups, teachers should first know why they have been grouped as they are. If teachers find the criteria satisfactory, they can then ask how well their grouping works and proceed to study its effectiveness.

Teachers who have used traditional homogeneous grouping may want to study the effects of changing to a heterogeneous arrangement. To study the effects of this change, teachers may keep daily records of progress on checklists or jot down quick notes. The teacher probably will record not only academic progress but also any changes in ways children socialize with each other, exchange information, or behave with the teacher. Such documentation will need to be carried out over a period of time so that both detrimental effects and benefits may be considered before the teacher decides which way of grouping is preferable.

Sociograms

In classrooms in which groups are not fixed, teachers may find it useful to "chart" the formation and development of groups of children. Sociograms are charts designed to give a graphic picture of group relationships. They have been used as a research technique to depict patterns of friendship and preference among people. When used in this way, they are elaborate and probably not feasible for most classroom teachers. But as we present them, they are simplified to show possible friendship patterns and groups that form around common interests. Figure 5.3 provides two examples, which show how the makeup of a group changed slightly over time while children worked on group projects in social studies.

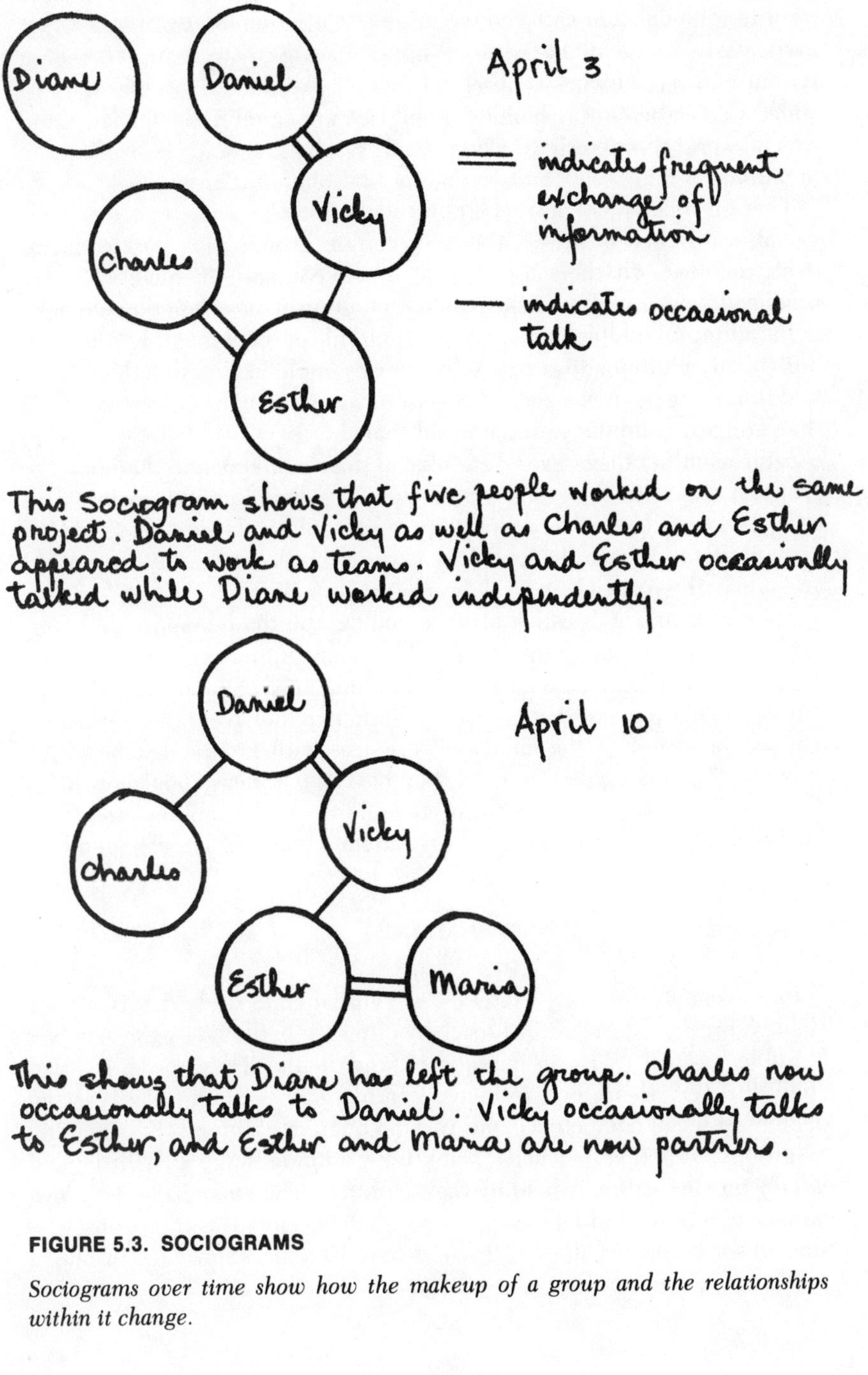

April 3

Diane   Daniel

Vicky

Charles

Esther

$=$ indicates frequent exchange of information

$—$ indicates occasional talk

This Sociogram shows that five people worked on the same project. Daniel and Vicky as well as Charles and Esther appeared to work as teams. Vicky and Esther occasionally talked while Diane worked independently.

April 10

Daniel

Vicky

Charles

Esther   Maria

This shows that Diane has left the group. Charles now occasionally talks to Daniel. Vicky occasionally talks to Esther, and Esther and Maria are now partners.

FIGURE 5.3. SOCIOGRAMS

Sociograms over time show how the makeup of a group and the relationships within it change.

The same information may be gathered by listing children's names and recording how each related to the others. With a sociogram, the teacher, particularly if she or he is visual-minded, can create a simple coding system and record what is observed quickly. Additional symbols may be added that indicate which child or children appeared to be in charge and which were uninterested. Codes and symbols should be kept to a minimum so that the technique does not become burdensome.

The information that sociograms yield may provide teachers with valuable insights into the stability of certain groups that work cooperatively together. Teachers also may be able to compare the quality of work produced when children choose their own groups and when they do not.

In addition, sociograms may be helpful in documenting the way individual children adjust to groups. For example in a class with children of different ages, the teacher, Mrs. Jason, was particularly concerned with the youngest child, Guy. She noticed that the six-year-old "loner" was as capable as most of the seven-year-olds in the classroom, and therefore she grouped him with three seven-year-olds for a math activity. A few days later, however, she noticed that Guy worked alone despite her grouping plan. Left to his own devices, Guy chose to work with a seven-year-old and two eight-year-olds several days later.

Another instance in which teachers may graph the relationships affecting individuals is the entry of a disabled child into a regular classroom. Teachers are especially concerned that the new child does not avoid groups of children and that groups of children do not avoid the newcomer. To keep a record of the child's experiences with groups, teachers may make sociograms frequently until they have some ideas about how he or she is adjusting socially, how the other children are responding, and if the quality of children's social as well as academic behavior has changed.

SUMMARY

In this chapter we have examined a realm of child study that is at once challenging and elusive. Most teachers often are baffled—by the group as a whole as well as by its members individually. They recognize that children exert their own influence. Individual children show varying degrees of social competence and varying degrees of interest in belonging to groups. Whether teachers' plans for grouping succeed will depend largely on views already held by their children. They may have their own notions of who should be leader, who else should join the group, and who should not be part of it. And teachers may have no knowledge or only a partial knowledge of these preferences as they set their goals for children's activities and learning.

Only as teachers become professionally experienced, only as they test out some of their hunches about the relationships between the group and the individuals in it, do they reach any degree of sureness about the nature of its complexities.

For group relationships are complicated, and the teachers themselves add to the complexity. No matter how scientifically teachers study the other elements of their schools or centers, how well they analyze and rearrange space, materials, and numbers of children, no matter how masterful they are in managing the group, they too contribute to it.

The group's response to a teacher is affected by the interpersonal relationships that prevail among group members. Their response is also influenced by how they interpret the teacher's actions and motives.

In presenting ways of looking at what affects the thinking and feeling of children in groups, we have suggested that teachers raise questions about how they group children and why. Are the teachers' reasons based on tradition, conventional wisdom, knowledge of development, or their own intuition and experience?

Finally, we see the teacher's concern for the group reflecting concern for the individual. The more that is known about the individuals in the group, the more effectively the teacher can deal with it. Correspondingly, the more the teacher knows of the group, the better individuals can be understood. In the next chapter, we consider children's expression and what it reveals about them as individuals.

NOTES

1. See S. L. Lightfoot, "Politics and Reasoning: Through the Eyes of Teachers and Children," *Harvard Educational Review* 43 (1973), pp. 197-244, for a study of two second-grade classrooms taught by black women in which the researcher discusses the relationships between the teacher's beliefs and the quality of her children's responses to interview questions.
2. Elizabeth Prescott, with Elizabeth Jones, Sybil Kritchevsky, Cynthia Millich, and Ede Haselhoef, *Assessment of Child-Rearing Environments: An Ecological Approach* (Pasadena, Calif.: Pacific Oaks College, 1975).
3. That manipulation of space affects the frequency of children's running is documented in W. C. McGrew, *An Ethological Study of Children's Behavior* (New York: Academic Press, 1972).

SUGGESTED READING

Bronfenbrenner, Urie. "The Experimental Ecology of Education." *Teachers College Record* 78 (1976): 157-204. This article deals with an approach to research that takes into account the many overlapping contexts in which children live. The author advocates studies that consider the reciprocal relationship between the child and the many aspects of his or her environment. He points out that even under experimental conditions, features of the situation are always changing.

Denzin, Norman. *Childhood Socialization.* San Francisco: Jossey-Bass, 1977. Denzin, a sociologist, highlights the importance of looking at children's social development from the point of view of the child. The author emphasizes the role of the child's own interpretation of social situations and the need for adults to see children as capable interpreters and not as incomplete adults. He also discusses the importance of language in the process of socialization. Research cited was done in naturalistic settings at the preschool level.

Gearing, Frederick et al., "On Observing Well: Self-instruction in Ethnographic Observation for Teachers, Principals, and Supervisors." Mimeographed. Amherst, N.Y.: State University of New York at Buffalo, 1975. This is a manual for school personnel who would like to study what they do in classrooms. They may focus on groups of children or on their own behavior with groups of children. Guidelines are presented for specifying a problem and systematically studying it. Written by anthropologists, it presents the teacher as an observer and researcher and suggests procedures that vary in complexity. Readers have the opportunity to choose the procedures that they have time to use.

Gronlund, Norman E. *Sociometry in the Classroom.* New York: Harper & Brothers, 1959. The author gives a thorough presentation of the uses of sociometric techniques in classroom practice and research. Teachers may want to modify or simplify suggested techniques for their own purposes and will find Part 3 the most helpful. It focuses on applications of sociometric techniques to educational settings. The author discusses the value of studying which individuals children prefer or don't prefer and the social relationships that evolve in groups. He also briefly addresses specific cases, for example, isolated children and handicapped children in regular classrooms.

Kounin, Jacob S. *Discipline and Group Management in Classrooms.* New York: Holt, Rinehart, & Winston, 1970. The author presents' results of studies of videotapes from kindergarten, first-grade, and second-grade classrooms. He concludes that certain characteristics of teachers as group "managers," such as the ability to handle transition periods smoothly, are associated with effective discipline. The book is not about ways of studying children but about the complex role of the teacher as he or she copes with children in groups. Kounin finds that the classroom teacher who works well with individual children has first been successful in working with the group.

Newman, Ruth G. *Groups in Schools*. Simon & Schuster, 1974. This book is written from a broad, psychological perspective. The author considers not only the roles of children but also the groups that may share goals in their work with children, including teachers, parents, and clinicians. She also points out the conflicts that arise among and within such groups. (The content of the book also is relevant to chapter 7, "Study the Child through Others.")

6 STUDY THE WAYS CHILDREN EXPRESS THEMSELVES

Young children's ways of expressing themselves are numerous and rich. Through play, language, movement, or the arts they reveal their feelings and thoughts, usually with ease and spontaneity. At times it appears when they willingly engage in any activity, it becomes expressive, particularly in the preschool years, although individual children prefer different means and have different styles of expression

The nursery school teacher who allowed children to "just talk" into a tape recorder heard four-year-old Richard's recording:

> Well, it's good to have you here Jack and Bat Kite. I like you a whole lot. And you two are great, first of all. And I'll never let you go away because I like you. This thing is really complicated so you can't do it. So you'll have to go in my pocket. Well, if that's all right, if they catch you, I'll save you. O.K.? Jack and Bat Kite, I like you.

Richard's "talk," well developed in vocabulary and structure, is imaginative, personal, and fluent. Curt, on the other hand, seldom took the opportunity to record his own speech, and when he did, he said "hello" two or three times and ran off. Delia, whether she used the tape recorder or just talked to someone, often spun tales that were remotely related to stories she had heard in books or seen on television. She sprinkled her rapid narratives with, "Boy, was I *sca-a-red!*" or "She was bad—she was a *re-ee-al* bad witch!"

Each child's oral expression has its unique qualities. Listen to children talking about a trip they have taken together. Some of them enumerate: "Well, we saw the cows and the milking machines, and the pigs, and . . . ." Some of them concentrate on statistics: "*forty* cows," "five

128

miles." Others reflect on people: the man who put the milking machines on the cows and was "careful not to hurt them," the booming laughter of another man—"Wasn't he funny?"—or the stern prohibitions of still another, "the mean one, the one who kept telling us to 'keep back.'" Certain children savor the sensory aspects of the experience: the "prickly" straw, the smoothness of the cows' hair, the differing smells of the barn and the poultry house, the fun of rolling on a grassy slope. Many children have absorbed much from the trip, but there also are those who seem to have been present without taking the experience into themselves. Some youngsters struggle to tell about the trip; to others words come readily and aptly.

A second-grade teacher asked the class to write an ending to a story that began, "We went to the woods for a picnic. I took a walk, and all of a sudden I was all alone." Most of the children wrote two or three sentences while Joey and Marian wrote many and appeared to be engrossed in the activity. The work of the class reflected as many different styles as the nursery school children exhibited when they expressed themselves orally.

Some papers were tidy. Many had erasures, scrawls, and almost undecipherable printing. The briefest was a few words in length. Longer ones ran to a page or more. Occasionally, papers had elements, crude but real, of humor, drama, or fantasy.

Language is only one mode of expression. Play is another. At the day-care center three-year-old Philip and four-year-old Mark played with the "dress-up" clothing in the doll corner. Philip put on a plaid shirt that he called his "coat," and Mark got into a pair of high heels. Mark then suggested, "Let's turn into Superman!" They stripped off their shirts, found some scarves to use as capes, and left the area.

As children grow older, the content of their dramatic play changes. They often are interested in playing a story they have heard or read. A few youngsters can portray the Wicked Wolf as readily as the unfortunate Red Riding Hood. More often a child takes one role with zest but plays the others without enthusiasm. Contrast the child who states, "What pretty flowers," picking them automatically, with the youngster who appears completely arrested by the invisible blossoms. The latter child not only "sees" them, he or she feels them and smells them; they have become completely real.

Subtle differences in expressiveness also are revealed in music and the dance. Watch a group of three-year-old children when the teacher suggests that they move with the music in their own ways. Some children's movements are stereotyped and rigid, others are free and open.

One seems disciplined by the music, another is released, still another appears frenzied. Look closely at older children in more formally structured dancing. All of them may do the steps correctly, but one child is light and graceful, another heavy and almost clumsy.

Equally diverse are children's ways of using art media. Give a second grade the problem of making a saucer. Each starts with a similar ball of clay. Richard pounds his clay against his clayboard long and noisily, ostensibly to smooth what is to be the bottom. Susan scratches little bits from the center of her ball. Peter adds water and quickly makes his clay too sticky to handle easily. Mary Ann is one of the first to say that she is finished. The outside of her saucer is smooth and well rounded, but, as the teacher quickly notes, the top surface is still rough and scratchy. In contrast, her best friend, Betty, is reluctant to stop when the period is over. She points out the places where she thinks she could improve what she has done.

What do children's ways of expressing themselves mean to teachers? How can they study children's expression and use it to help them in their learning?

THE MEANING OF EXPRESSIVE ACTIVITIES

In the largest sense, everything that children do is self-expressive and tells something of the kinds of persons they are. In this chapter, however, we are concerned with those areas of the curriculum in which children are explicitly encouraged to reveal their individuality; we will use the words "expressive" and "expression" to refer mainly to these kinds of self-expression. Notable among these are some activities we already have discussed (journals and interest finders, for instance) and also those activities often called "creative."

As children play, or make up their own stories, or dance, or paint, they live through—and to an extent transform—some of the pleasure and the pain, the joy and the anguish that are inevitable concomitants of growth. In ways we do not fully understand, the emotional freedom that is gained in these creative areas may relate also to the child's freedom to learn in other areas.

Thus, the expressive activities the school or center provides contribute in important ways to children's realization of whatever potentialities they may have. In addition, children's expression affords the teacher many opportunities for child study. Whenever children confront a situation that is not clearly defined, or create a story, a song, a dance, or an art object, they invest something of themselves in it. Children's expressive activities reflect their feelings, the way they see the world and the way they see others.

On one level, children are fully aware of the concerns and attitudes apparent in their self-expressions. On a deeper level, they are learning to cope with desires and feelings revealed in their expression; many of these desires and feelings may be concealed even from themselves. In trying to understand children, the teacher can be sensitive both to the emotional concerns of which children themselves are aware and to the significance of the deeper levels of personality.

As we read children's stories, watch their play, and look at their drawings, patterns sometimes emerge. Each child's creative expression has certain characteristics that we identify as unique. Many times it is impossible for a teacher to recognize the feelings the child may be expressing. Frequently, however, the intuitive teacher can sense from the child's expressive activities something of the nature of the child's inner world.

Outward performances may be similar. Several children may be equally competent intellectually and in their relationships with their peers. But of these youngsters, one may seem inwardly serene and comfortable while another appears to seethe with conflicting feelings. Sociability may reflect inner warmth or it may provide a facade for hostility. One child learns readily and with evidently deep satisfaction. Another learns equally well but with an underlying apprehensiveness. That child seems to lack self-confidence.

The inner world, which is reflected in the varied forms of expression, stems in part from what children feel, along with what they do, and what they learn. We have stated earlier that children learn best through direct experience. Whether children are developing concepts about the physical world while playing with blocks or about social relationships when they first attend a center or school, they learn through their own actions. What expressive activities provide is further opportunity for children to reconstruct or re-present a new experience so that they can integrate it into what they already know and understand.

Play and the creative arts aid learning as much as traditional academic tasks through which children might assimilate new experiences by representing them in words or numbers. In expressive activities, new experiences are translated into more personal forms. If those forms become inadequate, no longer make sense, or are not aesthetically pleasing to children, they will seek another way to re-present those experiences or developing concepts.[1] A child who draws people as tall as the houses next to them, for example, may one day demonstrate an understanding of relative size by drawing a house twice as tall as the person next to it.

When we study children's play, artistic efforts, and language, then, we can tell something about how a child organizes past experience, and how the child thinks as well as feels—an important dimension is added to our picture of each child.

ORAL EXPRESSION

In early childhood, almost all children talk more easily than they write. They express themselves orally in a variety of ways, whether they are singing to themselves, conversing, or sharing jokes with each other.

Young children, particularly preschoolers, are in the process of learning their first language or languages. Often they attend more to the form and sounds of language than older children and adults do. Consequently, what they say at times is playful. They experiment with words and sounds that are becoming part of their repertoire of language. A two-year-old, for example, may spontaneously chant short utterances while playing, "My ball. Here the ball. Want ball." The exact sounds produced probably will not match adults' pronunciations, but the child is expressing what he or she knows or is learning about the structure of language.

A three-year-old who gleefully held up two pieces of cereal between two of his fingers exclaimed, "Sandwich!" and then laughed. He understood the concept of a sandwich and, in addition, could express satisfaction with his own humor.

Four-year-olds who have already developed many of the forms of their language often make up simple rhymes, as this child, Robert, did:

> "Can you read my shirt? It says, 'Thick or thin at Pizza Inn,' inn, min, pin, pin, kin, kee, kee, bee, bee," and then he giggled. The teacher said, "Those words rhymed with *inn*." Robert: "They what?" "Rhymed." Robert was silent a moment, then said, "Oh, yeah, they sound like it, right? Like yum, yum, num, tum, tummy!" and he chuckled a little at his understanding of it and patted his stomach.

Teachers hearing such verbal play recognize that children are sensitive to the sounds of words. The children's expression reflects how they think about words and that their own manipulation of sounds and words is pleasurable.

Children in the primary grades often have fewer opportunities to share their personal responses to the sounds of words. A six-year-old child, Karen, used an opportunity to tell a story about some pictures she had drawn in a small booklet. She told part of her narrative, based on her drawing of a tree, to a tape recorder in this way,

> But one day, he had some apples on his tree. He picked them, picked, picked, picked, picked, plucked, plucked, plucked, plucked. And first the little boy said, "Can I eat an apple, mommy?" And his mother said, "Oh, well, I guess so, 'cuz it really is your apple tree." And the little boy said, "Oh, hurray, hurray, I love apples," and when he said that, he said, "Hurray, for me!" And then he started going for a walk to look for a duck, and it, the duck, said, "Quack!" "Who are you-uu, mooed the cow? Who are you, buk, buk, buk?" "I'm the fairy godmother."

Karen delighted in storytelling as well as in repeating words for the pleasure of hearing their sounds.

The teacher, listening to such tales, learns much about the extensiveness of the child's vocabulary, about the degree of fluency and the purposes— imaginative and expressive—in the use of language, and probably something about the child's reactions to literature and prior experiences with it. By contrast, the child who draws a picture of a tree similar to Karen's drawing and says, "There's a tree. It's got green leaves, and there's some grass," has a different notion of how language can be used in that setting. Previous pleasant experiences may be lacking; spoken language may not be this child's preferred mode of expression; or something other than a drawing may encourage talk. Teachers' own conversations may more successfully engage certain children in expressing themselves orally.

Teachers who especially enjoy the spoken word, who like to read poetry aloud and who have mastered the art of storytelling, encourage similar interests in their children. Stories teachers create as well as trade books can prompt children to express their feelings about events within the stories. They may feel free to talk about times when they are angry after hearing that a storybook character has suffered an injustice. Or they may raise questions about death if a character dies. Young children will not have a full understanding of the phenomena they ask about, but expressing uncertainties or fears may support their eventual ability to cope with them.

Children who would not feel comfortable expressing themselves individually often enjoy choral speaking. If youngsters can choose from a considerable variety of stories and poetry, their selections will reveal something of the kinds of persons they are. One child chooses a "spooky" story, another a humorous one, while a third prefers a glamorous fairy tale. One youngster searches out poems with a strong rhythm; a neighbor chooses those with vivid images. Although such differences among children are subtle, they are nonetheless real.

Because speaking develops naturally in almost all children, we may overemphasize its importance as an indicator of how children think and feel. Particularly when children are just beginning to produce language, adults anxiously await their first utterances. If these are not heard with some frequency within the first two or three years of life, there is often concern about whether the child is "on schedule."

Research on children's language has become a large and rich field, but at present researchers do not know precisely what is a "normal" rate of acquisition. There are linguistic structures that are acquired in a specified order, but individual variations are so broad that ages cannot be predicted for their appearance. And, as we noted in chapter 3, what a child actually *says* may give the listener only a partial picture of abilities. Words may exaggerate or mask what is known or felt.

Although many children express themselves freely through speech, some do not. A few of this second group may eventually need the help of a language therapist in order to develop oral expression. Others, however, may find music, art, some form of motor activity, or later, writing, more satisfying than speech. For this reason we believe teachers will want to consider the other modes of expression as attentively as they do children's speech.

"STRUCTURED" EXPRESSION

Centers and schools often include in the daily schedule a time for "sharing" or "show-and-tell." Less often a time is reserved for expression of individual or group concerns during which children and teacher listen to each other with the aim of understanding others' feelings. There are a number of published curricula available for this purpose.

One program concerned with children's emotional and social development has as its general goal the prevention of mental health problems. Guidelines are presented for children from age four through grade six. Such a program, under the guidance of a skillful and sensitive teacher, may promote positive feelings in children toward themselves and others through the discussion of topics such as "What I Feel Good About" or "Something Beautiful." Teachers, at the same time, can gather information about individual feelings, which they may periodically document in anecdotes.

Carried out on a daily basis with children as young as four years, however, any program of "structured" expression may eventually become less than productive either for the free expression of feelings or for the teachers' purposes in studying these feelings. The discussion of feelings and appreciation of others' viewpoints may be beyond the abilities of many four- or even six-year-olds, particularly when the discussions take place in large groups. Young children may learn more about others' feelings from incidents that commonly occur in the course of a day or a week than in talks *about* feelings. In addition, the routine quality of some programs may discourage spontaneous discussion of feelings because the children tire of the teacher so often urging them to express what they feel.

When children express themselves in a group situation, whether they are talking on such a topic as "My Birthday" or "A Time I Felt Worried," the responses each child makes influence the others. These patterns of influence in themselves tell the teacher something about the children. But many children, whether consciously or otherwise, will mask some of their own personal feelings to conform to what they perceive as the expectations of the group. Thus the feelings children express to other children may reflect a somewhat different aspect of their personality than what is written or told to the teacher alone. Important aspects of their personalities are also revealed in their play.

DRAMATIC PLAY

In their free and spontaneous play, young children express what they *know* and what they *feel*. They make of the objects around them—dolls, sand and water, boxes and boards—the world they have experienced. It is a world of houses to be lived in, buses to be ridden, cars to be driven, food to be cooked, babies to be cared for, and so on. How directly play may reflect what children know is suggested in the following incidents.

David and Jimmy had been playing "house" at their Head Start center. David said, "We need to go to the movies tonight. I'm gonna get my wife." He then said to a girl standing nearby, "Come on, wife. Can Aunt Faye stay and be the baby-sitter?" He added, "Get into the car," and Consuelo, Patty, and Jimmy climbed on.

In another center, five-year-old Veronica authoritatively told Jerry and Teresa to get dressed, "Hurry up! You have to go to the center for breakfast, and I can't be late to work. Lookit, here comes the bus. You guys are making me late." She quickly put a scarf on Jerry and tried to pick up three-year-old Teresa so as not to "miss the bus."

In a day-care center where many children's parents were university students in a large city, the pattern of living was different. A group of children were playing house. One of the boys was "father" and decided to take the "children" for a walk. He got ready for the walk by placing dolls and a campstool in the doll carriage. Then he called the "children." After admonishing them to stay close by him, not to run into the street, not to get too far behind, they started out. After walking about the room, presumably around the block and up the street, they came to a sidewalk of a main thoroughfare. There "father" pushed the baby carriage against the wall, adjusted the brakes, sat down on his folding chair, and pretended to read his book. He watched the "children" as they played on the walk, giving frequent admonition and direction about where and how to play.

These three incidents illustrate the manner in which the play of children reflects patterns of their lives. Such glimpses are helpful to a teacher who tries to guide the learning of children by beginning with experiences that are familiar and meaningful to them.

But children's dramatic play also expresses what they feel, sometimes directly, sometimes indirectly. The care a child lavishes on a doll may represent love previously felt, but it sometimes symbolizes the cuddling that the child longs to experience. The "spanking" a small boy in his role of "father" administers to his "little boy" may reflect a punishment he actually has received or merely his perception of his father in a disapproving mood. The girl who plays "doctor" and assures .the "patient" that "this won't hurt you," may herself have been either a brave or a timorous patient.

In any case, through play children re-present both unpleasant and pleasurable experiences. Children may change the outcome of a real event to deal with fears or to make their own past behavior more acceptable to themselves. When others are involved in the drama, a child may have to transform an experience to accommodate the wishes of others. Play is, then, a way to express feelings as well as to learn something about social relationships.

A single episode of a child's play tells little, but recurrent themes and patterns found in many observations are significant. The themes and patterns provide important clues about the ways the child is learning to cope with feelings and to find satisfactions for needs.

School-age children may not reveal themselves so openly, but the roles they choose spontaneously and the ways they play the roles they are assigned often tell a good deal about them. Many of the fairy tales and legends that teachers long have used for dramatic interpretation have elements in them that can be meaningful to children. They often represent symbolically conflicts that most, if not all, youngsters struggle to resolve. Thus children identify readily with some of the parts. At the same time, the situations are so clearly fantastic, so obviously not "real," that they are not likely to be threatening. A youngster can safely invest strong feeling in a role when the outcome is known in advance. In this respect, plays that are obviously "make-believe" have a certain advantage over those that more closely parallel real life.

Just as some children enjoy telling stories, some like to watch plays or even make them up as they go along. Often these bear marked resemblances to stories or comic strips the children have read or television shows they have seen. But always they exhibit something of the personalities of their child creators, producers, directors, and actors.

The outcomes of an unfinished story, or the plot evolving from a picture, can be developed dramatically as well as narratively. Teachers gain insight into the personality and the imagination of children when some easily adopt happy, carefree poses to enact the end of a story while others scowl and some abstain from the activity altogether.

With those children who do not readily take on roles, teachers sometimes use puppets. Particularly for preschoolers who are reserved about their feelings, puppets provide a safe medium that appeals to children and allows the expression of joy, anger, or aggression as they play. Skillful teachers throw themselves into roles to engage children in this special kind of dramatic play, and to observe the emotions that the children reveal in secure settings.

WRITTEN EXPRESSION

Young children do little of what we can properly call "creative writing." In this section we deal with forms of expression that are written either by the children themselves or by teachers who transcribe what children say. Many teachers view these transcriptions as necessary intermediaries between oral and written expression. They serve an academic purpose as well as an expressive function. Children will be helped in learning to read and write while they have opportunities to express themselves and reveal something of their personalities.

"Invented Spelling"

Educators traditionally have dealt with children's writing as something distinct from their oral expression. Spoken language, according to the conventional view, precedes the ability to read, and the writing process follows the acquisition of basic reading skills. (At the beginning of this century, however, Maria Montessori treated writing as a process natural to children that paralleled learning to read[2]).

Recently, some researchers and classroom teachers have pointed out that children's interest in making letters and words may precede actual decoding or reading and may not be a direct result of our teaching.[3] Children's early writing, instead, may be closer to other graphic forms of expression. The two-year-old's familiar scribble may be viewed as a precursor to drawing as well as to writing. Children themselves demonstrate that they perceive the two processes similarly when they say, "Draw my name for me."

Teachers who have observed children's "invented spellings" have not formally instructed them in writing letters of the alphabet, and the teachers do not insist on well-formed letters. The children seem motivated to write by the pleasure inherent in the activity. Writing down a "word" is an end in itself, and very often children show no immediate interest in reading what they have written. The junior author recently received two cards from a four-year-old named Victor who had written in various ways and places: "HICBO," "SILTOE," "SIO," "WICLT."

After reading the first combination of letters as "his bow," Victor said he didn't know what the other words were and pursued a new activity. Although Victor was already beginning to read, he had created his own words and spellings with no prompting from adults and with the pleasure and deep concentration that so often accompany drawing and painting.

Children who invent their own words or spellings put pencil or crayon to paper to express themselves. They may care little about using the words as a means of communication even if many of their forms are representations of conventional words. They are playing with words graphically much as they manipulate and play with words orally. Teachers in centers or schools may find it informative to keep samples of children's early writing. Spelling patterns that several children use may reflect their growing knowledge of relationships between sounds and letters. A kindergarten teacher, for example, found certain regularities from child to child.[4] Single letters were used to represent the sound of the letter name, as in PPL for *people* and FRN for *friend*, or one letter stood for a syllable, as in GRIF for *giraffe*.

Language Experience Stories

"Write about what you know from your own experience." The advice that veteran novelists and playwrights customarily offer the novice seems no less appropriate for children who are acquiring the basic skills of written communication. They are likely to write best about situations they have participated in and that have been most meaningful to them. Even a child who is not ordinarily expressive may be intrigued by a familiar topic. Experiences that have been strongly tinged with feeling, whether of pleasure and affection, or of anger, fear, or sorrow, are likely to be significant. There may be something important to say about these experiences, provided the class is one in which a child feels safe to express feeling.

Teachers often write down children's comments about a shared experience, such as a trip to the fire station, and call the collection of comments a "language experience story." Such a story can also consist of individual children's experiences or feelings. Topics teachers use to encourage free expression may be similar to those used to stimulate oral expression, for example: "My Last Birthday Party," "My Favorite Television Show," "My Baby Sister or Brother."

In suggesting topics such as these, teachers are not primarily concerned with the factual information they may gain about a child's home life, experiences, or interests. Rather, they are interested in the feelings the child expresses. They not only pay attention to the child's explicit statements but they also consider implied meanings. In a sense, they try to "read between the lines."

Preschool children who are unable to write down any of their feelings or imaginings often are the least inhibited in expressing them. When they do so, the teacher can write down what they dictate.

One four-year-old, Erin, dictated a letter to her "favorite" teacher, Mr. Kohn; she customarily looked to Mr. Kohn for comfort. It read:

> Dear Granma,
> I am being a good girl. Why don't you come home now? I don't like when you're on your trip. I want you to come home now.
> Love,
> Erin

The following day Erin dictated a similar letter, and the day after, she told a story about the present her grandmother brought back for her. Mr. Kohn knew of Erin's close relationship with her grandmother, who from time to time took short trips. Knowing something of Erin's family, he did not become alarmed at the clear feeling of loss that Erin expressed in her letters. Instead he allowed her to express those feelings and perhaps realize that although her grandmother's absences were not pleasant, it was possible for Erin to cope with them.

Other children struggle with problems that are not as easily resolved. Les, a boy who just had his fifth birthday, came into his nursery school one day with the news that his cousin was in the hospital. According to his mother, there had been an automobile accident, and Les was upset by it. For several days afterward, Les asked his teachers to read a book about children preparing to go to the hospital and another book with a protagonist who was punished by having to spend some time alone. He also told a long story, part of which a teacher wrote down:

> Then we went to the hospital. And there was blood all over. And the doctor was there, and he said, "We're gonna clean up all the blood. You stay right here. There won't be no more blood."

Les had never gone to the hospital, but his teacher wrote down what he said without questioning him. Whether or not Les had seen the accident or its aftermath was not as important as his willingness to express fears aroused by thoughts of accidents, bleeding, or the loneliness of hospitals.

In the primary grades, children begin to write down their own thoughts and feelings. The ability as well as the willingness to be self-expressive in writing, of course, varies from child to child and from group to group. But even first graders can write something about their likes and dislikes when encouraged by teachers who help with spelling and tolerate errors. A first grader, Liz, with help from her teacher, produced this after a lesson on the days of the week:

> I like Saturdays because Saturdays is not school. I don't like Mondays because Mondy is no cortoon.

A second-grade teacher, Mrs. Ferne, believed that most children have feelings, wishes, and stories to share when they are given opportunities to write them down. Children in her class could write about any topic that occurred to them, or they could use "story starters," such as "Some things that make me laugh are . . . ," "My parrot gave my secret away . . . ," and "I woke up one morning and looked outside. . . ." To stimulate thinking, the teacher asked children questions about topics related to the "starters" before the children began to write.

Some children wrote barely a sentence and relied heavily on stories they had heard before. Linda, for example, wrote, "one nite all thow the haws not a creature note." Mrs. Ferne included this in the week's collection of children's writing along with more complete and imaginative samples.

Bert's contribution of "I woke up one morning and looked outside . . ." was "The Fabulouse Morning":

> I woke up and looked outside. I saw 500,000,000,000,000,000,000,000 fooball cards and cluding all the Dallas cowboys. And I fanted. And then I told the Ginnies book of the records.

This short piece comes from a child with an active imagination. Bert neatly combined everyday things, football cards, with his fantasy to be included in the *Guinness Book of World Records*. After reading Bert's story, the teacher knew something of his interests and fantasies. As with the other children's writing, she corrected none of the spelling errors to help maintain fluency and enthusiasm for the activity. Judging from Bert's tale, she could be pleased that providing the children with opportunities to write was effectively nurturing their creativity.

Another second grader in the same class expressed himself in a different way. A world of witches and warlocks came to Arlen's mind, and he wrote about them in this way:

> One time there was a worlock named worlock king. And he was maried to a witch named witch queen. And they had 2 motercicles that had telephons in them, and the numbers on it weren't called telephone numbers. They were called worlock witch numbers. They got them as a wedding present. There Uncles and Ants put in there money in to buy them. And they were gladd that they were that nice. One morning they went out to ride them. And they met a bunch of witches. And they asked if they could ride with them. And they went a little further and met some worlocks. And they wanted to have a ride so they hopped on. And they met another cuple and another and another finly the worlock said why don't all of you go and call your broom and ride. & so they all got there broom and they rid of and that is the story of the only worlock and witch that ever had two motercicles.

Arlen's warlock and witch were products of his imagination, and he was able to weave a tale around them. Like young children's dramatic play, however, this story contains realistic elements that reflect what Arlen knows about marriage and weddings. At the same time, he may be dealing with fears held about witches by transforming them into ordinary, pleasant characters.

Reactions to Pictures

Sometimes the beginning of a story can be furnished by a picture, a filmstrip, or an excerpt from a film. One teacher of four-year-olds asked the children's parents to bring in photographs, showing the children at different ages from infancy to age four. She then made "books" about each of them, using the pictures as a stimulus for talk and expression of feelings. Not everything the children said was included in their books, but the project demonstrated that a young child can respond with ease when he or she is the topic at hand.

Teachers sometimes use Polaroid cameras to take pictures of children engaged in various activities at school, center, or on a trip. The photographs are quickly available, and either the teacher or the child can write down the child's reactions. Along with factual descriptions, children may include feelings about themselves or others.

Other teachers use illustrations in children's literature to encourage writing. Second graders drew their own illustrations of a monster they had read about before writing short stories of their own. Some children made their monsters seem nonthreatening and ordinary while others created more fantastic characters. Two stories with teacher-corrected spellings from very capable writers follow:

> Vik has a monster called Fred. He is 3 years old. He lives in a cave in Austin. He is 10 feet long. He likes to sleep in a closet. He likes best of all to kick girls. He hates GIRLS and is not very good at hiding.

Another child wrote:

> King Thing belongs to Yvonne and is 628,900 years old. He likes to eat books, but don't tell Mrs. M. [the librarian]. Yvonne can't have any dogs or cats because he hates them. He can run faster than a deer and yell louder than a gorilla.

A single composition does not tell a teacher a great deal about a child, but a series of compositions with many different subjects may. The way a child notices details and organizes them into a meaningful story indicates something of the quality of intellectual functioning. Are situations seen in rather conventional ways, or is there evidence of inventiveness? When a child departs from direct experience, what kind of world is created? Is the writing limited to surface descriptions or is there concern with the feelings of the characters?

Several teachers used pictures to help them understand more about how children might feel toward various aspects of their school and group life. The teachers showed photographs of situations that might arise on the playground or in the classroom. They assumed children would write more freely about the unidentified children in the picture than they would about themselves. It seemed likely that the kinds of reactions they would ascribe to the children in the pictures would resemble their own reactions to similar situations. We presented examples of children's spoken reactions to pictures in chapter 4. Teachers or primary-grade children may also write down such comments.

There is much that teachers can learn about the children in their own centers or classrooms by studying their written or dictated expression. Part of what can be learned depends on the teacher's skill in providing opportunities in which children feel free to express themselves. Part depends on the teacher's sensitivity to the personal meaning of what the child writes, and the ability to relate it to other information about that child. Inevitably, however, more will be learned about some children than about others; for written language, although an effective medium for certain children, is not so for all.

MOVEMENT, MUSIC, AND DANCE

Children's movements, like spoken or written products, can express feelings held about themselves. Two-year-olds exploring the world around them can walk with confidence and purpose, or they can be relatively still, waiting for an adult to serve as their guide. Three-year-olds, when given colored scarves to take outdoors with them, may gracefully run with them or do a rigid march, turning the scarf into a flag. Children in the primary grades, when given the opportunity to move freely, may do exactly that—joyfully—or they may watch what others do and move in a stilted manner.

Moving freely and comfortably in a variety of ways is often a major part of programs in creative dramatics. Teachers who use such programs can see which children are consistently cautious and restrained in their movements, and which children use their bodies as a means of expression with no apparent self-consciousness. The lessons teachers select might encourage relaxation or vigorous running, or they might specify roles for children to "play," such as that of an elephant, a leaf blown in the wind, or a tired person.

Many exercises of this kind are set to music, and often the movements children create are indistinguishable from dance. Music is evident in the rhythm of children's body movements and in their spontaneous chants. Although young children are not always able to keep time, their walking or running or skipping has its own pattern and represents the basic material that they can later elaborate into dance, given the right opportunities. Similarly, the vocal accompaniments to their play, though not always tuneful and often wordless, are fundamental musical expressions.

Whether children continue to express themselves freely in music and the dance as they grow older depends on a number of factors, including the kind of guidance they are given and their feelings about themselves. Some children in the process of development impose such rigid controls on their feelings that even their response to music is constrained. Others seize on the opportunity for release.

Teachers listening to children sing or watching them in an interpretative dance cannot know the depth of their experiences. But they can look for freedom or rigidity, absorption or passivity, and perhaps add some insight to whatever knowledge about the children they may already have.

ART

Like music and dance, children's art—their drawing, their painting, their use of plastic materials—is body expression in the beginning. It is children's nature to be active; they scribble, or slosh color across the page, squeeze and punch the clay for sheer sensory and muscular enjoyment. But as they grow and learn, these activities take on new meaning. They become media for emotional and, eventually, intellectual expression.

Like the quality of their movement, the quality of children's engagement with materials, as well as what they create, tells us something about them. Five-year-old Ellen, for example, explores the medium of finger paint and talks about her discoveries, which interest her more than the final product:

A blob of yellow paint placed on her wet paper by teacher. She immediately begins to mix the paint on the paper with both hands. "It's cold! Look at my finger marks." (She is making swirling marks with her fingers.) "Look at my hands. I'm gonna write my name with my finger marks." (She uses her whole hands, with palms, and uses her fingers alone. Makes fast movements in circles.) "Look at my hands. I rub them together." (She writes her name, spelling.) "E,L,L" and trails off. She makes zigzag motions and counts "1,2,3,4,5,6,7,8." She is given a piece of sponge. "Hey look it." Squeezes the paint out of the sponge. She uses the sponge in swirling motions, very rapid circular movements, and then squeezes it. A blue blob is added. "Now look at mine. It's green and blue. Now look at my green hands. I'm gonna rub this all over my hands." (Rubbing sponge into hands. She wildly uses hands to make symmetrical motions on paper. Paper tears down the middle. She smooths it out. Leaves work.)

In contrast, Martin, also age five, spends half as long at the art table and appears to view the activity in a completely different way from Ellen:

Given sponge, starts carefully with sponge, spreading paint on paper. Using left hand, makes circular movements. Holds sponge delicately with three fingers. Switches sponge to right hand—uses either hand to hold sponge. Yellow blob added. Approaches yellow area with sponge, from green and moves sponge around and around, rather slowly. Makes sounds softly, along with the motion of his hand. Uses the sponge in the palm of his hand now. Every few moments stops to look at his hands. Uses one hand at a time to hold sponge, no fingers or hands directly on paper. "I'm finished!"

Clinical and developmental studies show that the emotional ups and downs of many children are clearly reflected in their art work. One pattern in the use of form and color parallels the periods when the child's life is relatively serene; different ones appear during times of trouble or anxiety.

The child's art also reflects the struggle and growing ability to understand the world. Those who have studied children's drawings, for example, see a progression from scribbles that go back and forth across the page, to lines deliberately placed in a variety of ways, to shapes (circles, squares, and so on), and finally to representations of objects and people. Not surprisingly, the human figure is frequently drawn at this stage. Early pictures of the child-artist and the people and things around him or her appear to emphasize those details that are most personally meaningful. Figures 6.1 through 6.6 illustrate the growing complexity and organization of children's drawings and paintings.

It is often said that children of five years or under draw what they *know*. Accuracy of representation and proportion are not found in their work. Not until they are seven or eight do they usually become concerned with renderings that are "realistic." At this time, children try to capture what they *see*; they reduce the discrepancies between what they perceive and what they produce. Even then what each child sees is different from what anyone else sees, and artistic work continues to be highly personal.

Because some children appear to express themselves more readily in drawing or painting than they do in speaking or writing, art work may sometimes be used to gain information about these children's interests and background. Many preschool and kindergarten teachers ask children

FIGURE 6.1

Done by a three-year-old girl.

CAtherine

FIGURE 6.2

Done by a four-year-old girl.

Marion

Mom and the little girl
are having a party. Ribbons
and balloons are flying around.
The party is in the summer.

FIGURE 6.3   *Done by a five-year-old girl.*

Van

Mighty Mouse is going
to attack a cat.

FIGURE 6.4   *Done by a five-year-old boy (caption written by kindergarten teacher).*

FIGURE 6.5 *Done by a six-year-old girl.*

FIGURE 6.6 *Done by a seven-year-old boy.*

to talk about their drawings and paintings and then write short captions on the work that reveal interests of the artists.

Primary grade children may draw "Favorite Activities," "My Family and Me," "What I Like To Do after School," "My Best Friends," as they might write compositions on these topics. The information they furnish is, of course, subject to the same limitations as apply to any self-report techniques. A further limitation is that the child's "report" may indicate more about what he or she likes to draw, or can draw, than it does about the topic assigned. A child may enjoy bicycling but make a picture of a ball player because a bicycle is too difficult to draw.

At all ages, the child's art work provides important clues to individuality. What the child chooses to paint or draw or model, whether the primary interest lies in form and design or in telling some kind of story, the freedom or constraint with which the medium is approached, the carelessness or meticulousness of technique, whether the work is large and expansive or tiny and restricted, the use made of space, the number and kind of details, what is said about the work—all of these are relevant to understanding the child as a personality.

The teacher must remember, however, that some of these factors may be influenced by children's environments as much as by the kinds of persons they are. Some children are taught to "fill the page," colors a child might choose spontaneously are not always available, inadequate tools or crowded work space may hamper freedom of expression, and other restrictions may affect the child's art. Further, some of what is revealed in the child's art work has to do with the deep and often unconscious motivations that the teacher is not professionally equipped to interpret. Whatever seems significant in children's art consequently must always be related to other information the teacher has about them.

USING INFORMATION FROM EXPRESSIVE ACTIVITIES

We emphasize that the primary purpose of the activities described in this chapter is to provide for child *expression*. Even if they are never used for child *study*, they have important values for children.

We have said little about techniques for evaluating children's forms of expression. We believe it is important simply to provide many opportunities for expression and to encourage children to take those opportunities, particularly in times when academic skills receive the greatest emphasis in programs—even at the preschool level. Such provision will lead to a more balanced curriculum. Consequently, children not only will experience school or center as a place for learning through a variety of media, but also as a place where their expression of individuality is valued. In addition, expressive activity allows for *all* children to have successful and satisfying experiences, whether they are academically slow or quick, gifted or handicapped.

We have tried to alert teachers to some of the questions they may raise about the significance of the ways children express themselves. We have suggested some of the clues to look for. We have, however, tried to avoid implications that a particular kind of expression (the use of certain colors in painting, for example) necessarily has a particular kind of meaning. The literature of child and clinical psychology provides some evidence about what different kinds of expresson frequently do mean. But each child is unique, and the significance of his or her own modes of expression lies not so much in their resemblance to those of other children as in the pattern of individuality they present.

Teachers faced with the responsibility for guiding the learning of many children cannot possibly understand all the complexities of each child. Inevitably they are confronted with more clues than they can pay attention to; it is far more difficult to synthesize these clues into a complete personality picture.

As teachers think about a child's learning, however, they can draw, often intuitively, on their knowledge of the child's self-expression. The teachers' hunches about the child's motivations, the satisfactions being sought, may suggest to the teachers the possibilities for making learning more meaningful and more rewarding. Their insight into the children's pictures of themselves and what they would like to be may present clues for helping children to find a greater degree of self-realization in learning. At the same time, it may help to understand the kinds of learning situations in which children are likely to feel comfortable and ready as contrasted to those in which they are likely to feel too threatened to perform adequately. Teachers may vary the way they introduce a new area of learning, a new concept, or a new skill, according to their understanding of children. They also may vary the conditions for learning, setting a small and very specific task to be accomplished independently or giving a larger area to explore, supervising closely or casually, having a child work alone or with another child or in a group, encouraging or discouraging competitiveness, and other variations related to the teachers' understanding of children.

SUMMARY

In this chapter we have concerned ourselves with the meaning of those activities in which children are given freedom to express themselves. We have looked particularly at the opportunities for self-expression that are inherent in the language program, dramatic play, movement, dance, and art. Through these activities, children reveal many things about themselves that they are aware of; they also reveal something of desires, wishes, strivings that are more deeply buried. Teachers cannot deal directly with much that goes on beneath the surface, but they cannot escape its influence on the child's learning.

Expressive activities tell us something not only about the feelings of children but also about their thinking. All forms of expression permit the child to integrate unique past experiences, to re-present a growing knowledge of the world. That knowledge may be aesthetic as well as physical, mathematical, or social. Aesthetic development, no less than emotional and cognitive development, is regulated by the mechanism of equilibration, described in chapter 3. Children seek appropriate ways to express what they feel and know so that there is a balance between their conceptual understanding and their mode of re-presenting it.

In the process of giving form to concepts children are acquiring or have acquired, they develop their own aesthetic standards. These are not adult standards, but they provide a basis for children to judge whether their own movements, stories, or paintings are adequate and personally satisfying. What satisfies one child, of course, may not satisfy another; what is significant for one may have little significance for another.

Teachers relate whatever hunches they may have about the significance of a particular child's expression to other aspects of their knowledge of the child. Sometimes they verify their hunches through continuing observation of a youngster. Frequently, however, in order to get a more complete picture and to correct some of their personal bias, they need to share the thinking and observations of other people. We shall turn to this aspect of child study in the next chapter.

NOTES

1. For an elaboration of the relationship beween aesthetic development and Piagetian theory, see David Elkind, Donna Hetzel, and John Coe, "Piaget and British Primary Education," *Educational Psychologist* 2(1974): pp. 1-10.
2. Maria Montessori, *The Montessori Method* (New York: Schocken, 1964).

3. Carol Chomsky, "Invented Spelling in the Open Classroom," *Word* 27 (1975):
   pp. 499-518.
4. Rhea Paul, "Invented Spelling in Kindergarten," *Young Children* 31 (1976):
   pp. 195-200.

SUGGESTED READING

Cazden, Courtney B., ed. *Language in Early Childhood Education.* Washington,
D.C.: National Association for the Education of Young Children, 1972. This is a
collection of papers, some by Cazden, about language and language programs for
young children. Like current researchers in language acquisition, the authors
emphasize the view that language development is a natural process in which
almost all children learn language—and the specific dialect of the people around
them—without formal instruction. Topics include the selection of preschool
language programs, the attitudes of blacks toward different dialects of English,
language in day-care programs, and children's early writing.

Chukovsky, Kornei. *From Two to Five.* Translated and edited by Miriam Morton.
Rev. ed. Berkeley: University of California Press, 1968. Written by a Russian poet,
this fascinating book contains numerous examples of young children's inventiveness with language. Although the focus is on creativity with words, the author also
shows how children's poetic and charming inventions reflect their thinking and
their ability to see relationships in everything around them.

Gardner, Howard. *The Arts and Human Development: A Psychological Study of
the Artistic Process.* New York: John Wiley & Sons, 1973. This is a comprehensive
synthesis of research on artistic development, which takes into account several
theories of human development, including Piaget's. Gardner discusses the artistic
process and its relationship to symbolic processes as well as research on music,
language development, pictorial art, and literature. Some examples of children's
music, art, and writing are presented.

Hartley, Ruth E., et al. *Understanding Children's Play.* New York: Columbia
University Press, 1952. This classic book, Freudian in orientation, is based on
extensive observations of the play activities of children, with particular attention
to ways in which various activities—dramatics, block play, water play, painting,
music, and movement—are related to personality development. While the study
involved only preschool children, the discussions of the function of play, what we
can learn about children from their expression in play, how we can help their
growth through giving opportunities for play in different media, and what
different functions these various media serve for the child, are equally pertinent
for the older child.

Kellogg, Rhoda. *Analyzing Children's Art.* Palo Alto, Calif.: National Press Books,

1969. There is an abundance of black-and-white illustrations primarily of children's drawings and paintings in this interesting and readable book. The author traces the development of shapes and forms, devoting several chapters to children's scribbling and prepictorial representations. Related research and discussion of cross-cultural and theoretical issues are also included.

Lowenfeld, Viktor, and W. Lambert Brittain. *Creative and Mental Growth*. 6th ed. New York: Macmillan Publishing Co., 1975. This textbook is full of illustrations, most in black-and-white and some in color, which give the reader a sense of how children's art reflects their cognitive development. The first seven chapters are of particular interest to early childhood teachers. They deal with classroom procedures as well as the child's treatment of color, form, and space from age two through nine.

Read, Charles. "Pre-school Children's Knowledge of English Phonology." *Harvard Educational Review* 41(1971): 1-34. This is a report of one of the early studies of preschoolers' "invented spellings." Read discusses how children's writing reflects their unconscious knowledge of the sound system of English. Like other recent studies in child development, this research highlights the child-as-thinker and hypothesis-tester. In addition, it has implications for the natural integration of oral and written aspects of language in school settings, starting with preschool.

7 STUDY THE CHILD THROUGH OTHERS

Much can be learned about a child and much can be done to facilitate his or her learning and development when child study is confined to what goes on in the school or center. If our study of the child is to approach any degree of completeness, however, we must go beyond what we can observe in the classroom and what we can find out from the children themselves. We must seek information from others who know about their growth and development.

In doing this, we have at least three purposes in mind. First, we want to discover how each child behaves, responds, reacts in various environments—at home, in the neighborhood, at church, and in other places. We need to know something of the children's developmental histories. We want to discover the values and expectations that people other than ourselves have held for them, so that we can put our own values and expectations in proper balance.

In addition to getting such specific information about a particular child, we want to check our own ways of perceiving the child. How closely do our notions of abilities, interests, and concerns correspond with those of others, who know the child in situations different from those we experience with the child? To what extent has our own personal bias entered into our appraisal? Whenever our way of seeing a child differs strikingly from the way others see him or her, bias is likely. Finally, we often need help in discussing and setting up goals that will be reasonable and appropriate for a given child.

We turn to our co-workers and to parents and other community members for exploration of the significance of the educational goals that are commonly held for all children, to see how they should apply in this particular community and with this group of youngsters. Many persons who have an interest in children can contribute to our study: parents, both the child's and others who know the child, grandparents, maintenance people and cooks, school bus drivers, doctors, nurses, social workers, psychologists, psychiatrists, religious workers, community leaders, and others. But the key resource is the parent. In this chapter we devote most of our attention to the ways the teacher studies children through and with parents, though we also consider briefly the other persons who can help in such study.

Although teachers recognize that child study through other persons often yields important insights, many teachers are hesitant about undertaking it. They have good reasons for their reservations. Some of these they state quite openly; others are more personal.

SOME DIFFICULTIES

A major problem confronting many teachers who would like to confer with parents or consult others about children is finding time to do so. Some schools provide "floating teachers" or dismiss classes early on certain days to free the classroom teacher for conferences and home visits. Occasionally two teachers work out a plan whereby one of them takes two groups while the other is freed for a short period. More often, however, conferences must be arranged at the end of the day; and this is not easy, since parents' free time does not always coincide with the teacher's after-school hour. Although many teachers manage to hold a considerable number of conferences despite the lack of any time provision for them, they are keenly aware that such hurried meetings are not very effective.

Many teachers, if they were to be completely honest, would indicate that they do not particularly relish the idea of conferences with other adults. Some who feel this way are people who have chosen to work with children knowing that they are more comfortable with them than with older people. Others, probably the majority, recognize that their professional training has not equipped them very well for this aspect of their teaching. A teacher's preparation usually includes assuming major responsibility for the conduct of a class. Less often, however, does such preparation involve conferring with parents.

Insecurity stemming from lack of preparation is heightened when the parents come from an ethnic or cultural group unfamiliar to the teacher. Further complications arise when the teacher assumes knowledge or understanding of a particular group but is actually dealing with stereotypes.

Another difficulty stems from the teacher's uncertainty of the definitions of the teaching role in relation to the roles of the other adults who are interested in the child. This is particularly true of the beginning teacher, but many experienced teachers are equally unclear in this matter. The teacher's specific function is to help the child acquire the skills, knowledge, and attitudes the community believes will be needed for useful work and good citizenship.

Though parents contribute to this also, their most important function is providing the child with affection and emotional support. Teachers cannot possibly assume this function, but they may in a limited way augment it.

Similarly, the teacher's role differs significantly from that of the psychologist or psychiatrist. Teachers working with children in a group must help the children curb certain of their impulses and keep their attention directed to the learning at hand. In contrast, the therapist, usually working with an individual, although sometimes with a small group, at certain stages in treatment may find it necessary to permit, or even encourage, expression of feelings that could not be tolerated in the classroom.

The distinctions we draw between the teacher's role and the roles of the parents and colleagues in other professions are not hard and fast. The roles do overlap at many points. When teachers realize clearly their own unique functions, they appreciate more fully the contributions that other people make to the child's development. Secure in the knowledge that in certain specific ways they are better prepared to help the child than any of the other persons who are interested in the child, teachers are less likely to be beset by feelings of inadequacy or jealousy.

Feelings, all kinds of feelings, toward themselves, toward other adults, toward children, necessarily influence not only the kinds of information and help teachers seek from other adults but also their ways of seeking help and the use they make of whatever help they receive.

Just as a teacher sometimes sees in children the child he or she once was and becomes overidentified with them, so the teacher may regard the other adults who are interested in the child not so much as peers but more as the parents and other authorities known as a child. The teacher does well to face as honestly as possible the kinds of feelings he or she brings to attempts to study children through others. Many feelings, concern for the child, sympathy for the complexities of parenthood, and more, further the teacher's relationships with other adults. Other feelings hamper them.

When teachers feel that they can be all things to each child, or that they should somehow find some way of helping every child, they will find it difficult to value sufficiently the contribution other adults make.

Occasionally, teachers unconsciously derive so much satisfaction from the authority they hold in relation to the children that they cannot bear any suggestions that appear to threaten or question their prerogatives.

Teachers who have the courage to examine their emotional reactions toward the adults with whom they share responsibility for children are likely to confront a mixture of positive and negative feelings. This may help them to understand the aloofness, the defensiveness, and even the open hostility they sometimes encounter. Insight into self often leads to increased understanding of others. Such understanding is especially important in working with parents.

PARENTS, IMPORTANT RESOURCES

The teacher may not readily see that parents typically know more about their children than anyone else does. A little reflection may be needed to make the point clearer. The parent's substantial acquaintance stems from the moment of the child's birth and before and includes most of the child's waking and sleeping hours. Parents know children at their worst and at their best. It is true that the parents' strong emotional involvement often precludes objectivity, but the nature of the parental bias probably is one of the most important facts to be learned about the child.

An increasing number of children whose mothers are employed outside their homes spend a considerable portion of their early years with teachers and other day-care workers. Nevertheless, the parents' continuing responsibility for the child carries with it the most intimate and complete knowledge of the development of the child as a person.

Most early childhood teachers, whether in day-care centers or in schools, have some contact with parents. The parent brings a child to school, stops by with rubbers, writes a note to explain an absence, comes to meetings, and sees the teacher at other times. These casual encounters, although they provide little information about a child's history and few details about the present living situation, may provide clues to the nature of the parent-child relationship. The youngster whose mother is always on hand for meetings, who checks on such matters as arrivals at and departure from school and whether a sweater is worn at recess time, and who comments at length on each report card, appears to live in a different world from the child whose mother rarely comes to the school or calls and merely returns the report card with her signature. It would be dangerous, however, to infer from such limited information that one child was more cherished, or more harassed by parental supervision, than the other.

The Casual Meeting

Casual meetings occur as the teacher encounters parents in the community or when parents come to school to meet their children or to attend school functions. The distinctive feature of casual meetings is their unplanned, spontaneous quality. Having no particular focus, they often reveal the parent (and the teacher) in a different light from that cast by the situation in which each is intent on making a good impression or on getting some point across. Sometimes parents in such unguarded moments mention matters of really deep concern to them. The way the teacher responds to these concerns, brushing them aside or responding with genuine interest, may be crucial to the further development of the parent-teacher relationship. Even if the parent has raised a question that cannot be dealt with at the moment, the wise teacher will see that the way is left open for the parent to discuss the matter further at a more appropriate time and place. Perhaps the major requirement for the casual meeting is that it leaves the parent with the feeling that the teacher is an approachable person who appreciates the parental role.

Most schools and many centers are not willing to leave the opportunity for teachers and parents to get together completely to chance.

An old and tried method of approaching parents is through meetings at which the goals and purposes of the school are discussed. Perhaps the main value (necessarily limited) of such meetings lies in the feelings of friendliness, understanding, and warmth that they may generate. Through these meetings, teachers frequently have the opportunity to identify the parents of the children in their rooms and to meet them in a more or less casual manner. This provides a kind of undergirding for any further contacts that may develop.

Parent Involvement

Under federal programs or in cooperatives, parents, in varying degrees, are involved in the determination of policy. They also assist in the implementation of the program, serving as volunteer classroom participants or in some instances as paid aides. In these situations the relationships of parents and teachers differ from those prevailing when most of their contacts are of a more casual nature. These relationships appear to be most fruitful when the school or center is able to promote an atmosphere of mutual respect and make ample provisions for the confrontation and resolution of whatever differences may arise.

The Parent-Teacher Conference

The parent-teacher conference focused on the parent's child differs from both the casual meetings teachers have with parents and the meetings that relate to policy or the implementation of the program. The conference is held at an appointed time and place and is planned in some detail. Conferences may take place at home, at school, at the center, in offices, or in some other place mutually agreeable to parent and teachers. Conferences in children's homes have the value of enabling the participants to see the environment in which the child lives, works, and plays, and to note such attitudes and values as may be indicated by furnishings, routines, and disciplinary measures carried out during the visit. Whether the child or other children are present during the interview and how they are related to the conversation are also significant factors that give clues to the child's behavior and development. There are also some disadvantages to home conferences.

The following report of a home conference illustrates the kind of information and understanding that may be gathered from such an experience. The teacher was making routine visits to all the children in her kindergarten. She writes:

> Visited Gary W's home today. Gary met me outside, welcomed me, took me by the hand and led me upstairs to see his baby sister and his mother. Mother seemed glad to see me. Said she was sorry she hadn't been able to visit the Kindergarten or come to any of the meetings at school but perhaps she could a little later in the year. The baby is just a month old.
>
> During the visit Gary was running in and out bringing me toys to observe. Once he brought in two oranges and asked me if I'd like one. I thanked him but said I didn't believe I did. He sat down, peeled one, and ate it. His mother commented on his dirty hands, but did not suggest that he wash them. She asked him if the orange tasted good when he ate it with such dirty hands. He said, yes, it tasted all right. Mother said they had a battle every evening when they asked him to wash his hands before dinner. I asked what he did at school every day before he ate his piece of fruit. He said he washed his hands. Mother said he never wanted to at home. Mother asked me if he was mean at school. Since Gary was in the room at the time, I replied that sometimes he helped us but other times he needed help. She replied that he was that way at home. Some days he was real mean, but she smiled when she said it. After Gary had showed me his toys, he showed me a picture of his father. His father's picture

showed a young, cheerful looking person of whom one might say, "He has personality."

Gary sat down to peel and eat his other orange. His mother said when he finished eating it he could take his peelings to the kitchen, but he said he guessed he'd just leave them there—which he did.

I was sitting on a couch and Gary told me that's where he slept. His mother told him to tell me what happened to his bed. He said it got broken. I expressed sympathy and asked how it happened. He said he and another kid were jumping up and down on it and it just broke. His mother said she was having it fixed.

The baby slept during my visit, but I admired her to Gary's satisfaction.

When I mentioned leaving, Gary asked me if I was going to see Richard and Marvin. (They live in the same duplex and are members of our morning Kindergarten class.) When I said yes, Gary offered to go with me. Mrs. W. asked me to come again. Said she was almost always at home. Said she would probably start walking to school with the boys soon and let Mrs. M. (Richard's mother) stay with the baby. She usually comes after Richard, Gary, and Marvin. They need to cross 12th Street (the traffic is heavy). However, there's a policeman there to help the children across.

I said goodbye to Mrs. W. and accompanied by Gary went to visit Richard and his mother.

The teacher felt that the conference gave her a number of clues to understanding Gary. Despite the mother's comments about Gary's dirty hands and his meanness (what did she have in mind here?), the teacher got the impression of warmth and affection. She was struck by the mother's indefiniteness and apparent lack of consistency. (This may reveal as much about the teacher and her values as it does about the mother.) The teacher also noted Gary's seeming acceptance of his new baby sister, and the apparent neighborliness among the families living in the duplex. Evaluating the conference in the light of its purposes, which were primarily to get acquainted and to establish a friendly basis for further contacts, she felt the conference had gone rather well.

Sometimes it is interesting to reverse roles—to consider the impression the parent may get from the teacher. In this instance it seems likely that Gary's mother felt that the teacher was friendly and interested in her child. Did she wonder about and perhaps resent that the teacher succeeded in getting him to wash his hands so readily? (The teacher's implicit assumption that a child's behavior in school is likely to be carried over into the home is questionable. Indeed, the child's home behavior sometimes represents rebellion against school regimentation, restriction, and constraint.) Did the mother really care about the hand washing? Perhaps she assumed this concern because she anticipated the teacher's disapproval. And what about the teacher's comment that "sometimes he helps and sometimes he needs help"? Did this satisfy the mother that Gary was pretty much the same in school as at home? Or would she wonder about this and want to get a more definite answer? (The teacher wisely intended to leave this matter open for discussion at a later and more appropriate time.)

Whether or not this conference would have developed any differently had it been held at the school is not known, of course. Ordinarily, the home visiting procedure is considered more acceptable at the early childhood levels, where the school's function more closely parallels that of the family, than it is at other grade levels.

In certain circumstances, home visits may be regarded as an invasion of family privacy. Some cultural groups welcome others to their homes only when they feel they know them extremely well. Some poor families have learned from bitter experience that the would-be visitor, usually social welfare worker or policeman, only comes when there's a problem to be investigated. Certainly home visits should not be attempted unless there is general agreement in the community that teachers routinely visit homes. If home visiting is not a usual procedure, teachers probably will wisely prefer to make appointments with parents at the school or center unless the parent clearly and spontaneously indicates that a conference at home would be preferable. When the conference is held at the school, whether in the classroom, office or conference room, the teacher emphasizes that the matters of concern are professional rather than merely social. At the same time the conference more readily stays on its main focus, the child's learning in school or center.

When the teacher senses that the parent, on the basis of prior experience, regards the school as an unpleasant place, an alternative may be suggested. A nearby community center, or park, even the parking lot of the supermarket may serve.

Characteristics of a Successful Parent-Teacher Conference

As the previous illustration of a conference suggests, success is a relative matter. Somewhat too often, the conference is seen either as a magical key to "understanding" the child, or as a last desperate measure for solving a problem. More realistically, the conference, like most other child study techniques, usually does little more than provide the teacher (and the parent) with clues that have to be tested and verified in working and living with the child. A conference may meet all of the criteria for success that we set forth here and still raise as many questions as it answers.

A Good Conference Is Purposeful.   The teacher's reason for wanting to talk with the parent is made explicit. If conferences are held routinely, either at the beginning of the year to get acquainted with parents, or at intervals to report to them on the child's progress, the teacher makes sure that the parent knows that this is the purpose of the conference. When the parent is asked to come in for a special conference, the reason is specified. The teacher may say, "I find I can help the children in my class more effectively if I know a little bit about their interests outside of school, whether they talk about school at home, and so on. I hope you can help me to get better acquainted with Richard." Or, "George is having trouble with his reading. He isn't responding to the help I've tried to give him. I wonder if he's said anything about it at home, or whether you have any clues as to what may be the matter?"

Statements about the purpose of a conference should not be so vague as to leave the parent wondering what it is all about, or whether the teacher may not be subtly digging for something the parent does not want to reveal. On the other hand, teachers should guard against statements that are sure to antagonize parents or make them feel guilty. Sometimes it is helpful to consider whether the purpose the teacher has formulated is one that would seem acceptable and reasonable to her if the parent and teacher roles were reversed.

Although parents and teachers may differ as to the *methods* of child-rearing and education, it usually can be assumed that they are in agreement about their goal, which is the optimum development of the child. A conference is based on the supposition that they both have something to contribute to the realization of the goal.

Teachers and parents often find it difficult to recognize their common goals. Both, subject often to pressures and sometimes to criticism in their respective roles, find it easy to place blame on one another. The responsibility for keeping the mutual goal clearly in view, however, seems to rest primarily with the teacher.

One teacher, who had not yet had much opportunity to get to know a child's mother, handed her a package of wet clothing, with the explanation, "Suzie *accidentally* spilled some paint on her dress so we washed it out for her." The mother, paying no attention to the explanation, immediately slapped the child. The teacher, belatedly, realized the importance of being certain that the child's clothing was always protected and the necessity for getting to know more about the mother and her expectations for Suzie. She decided to ask the mother to come in for a conference but thought it best to wait until a time when she was not upset.

A second-grade teacher, who was inexperienced, was angry when a child brought back his homework with, "This is a stupid way to teach subtraction" scrawled across it. Without waiting for her wrath to subside, she called the mother, insisting that she come to school that very afternoon. As soon as the mother arrived she gave her a lengthy explanation of the method she was using. As she commented later, the mother "paid no attention." She did not think that she had convinced her.

In both cases, the immediate goals of parent and teacher seemed at odds. In the second instance, however, both mother and teacher shared the longer term goals of wanting the child to master subtraction. Had the teacher been less defensive she could have found out what had happened to make the mother question the teacher's method. Was the mother angry because the method was new to her? Or was it that the child did not understand the method? Unfortunately, the teacher never gave the parent a chance to explain.

In the first instance, the compatibility of the teacher's and parent's longer term goals for Suzie is less obvious. Perhaps Suzie's mother had had a frustrating day at work, and the wet clothing was the last straw. It may also be that she really did not understand that the paint spilling was not intentional. Or the slap could be the mother's message to Suzie that she should not make extra work for the teacher. There is also the possibility that slapping Suzie is habitual and the mother is having a hard time being a parent. The teacher was wise to postpone discussion until a more propitious time since she felt upset by the parent's behavior and there was so much uncertainty about the meaning of the behavior.

A Good Conference Is a Two-way Process. As the incidents described suggest, the teacher's preoccupation with his or her own point of view frequently prevents a joint quest for mutual understanding. The parent surely regarded the conference on methods of teaching subtraction as an imposition.

Sometimes conferences also take on the character of an inquisition. The teacher asks a battery of questions when fewer but broader, more open-ended questions would serve more effectively to help the parents feel that their feelings and opinions are genuinely respected.

In conferences with parents or other adults, just as in conferences with children, *listening* is important. Paying attention to what the other person is saying and how it is said, to the accompanying facial expression, gestures, and voice, leads to much more understanding than concentrating on what one is going to say next.

If the conference is to be a cooperative exploration, the teacher cannot presume to know the answers and thus be in a position to tell the parent.

The teacher can take clues from parents' comments. If parents suggest that the child is difficult, the teacher may explore their views further, asking, "Why do you say that?" or "Can you tell me just what he does?" If parents suggest causes, they can be accepted and perhaps other possibilities suggested. Behavior is complex. There are many causes, and parents' hunches are often as good as and sometimes better than teachers' hunches. When parents suggest plans of action, they can be accepted at least for a try. They may work; and, if not, other plans may evolve from them. If the aims of the conferences are to secure cooperation and develop parent responsibility and initiative, it is important to encourage parent response, certainly not to do anything that will defeat it.

If a conference is truly two-way, the teacher does not do *all* the talking, but the teacher does have a contribution to make. Just as the teacher expects to learn from the parent, so the parent has certain expectations for receiving information. The parent knows the child at home; the teacher knows the child at school or center. The more concrete and specific the teacher can be about the child, the more likely it is that teacher and parent will find a conference mutually profitable. Thus, "He's getting along all right in his reading" could apply to almost any child, and probably tells the parent little that is not already known. In contrast, "Bill's finished the second reader and has just read two story books about trains. He is beginning to be able to sound out new words he doesn't know, but he still relies mostly on the pictures or the other words in the sentence" gives a more vivid picture of the child's progress. The parent will still need to know whether this is about where the teacher would expect a child of Bill's ability to be and, specifically, whether he needs more help wih phonetic clues.

Unless parents get such information as this, or sense that the teacher does know the child this well, they are apt to go away from the conference feeling sure that the teacher is a ready listener and eager to get help from them, but the parents may not be at all sure about the teacher's effectiveness. This is particularly true when the conference is held for the purpose of getting acquainted or of dealing with something that the teacher sees as a problem, which is not so viewed by the parents.

A Good Conference Is Friendly.   Keeping the focus of the conference primarily on the child and bearing in mind the nature of his or her responsibility toward the child may help the teacher in establishing and maintaining the friendly relationship that is basic in a good conference. Friendliness here goes beyond mere politeness, a warm greeting, a comfortable place to talk without interruption. It is a matter of accepting the views of the other adults without being judgmental or critical. The relationship differs from the one the teacher has with the child, which necessarily involves evaluation.

The teacher may feel, and rightly, that if the parent were different, the child would be different. It is, however, not the teacher's responsibility to attempt to change the parent, but rather to use whatever insights can be gained through the parent to work more effectively with the child. Of course the teacher's acceptance and understanding may enable the parent to function more effectively with the child.

Genuine acceptance runs deep. It goes beyond toleration and involves appreciation for whatever human struggle the other person represents. This kind of acceptance comes readily to some people, only with difficulty to others. Some excellent teachers find it hard to be accepting of all kinds of parents and wisely select their teaching positions accordingly. Increasingly, many teachers are learning, through their experience with conferences, through consultation with other specialists, and through better understanding of themselves, the kinds of situations they can deal with effectively in a conference and the kinds that are better referred to someone else.

A Good Conference Moves Forward.   A good conference leaves the parent and the teacher with some feeling of what are appropriate next steps.

Sometimes the information seems fragmentary and tiresome, and the teacher feels the conference didn't "get anywhere." Some of the difficulty comes in expecting answers to problems to be in one piece, complete, rather than in small pieces as expressed in factual information, attitudes, family atmosphere, family relationships that must be fitted together to give a pattern. As has been stressed repeatedly, a child's personality and behavior are complex, and it may well be more harmful to feel impelled to "do something" about a problem immediately than to wait until there is sufficient evidence on which to base one's decisions and plans—even at the risk of seeming "not to get anywhere."

In the case of a conference to get acquainted, or to report on progress, there may be agreement, not necessarily explicit, that all is going well and that efforts in the child's behalf should continue in the same directions. Where some problem or difficulty has arisen, some statement of what has been accomplished is helpful, even if it is only the recognition that there *is* a problem and that the teacher, the parent, or both are studying it.

What May Be Learned from Conferences

The most important information to be gleaned from parent-teacher conferences probably has to do with the attitudes of the child and the parents toward the school or center. What kinds of concerns do the parents have? Are they interested in all the child's activities, or do they pay more attention to academic performance? Are they able to supplement what the school or center offers, or is their time too limited? Does the child talk about school or center at home, and if so, what does he or she emphasize?

Sometimes information about a child's attitudes in the past throws light on his or her current situation. One teacher recorded the following in her journal after a conference:

> Alice's mother reports that her feelings were hurt by the teacher when she was in kindergarten. The teacher reprimanded her for something that she did not do. From that time on, the other children blamed her for things they did. She disliked school and often cried that she did not want to go.

The teacher wondered whether so much dislike and difficulty really stemmed from one incident or whether it had become a symbol of a number of hurts she had received. In any event, the teacher had a clue that Alice might respond to more opportunities for success if she could find them for her.

In another notation the same teacher wrote:

> Mr. O. says Joan should be spanked when she has difficulty with reading. He still measures her progress by her sister Nancy's (Nancy had matured much earlier).

The teacher had been concerned over Joan's reluctance to attempt anything new. In view of this information it seemed likely that her reluctance stemmed from a fear of failing.

From conferences the teacher often gains an impression not only of the parental expectations for the child's schoolwork but also of their expectations in general. Caution is necessary, for the short time the parent and the teacher are together provides only glimpses of the parent-child relationship. Nevertheless, whether the parent describes the child in positive terms or emphasizes problems, recounts behavior in considerable detail or rather vaguely, sees the child as resembling some other member of the family or as somebody rather unique, concentrates the conversation on the child or focuses more on a brother or sister, the parent gives some clues to the place the child has in the family. Something of whether the youngster is living up to parental hopes or is somehow failing to meet parental expectations is revealed. Such information helps the teacher to understand some of the goals the child may be setting personally.

Looking at the parent-child relationship in terms of what the parents seem to want for the youngster, their methods of encouraging or discouraging him, and the ways they view his accomplishments and his difficulties seems likely to yield the teacher considerable insight that can be used in the classroom. If teachers are at all intuitive and sensitive, they will not overlook the deep feelings that underlie the parent-child relationship. Parent or child, or both, may be unaware of these feelings. Neither the conference setting nor their own professional training, however, is such that teachers can hope to identify the sources of such feelings. For the teachers' purposes, it is sufficient to understand the ways parent and child consciously view one another.

Parents' expectations for their children often are also apparent in the information they give about the children's home activities and responsibilities. Contrast the following excerpts from one teacher's notes on conferences:

> Joe's father is confined to a wheelchair. Joe spends all his after school time with him and never has an opportunity to play with other children.
>
> Peter and his dad have a workshop and a playroom downstairs.

The teacher saw the information about Joe as a clue suggesting that his relationship with the other children might be affected by his inability to spend much time with them. She might also consider the possibility that Joe's responsibility could be either a source of irritation or a source of pride to him, or even a combination of both. Similarly, the item about Peter gave the teacher an idea that Peter's dad might serve as a resource for a construction project she had in mind for the class. Taken at face value, this item certainly suggests mutual enjoyment between father and son. But one would like to know a little more. Whose projects are carried out in the workshop? How does Peter participate and what kinds of satisfaction does he derive? What about the playroom? Do Peter's friends share in it? Often, a single item from a conference provides not one but many clues that may be used to develop further insight.

Special Demands on Some Parents

In one sense, all parents have special needs since each parent, like each child, is unique. However, teachers need to be especially sensitive to circumstances that place special demands on some parents. These pressures make some parents prone to difficulties in their parenting and less open than other parents to collaboration with the school. Sensitivity to such possibilities should not lead the teacher to assume that the parents who belong to a particular group will necessarily respond in a certain way. To stereotype parents is always unproductive.

Parents who belong to cultural minorities often have values that differ from those of the teacher. Many have experienced discrimination. They may not understand the language spoken at school. Many think of the school as a forbidding, unfriendly place. When the teacher can find ways to open communication, based on an appreciation of the individuality of each parent and an awareness of their struggles, the chances of finding some mutually valued goals for the child are much improved.

Parents with handicapped children are particularly in need of conferences that enable them to express their concerns about their children. They can provide much useful information and usually want to ask many questions about the provisions that will be made for their children. Parents of handicapped children get needed reassurance from the feeling that the teacher wants to know what they know and is willing to share information with them. It helps them to cope more effectively with the anxiety and guilt that many parents of handicapped children experience.

Increasingly, many of the parents the teacher encounters are single. This is most often true of mothers, but many fathers also have sole or major responsibility for their children. Many single parents manage their situation extremely well. Some are deeply concerned about the ways their children may be affected and may look to the teacher for reassurance and help. Some try hard to respond to the teacher's requests for conferences or for attendance at meetings or assistance in the classroom although there is only one parent available to handle responsibilities otherwise shared by two. Teachers can avoid putting such parents in a difficult situation by simply assuming that all parents have different obligations and responsibilities, different time commitments and different preferences for parent involvement. Above all, teachers can avoid communications with parents that imply that all children have two parents, or that all parents are mothers.

A number of the parents in early childhood education programs are young. Teenage pregnancies sometimes mean that the mothers of three- and four-year-olds are still teenagers. While parenthood often is a maturing experience, the young person's adolescent needs for supportive peer relationships, for new experience and self-expression do not vanish with the birth of a baby. Accordingly, these parents may, consciously or not, look to the center or school, and the teacher, for a parent program and support that is different from that desired by older parents.

OTHER RESOURCES

Teachers often need to seek the help of persons other than the parents to provide for aspects of development that teachers are not equipped to handle. Conversely, other persons who are interested in the child may also seek out the teacher's help.

Ordinarily, teachers turn to their colleagues in the school as first resources. Whom they consult and for what purposes depends to a considerable extent on their knowledge of the functions each one performs. Some schools have a large staff and many specialists. Other schools and many centers have more limited resources, so that one person combines many functions, and certain kinds of help may not be available.

Principals and directors are strategic persons who know the resources of the school system and the community. Particularly when they have been employed in the community for several years, they can provide the teacher with a perspective on such matters as the usual expectations of parents and the meaning of certain community customs. The principal or director usually does not know a child as intimately as the teacher does, but may be aware of characteristic trends in a child's development, and know how the child has responded with different teachers.

The child's previous teachers, or teachers who currently work with the child in special situations such as art or music or physical education or in the library, also can provide the teacher with important clues to understanding. (Not to be overlooked is the casual information that may be furnished by other school workers such as secretaries and food service and maintenance personnel.) Knowledge of how another person sees a youngster may help the teacher to correct personal bias.

Supervisors, curriculum specialists, special educators, reading specialists, bilingual resource persons, and community workers, often provide helpful insights about a particular child. They may suggest new ways of presenting instructional material, or see possibilities for learning that have not occurred to the teacher. Some specialists are experienced in child study and will help the teacher to use it both in planning and in evaluating children's learning experiences.

School health personnel have much to contribute to child study. In many situations they have more direct contact with the parents and the homes than anyone else. In addition to helping the teacher follow through on matters directly related to the child's health, they often can verify some of the hunches the teacher may have or suggest other clues to be pursued.

The teacher's efforts to help the child learn often are frustrated by factors external to the classroom. Some of these may relate to the child's health and can be dealt with by the school nurse or doctor. Some of them may stem from the child's economic situation, as in the case of a child who lacks adequate food or clothing. In these cases the school usually has an established procedure for referring the parent to some welfare agency. The matter often is handled by the nurse, sometimes by a school or center social worker. Many of the factors that hamper a child's learning, however, stem from various kinds of emotional disturbances. Sometimes a social worker helps the teacher in dealing with these problems. Some schools and centers also employ psychologists and psychiatrists.

Each teacher needs to ascertain the resources the school or center has and how the specialists customarily function. Where the school has only limited personnel, the teacher will wish to find out what community agencies are available and discuss with the principal or director the possibilities for using them.

Potentially, individuals such as the psychiatric social worker, the psychologist, and the psychiatrist constitute the teacher's best resource for consultation about children's emotional difficulties. Many special education consultants who advise teachers on mainstreaming also can assist the teacher in this way. They can help the teacher to sort out the steps necessary to handle personal feelings about such difficulties. Unfortunately, teachers are not always fully aware of the ways these newer members of the school team work, and they in turn sometimes lack a precise comprehension of the teacher's job. Each has to learn from the other, much as teachers and parents do.

We may take the teacher's relationships with the school psychologist as an example of how to draw on the resources of a specialist in the treatment of emotional disturbances. Usually, the teacher is the person who calls the attention of the psychologist to a particular child. Customarily, referral goes through the principal's or the center director's office.

Many teachers have questions about this first step. Some children are in such obviously dire straits that there is little question about their need for referral. They are completely blocked in their learning, out of touch with the reality of the classroom, or so destructive as to endanger the other children. But what about others who, though they seem less acutely disturbed, are nevertheless functioning inadequately? The teacher may feel a failure with these youngsters, or think that a request for help reflects adversely on his or her teaching. Or the teacher may believe that the available psychological services are insufficient to serve any but the most pressing needs.

It is true that most schools and centers have limited psychological services. Psychologists believe, however, that time and money often may be saved if referrals are made before problems become overwhelming. Teachers often can help in this matter of when and whom to refer by meeting with the psychologist to find out the kinds of services that are or can be made available. Discussion of the sorts of behavior that signal serious trouble gives the teacher perspective on which youngsters should be referred. The psychologist also can help teachers to think through the best ways of presenting the matter of referral to parents. Some children do not seem to need referral, but the teacher may be concerned about them; meetings with the psychologist may further indicate whether the psychologist has any time available for consultation about such children. Where the psychological services are particularly adequate, the psychologist may occasionally observe such children in the classroom. The teacher also may call on the psychologist for suggestions of ways to plan for conferences with parents that the teacher finds difficult.

When it has been suggested to the parents that the child needs help or the child's name has been given to the psychologist, the teacher's responsibility does not end. Usually the psychologist asks the teacher for a more detailed report of the child's classroom behavior. This is where the teacher's anecdotal records and other child study techniques are especially useful. The more accurately the teacher can describe what the child has done and said under varying circumstances, the more helpful the report is likely to be.

The psychologist's next step will be a diagnostic study, which may include tests and other diagnostic techniques, interviews with the child and parents, and observation in the classroom. Following this, the psychologist will make recommendations, which may be for therapy for the child, counseling for the parents, remedial work, some shift in classroom procedures, assignment to a special training, and other possibilities. Whether these are arranged as part of the school services, through some other community agency, or privately will depend on the particular situation.

Often the teacher is brought into the plan for the child, and asked to carry out suggestions made by the psychologist. Occasionally when the arrangements for therapy are made privately or through some agency other than the school, the teacher is given little or no information beyond that the child or the parents are "getting help." This may baffle or annoy the teacher who feels that the child might make faster progress if the teacher knew more specifically what to do in the classroom.

The therapist, expecting the child to cope with the same kinds of situations as other children do, may feel that suggestions to the teacher are not necessary. The therapy sessions will then be used to help the child understand whatever feelings may have been aroused. Thus a therapist's apparent unwillingness to intervene in the classroom may only testify to a recognition that therapist and teacher serve the child in different ways.

The more experience teachers have in working with psychologists (and psychologists with the teachers), the easier it is for them to understand that different children may be handled in different ways and will respond in different fashions.

Therapy takes time. Some children will show an immediate improvement, later go into a slump. Some children get much worse before they get better. The reactions of some children in therapy are so disturbing that the teacher will want to discuss them with the psychologist. In general, if in doubt, the teacher does well to raise questions directly with the psychologist. Most psychologists are appreciative of the teacher's interest in the child and cognizant of the important contribution the teacher makes. Increasingly they value a reciprocal and cooperative relationship in which information about children is shared.

Important as colleagues in the school or center situation are in helping the teacher to understand individual children, the resources outside the school cannot be disregarded. Recreation workers, Sunday school teachers, group leaders, and others may be helpful, if the teacher is in contact with them.

Children spend only a part of their waking time at home and in school or center. What seems to be lacking in the child's life in one setting may be well met elsewhere. For example, a bright girl who had been accelerated in school, so that she was placed with children who were socially much more mature than she was, found deeply satisfying companionship in church and Sunday school activities where she sought out youngsters whose social interests corresponded closely to hers. Many youngsters who seem to have little drive or ingenuity in the school situation, where attendance is mandatory, are self-directed and inventive in the community center, where attendance is voluntary. At the early childhood level, also, some children from minority cultures behave differently in center or school than they do in the extended family, where they feel more accepted and adequate.

The individual teacher can hardly be expected to know everyone who knows the child. Perhaps it is well that teachers do not concern themselves about certain segments of the child's life. As we have indicated repeatedly, teachers study children in order to help them learn more effectively—this is their responsibility and their main concern.

On the other hand, adults may differentiate their responsibilities for children so sharply that they lose sight of the fact that each child is a total person. It is easy to assign responsibility for the child's physical development and economic well-being to the home or to certain health and welfare agencies, social development to the recreational agencies, spiritual development to the church, and academic development to the school. But such a breakdown is unrealistic. The whole child is a person, with physical being and thoughts and feelings, in every situation. The child can't be cut up—he or she must be seen as one piece. Parents and doctors, nurses, religious and social workers, and educators need to work cooperatively lest children become the pawns of a variety of professional people, all intent on furthering their particular aspect of development.

COOPERATIVE CHILD STUDY

Sometimes child study goes beyond the kind we have emphasized most in this book, the study that the teacher carries on to improve the learning of the youngsters in the teacher's group. Child study also may extend into the community, as various persons who are interested in a particular child or group of children pool their knowledge. In that event, parents must agree to the sharing of records and information.

The Case Conference

One technique used in working with others to study children is the case conference. Through this method a group of interested persons are called together to discuss the problems of a particular child. These adults are carefully selected either for what they can contribute as professional workers (social workers, nurses, psychiatrists, ministers, juvenile court workers, or others) or for what they can contribute as interpreters of community problems and needs. In planning such a conference, someone should be given the responsibility of preparing a brief resumé of the case study, pointing out the specific problems that the discussion should consider. If the conference includes individuals who are not immediately involved in the situation, the case material must be carefully disguised to keep it confidential. After the resumé is presented, the meeting is open for discussion and exploration of the problem involved.

Some highlights of a case that was discussed at such a conference follow. The summary was presented by the classroom teacher. Invited to the conference were the school social workers, the school nurse, the teacher, the principal, the recreation leader at the community center, and a child welfare worker. The teacher described Dolores, a second grader, as one of sixteen children in a family supported by public assistance. The father was ill and unable to work.

The teacher went on:

> Dolores often becomes frustrated and sometimes has a temper tantrum. For example, last week she attached herself to a group of which she was not a member and began making suggestions and giving directions which were resented; so I said, "Dolores, were you invited to help with this?" That was enough. She withdrew from the group, drawing a crayon mark through a child's drawing as she passed, pushing a child who was in her way, unscrambling a puzzle and sliding her feet noisily across the room. These tantrums gather momentum when they get started, and so does my impatience.
>
> Then the children left to go to the lunchroom. There Dolores had an accident and dropped her tray with all the food on the floor. The accident was partially June's fault, and she tried to straighten the problem out with Dolores, but Dolores would not look up. She sat in a very dejected way with head bowed and a few tears which she tried to cover up. She would not move even when June assumed the responsibility of the whole accident. After several minutes sitting on the floor, Jackie leaned over and whispered something to her. She looked where her new lunch was waiting for her—and in a few minutes she was eating and smiling again. I later found out that Jackie had in some way bargained with her about letting her take his place at the end of the table.
>
> Yesterday, a group of children came into the room at the early bell and were talking with me. As we talked, Joyce came in and started to tell us about Dolores, who was standing in the hall, crying. As we gathered more from the excited Joyce, we found that Dolores was being teased by some boys in the hall about her little doll without any clothes. I went to the hall to see what I could

do and suggested we bring a blanket from our doll corner for the doll. Dolores would not accept our help.

Here was a youngster whose life was beset with many problems, each of which concerned a different community agency. It was easy for the social workers to see her as one more item in an overburdened family budget, the nurse to see her as a patient needing dental work, the principal as another member of an already troublesome family, the teacher as a disruptive element in the classroom, the recreation leader as a child in need of help his agency could not offer, the child welfare worker as a candidate for a foster home not available. Someone must speak for Dolores, struggling for some kind of recognition and status. Someone must sense and help colleagues to sense the pathetically low self-esteem such a child often has, and her probable need for more adult acceptance.

A number of questions were raised. We examine them from the perspective of Dolores and her family.

The first three questions the case conference addressed were: What was the home situation? What agencies were on the case? What was the father's health problem? These questions reflect the complexity and categorical nature of our social and health services. A number of workers had had contact, sometimes in the home, sometimes in their offices, with various members of the family of Dolores. None had a full picture of the life of the family. Finding it necessary to cope with different workers and differing sets of regulations, the various family members had learned to respond as best they could in order to maintain themselves. One wonders whether the family as a unit might not have been strengthened had there been only one worker and one source of funding for them.

Another set of questions addressed possible ways of improving the situation for Dolores: Was foster home care a possibility? Could any further assistance be given this family to help them do a more adequate job of feeding and clothing the children? What about a temporary homemaker service? In difficult home situations, placement of the children elsewhere, at least temporarily, may provide parents a much needed respite. In the case of children who are severely neglected or abused, placement elsewhere offers the child the protection that seems essential for survival. Foster home placement is, however, a drastic solution. Too often the child's return home is delayed unduly with no permanent provision made for the child's care and well-being. The possibility of providing additional financial assistance to the family seems more reasonable. An assured, decent income is essential if families are to be expected to assume full responsibility for their children.¹ With an adequate income, the family of Dolores might manage without excessive difficulty. Or they still might need access to homemaker services. When such services have employed individuals sensitive to the family's cultural values and background, they have often been successful in helping families to function more effectively.

A final set of questions related to Dolores herself: Had Dolores been placed in the school group that was most advantageous to her? Did she have a reasonable chance to succeed in it? Was she making the most of the community center resources? The first two of these questions confront the school's responsibility for Dolores.

It is interesting that the teacher's summary says nothing about Dolores as a learner. She probably was having difficulty and needed special help, but it is reasonable to suppose that she may have found her school tasks lacking in interest and challenge. Curricula that provide a narrow range of experience may never involve certain children. It is also possible that the curriculum offered children little chance to work together, in a constructive fashion. Her teacher also might have considered whether there were any teaching strategies she might have used with the other children and with Dolores to improve the existing social relations.

The last question, relating to her use of the community center, is reasonable if the center has a group appropriate for a second-grader. A good experience there might help her to feel more positive about herself and improve her situation at school. Such improvement would, however, also be contingent on the nature of programs provided at school. So, in the long run, all three of this set of questions call for an examination of the school's effectiveness in meeting this child's needs.

The important gain for Dolores was not so much the answers to any of the questions posed. It was rather that in the process of looking at her as a person, the representatives of all the agencies involved could deepen insight and understanding about her. Plans for her no longer would be so piecemeal.

The plight of Dolores was, unfortunately, not unusual. She typifies many youngsters for whom schools have a shared responsibility. This case conference illustrates a way of seeing the work of the school and the teacher in perspective with the work of others who are also interested in the child.

Case conferences utilize the competencies of many different specialists, and enable them to see aspects of their work that they have in common with others. In case conferences, workers supplement, extend, challenge, and clarify each other's findings and understandings. They become acquainted with each other and identified in their particular area of service. Their combined insights, opinions, and judgments tend to improve community services related to children. At the same time, community workers have an opportunity to become familiar with the goals and purposes of the school or center.

Cooperative Study and Educational Goals

Cooperative child study often involves consideration of educational goals. What are reasonable expectations for a particular child to accomplish? Can he or she learn the same things and in the same ways as typical classmates? Is too much being demanded, or is the challenge to this child insufficient?

Questions such as these are asked not only about individual youngsters but about groups of children. Many of the concerns expressed in the case conference on Dolores apply to most of the other children in her neighborhood. Should the goals held by the school she attends differ from those held in a more privileged area? Should goals be modified in the light of what is known about children, their assets and their liabilities, or should similar goals be set for all the children in the community?

Obviously the answers to questions such as these go far beyond the realm of child study. The process of establishing educational goals in a democracy is undeniably complex. Nevertheless, cooperative child study almost inevitably raises such questions, and it can contribute relevant information in the search for answers. It provides opportunities for citizens who are not teachers to become familiar with the ways children respond to the school program.

In addition to the usual meetings and "open school" days, some schools arrange for more intensive observation, and in some instances for participation. A single classroom may be visited several times, or several different classes observed. The experiences are discussed with the teacher or some member of the school staff. In such an exchange, the "observer" understands better the complexity of the teachers' job; and teachers often gain fresh insight as they see the children and their work with them through the eyes of the visitors.

In the following descriptions of parent cooperative child study, it will be seen how naturally and often the consideration of educational goals figures either as a framework or a result of such cooperative study.

Child Study With Parent Groups

One school approached the problem of cooperative study by inviting the parents to an open house at a time when they thought a majority of parents would be able to come. The children showed their parents the work they had done, including their journals with entries they had dictated to the teachers or written themselves, their word dictionaries, and their math worksheets. They also pointed out various features of the room, such as the science center and some "experiments" in progress, their pets and plants, the variety of games used to strengthen mathematics and reading skills. After that, the children were excused to see a film and participate in other activities.

The parents and teacher then sat down together to discuss what they had seen and to consider forming a child study group for the year. The teacher began by asking them to comment on how what they had seen reminded them of their own early school experiences or how it was different. This stimulated some lively discussion and enabled some parents to express their reservations about the classroom's informality and diversity. The teacher then suggested that meeting regularly as a child study group would enable them to see how the classroom "worked" and how it affected individual children.

The group identified some of the topics they would like to discuss at later meetings. They agreed that if they had inadequate information about something, or felt they needed outside help, they would invite an expert to come in. Depending on the nature of the problem, they could go to the child guidance clinic in their community, the child welfare worker, the principal, school psychologist, reading specialist, doctor, or nurse. Here are some excerpts from the record of the discussion of the first group meeting.

> Discussing the big overall queston of what kind of education is necessary in these times, a father responded, "I don't see how you can teach understanding. That's something you either have or you don't. You get it from experience, and kids haven't had it."
>
> "Could we arrange to have such experiences happen to them?" the teacher asked.
>
> He hesitated, "We-l-l, yes, perhaps—but I don't get it."
>
> Another father responded: "I don't know what you're doing, but it's all right with me because my boy likes mathematics and I never did." When the teacher asked if he thought students should always like what they are doing, he replied, "No, but it helps."
>
> A mother responded: "I believe in drill. If Mary goes over a thing enough times, it will stay with her, and I want her mathematics to stay with her. Responsibility is all right in its place, but I think the school's job is to teach kids to read and write and add correctly. All of them could take more drill. Drill never hurt anybody."

The teacher stated that Mary was very good at addition. James, however, had not yet caught on very well and did indeed need more drill. She asked, "Should I keep on drilling Mary on what she already knows, just because James needs more drill?"

Mary's mother responded, "I hadn't thought of it like that, what do you do?" This led into a variety of ways of individualizing to meet different children's needs, and the role of games in providing needed drill.

In another school, cooperative study with parents was based on actual observation of classroom procedure. A teacher planned a series of three classroom observations in different areas of work so that parents would have an opportunity to get an overall view of the whole program. First he invited them to see reading activities, next to observe a free-choice period, and last to view the culminating program in a social studies unit. Each observation period was followed by a discussion period, at which time the children were sent to the playground with another teacher who worked cooperatively with the classroom teacher in the parent program.

One teacher seeking better communication with and understanding of parents about their children's school progress decided first to discover the parents' own attitudes toward school experience. She asked them to respond to the following questionnaire:

What do you expect your child to get from his school experience?
What about his physical development?
What about his social adjustment?
What about his emotional stability (mental attitudes, approach to work, ability to take suggestions)?
What are his special abilities?
What has been his development of special skills?

Their responses proved to be provocative for the teacher and useful to her in future discussions of reports on pupil progress. One eventual outcome was that conferences were substituted for the grade card as a means of reporting pupil progress.

Some of the other specific outcomes of this cooperative study, as seen by the parents, were stated by them as follows:

It helped to clarify (in my own mind) what I wanted my child to gain from school experiences.

I had an opportunity to explain any pertinent facts about my child that would enable the teacher to work with him more effectively. (Physical, social, emotional, etc.)

Maladjustments at home and at school were pointed out and we were often able to find some ways of handling our mutual problem.

Some of the values that may accrue from cooperative child study with parents are mentioned in the following excerpts from an evaluation of one such program:

1. Parents are deeply concerned with the social development of boys and girls and have an important contribution to make in the analysis and planning of better group living in school.
2. Parents of children about the same age probably form the best working group because of the similar problems and common interests.
3. Parents and teachers usually see the same goals for children if given a chance to get together and see the problems jointly.
4. Parents may be of great help in interpreting a program of experimentation to other parents and to the public.

SUMMARY

As teachers study children through others, their realization of their own specific and unique contributions to each child's development is important. Also important is the recognition that the parent is an excellent resource for ideas and information helpful in understanding the child. The teacher's colleagues and other professional workers also contribute such ideas and information.

As teachers study the child through and with others, many stereotypes are broken down. Teachers discover how much they have in common with other people, and how to use others' competencies and their own in the common cause.

Three main purposes are fulfilled by studying the child through others: first, such a study makes possible extending one's information and insights about a child to a number of different situations; second, the persons who are affecting the child's growth and development are involved in a more deliberate and personal way in defining the goals and purposes of the child's education; third, persons outside the teaching profession gain some knowledge of the magnitude and complexity of educational problems.

NOTES

1. This issue is discussed at length in Kenneth Keniston and the Carnegie Council on Children, *All Our Children: The American Family Under Pressure*, (New York: Harcourt Brace Jovanovich, 1977).

SUGGESTED READING

Almy, M. *The Early Childhood Educator at Work.* New York: McGraw-Hill, 1975. Two chapters deal with the early childhood educator's work with other professionals and with parents.

Baker, K.R., ed. *Ideas That Work with Young Children.* Washington, D.C.: National Association for the Education of Young Children, 1972. This compilation of articles from *Young Children* includes a section in which teachers report on their ways of working with parents.

Chess, S.; Thomas, A.; and Birch, H. *Your Child Is a Person: A Psychological Approach to Parenthood Without Guilt.* New York: Penguin, 1977. Drawing on their longitudinal research, the authors of this readable book show how the individuality of the child contributes to the effectiveness of parenting from the moment of birth. Many case studies, helpful to teachers in understanding child behavior from the view of the parent, are included.

Epps, E.G., ed. *Cultural Pluralism.* Berkeley, Calif.: McCutchan, 1974. Essential background material for the teacher working with minority groups is provided by this publication. A chapter by Alfredo Castaneda discusses issues of assimilation particularly related to the Mexican-American experience. Ralph Uido deals with Japanese-Americans. A long section on various aspects of the black experience includes a very useful chapter by Diana Slaughter.

Group for the Advancement of Psychiatry. *The Joys and Sorrows of Parenthood.* New York: Charles Scribner's Sons, 1975. This book is concerned with what it is to be a parent, and the expectations parents set for themselves. Teachers of young children have found it most illuminating.

Honig, A.S. *Parent Involvement in Early Childhood Education.* Washington, D.C.: The National Association for the Education of Young Children, 1975. This pamphlet briefly reviews the parent involvement in aspects of different early childhood programs. It also discusses the reasons it is sometimes difficult to involve parents. Extensive lists of informational resources are included.

Langenbach, M., and Neskora, T.W. *Day Care: Curriculum Considerations.* Columbus, Ohio: Charles E. Merrill, 1977. A realistic view of possibilities for the involvement of parents of differing backgrounds.

Morrison, G. S. *Parent Involvement in the Home, School and Community.* Columbus, Ohio: Charles E. Merrill, 1978. This book provides comprehensive and practical coverage of the many aspects of the teacher's work with parents.

Pickarts, E., and Fargo, J. *Parent Education: Toward Parental Competence.* New York: Appleton-Century-Crofts, 1971. Intended for teachers who carry major responsibility for parent education, this book provides suggestions for group discussions and other activities with parents.

Southwest Educational Laboratory Parenting Materials Information Center. "Parenting in 1977: A Listing of Parenting Materials." Mimeographed. Austin, Tex.: Southwest Educational Laboratory, 1977. Available from SEDL Parenting Materials Information Center, 211 East Seventh Street, Austin, Tex. 78701, this is an excellent and extensive bibliographical resource for the teacher involved in planning a parent involvement or parent education program.

Stevens, J.H., Jr., and King, E.W. *Administering Early Childhood Education Programs*. Boston: Little, Brown & Co., 1976. Chapters on basic strategies in parent involvement and models of parent education and involvement explain, in practical ways, principles and techniques for effective work with parents. The viewpoints of parents from minority groups are particularly well presented.

Talbot, N.B., ed. *Raising Children in Modern America, Problems and Prospective Solutions*. Boston: Little, Brown & Company, 1976. This book, a compilation of papers prepared by authorities in various fields, provides a comprehensive picture of the social, economic, and health problems faced by parents in America today. The chapter by Minuchin is especially recommended.

8 ASSESS AND DOCUMENT DEVELOPMENT

The many ways of studying children described in this book are directed toward a particular kind of assessment. Such assessment is ongoing and continuous. It tries to take into account the ways children differ in backgrounds, learning styles, and interests. This assessment looks at children when they are actively engaged in a variety of activities and settings, and concerns itself not only with behavior, but also with the thinking and feeling that underlie behavior. It tries to appraise development as it proceeds along different lines and to take into account the relationships among those lines. The focus, to use a cliché, is the development and learning of the "whole child." Such assessment relies heavily on the knowledge, understanding, and skills of those who teach the children.

Not all assessment is of this kind. In early childhood education, as at other levels, assessment often is a matter of specifying behavioral objectives or outcomes and appraising their accomplishment. The objectives are set by the teacher, or prescribed in a curriculum that may have been developed locally or may appear in a textbook. Some form of testing determines the children's level of performance at the beginning of the program. The tests may be teacher-made, or provided by the publishers of the curriculum; or the tests may be standardized. A similar kind of testing is used to check progress.

Programs using these kinds of assessment procedures may or may not be highly individualized. Some programs are built around the notion that individuals will vary in the rate that they accomplish objectives. Other programs also take account of differences in learning styles and provide different kinds of activities for different children.

Some of the differences between developmental and behavioral assessment are schematized in Figure 8.1. *(Top: Developmental)*

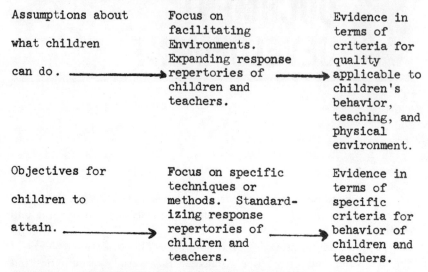

Assumptions about	Focus on	Evidence in
	facilitating	terms of
what children	Environments.	criteria for
	Expanding response	quality
can do. ⟶	repertories of ⟶	applicable to
	children and	children's
	teachers.	behavior,
		teaching, and
		physical
		environment.

Objectives for	Focus on specific	Evidence in
	techniques or	terms of
children to	methods. Standard-	specific
	izing response	criteria for
attain. ⟶	repertories of ⟶	behavior of
	children and	children and
	teachers.	teachers.

FIGURE 8.1. DIFFERENT APPROACHES TO ASSESSMENT

Adapted from Anne M. Bussis et al., "Alternative Ways in Educational Evaluation," in *Testing and Evaluation: New Views*, ed. Monroe Cohen, and coordinator Vito Perrone, (Washington, D.C.: Association for Childhood Education International, 1975) p. 11. Reprinted by permission of the Association for Childhood Education International, 3615 Wisconsin Avenue, N.W., Washington, D.C. 20016. Copyright © 1975 by The Association.

In developmental assessment, children are seen as individuals bringing different kinds of resources to their own learning. Initial assessment, getting to know each child, establishes what some of their resources as well as some of their needs are.

Behavioral assessment starts with the behaviors that are assumed to be appropriate for children of a particular age or grade level. The focus of the program is on the teaching of these behaviors, often with prescribed methods for teaching. Thus the behaviors of both children and teachers are shaped in specified ways. This contrasts to the variety of behaviors that may be encouraged in programs that apply developmental assessment. Here the focus is on providing an environment that encourages both children and teachers to draw on their own personal resources and develop new ones. Assessment is concerned with how the program meets certain standards of quality.

Standards of quality may apply to the learning of the children, from the standpoint of both process and content, and also to the context in which learning occurs. Process questions might have to do with the nature of the child's effort, including purposefulness, involvement, interest, and independence. Content questions concern the substance of the child's learning. For example, are the concepts to be acquired trivial, matters of the moment, or powerful—keys to the acquisition of further knowledge? Questions of context deal with the qualities of the human environment in which the learning occurs. Are the encounters of child and adult, child and child, open, honest, respectful of the other's efforts and feelings?

In developmental assessment evidence about the success of the program is sought in the behaviors of the children and the teachers. Can the children demonstrate the behaviors set as objectives? Have the teachers exemplified the methods and techniques that were intended to teach the expected behaviors?

Both kinds of assessment have their merits. Both have potential hazards for those who use them and for the children who are assessed.

Behavioral assessment appears to be more objective, less subject to human error, more clear-cut and definite. It represents an engineering approach that appeals to those who especially value efficiency. The hazards of the approach lie in the possibility that the behaviors selected as objectives may or may not be appropriate to the ultimate goals of early education. Beginning reading programs, for example, often prescribe behaviors that have little to do with the processes involved in grasping meaning from print.

Some typical examples are:

> Child will be able to follow with both eyes working in unison an object moving from side to side in front of him about 18 inches away.

> Child can point to and name the geometric shape that is different from the others.

While a child's inability to execute these behaviors may be symptomatic of certain developmental problems, both are peripheral to relating the black symbols on the white page to language and experience. A child may manifest behaviors like following an object with both eyes or pointing to geometric shapes with no awareness that they have anything to do with reading.

Developmental assessment is open to all manifestations of the child's learning and development. It looks not only for specific behaviors but for instances that reveal the child's way of thinking and feeling as well as his or her behavior. Accordingly, it is more flexible, better able to give the child credit for whatever breadth or depth of knowledge, or array of skills he or she manifests. But this kind of assessment also carries with it equally real hazards. Unless the teachers who attempt it are well informed about children's development and learning, unless they are willing to apply the standards of quality to themselves and to the program they provide, this kind of assessment can lead to trivia. It does, however, offer teachers possibilities for developing and learning along with the children. If we can assume that teachers, like children, respond to the expectations that are set for them, developmental assessment seems more promising.

SETTING GOALS

The initial step in any assessment is the setting of goals. What are the expectations for a particular group and the individuals in it? One newly opened primary school had a list of seventeen goals. The first year they chose to concentrate on the following three:

1. We want girls and boys to speak, listen, write, read and to deal with mathematical concepts effectively and confidently.
2. We expect that children will take more responsibility for their own learning in all areas—social, academic, physical.
3. We hope that children will increase their understanding of their individual rights and the rights of others.[1]

These goals, and particularly the first, are shared by many programs. Later in the chapter we will offer specific suggestions for monitoring progress toward them.

The goals set for a multiethnic center with younger children were:

1. To involve parents in the center in a way in which their ideas and concerns would not only be shared but would result in changes or modifications in the existing program or implementation of new aspects of the program.
2. To establish communication between parents and teachers so as to provide a more responsive classroom environment for the child and a more responsive home environment as well.
3. To set up a process whereby selected parents would be trained and involved in the evaluation of classroom curriculum.
4. To have the classroom curriculum routinely evaluated by parents and teachers.
5. To develop ways of using our videotape capability to undergird and enhance our total evaluation process.[2]

Who Is Involved in Goal Setting

Sometimes teachers are in schools or centers where the goals, as in the preceding examples, are being formulated for the first time. More often teachers find themselves in settings where certain goals have become traditional and accepted. They have to consider whether these goals are compatible with their own styles of teaching and whether they need to seek modification in the goals or in their own teaching.

The Administrator Sets the Tone.   Recently an experienced early childhood teacher moved into a new school. The principal at the first faculty meeting laid forth his "no nonsense, keeping them at the books and workbooks" philosophy. The teacher, who had been appointed for a short term only, planned a program that relied heavily on the children's own language ·interests, although it included prescribed books and workbooks. She felt that she was accomplishing the goals set by the principal, but in a way that was appropriate to the children she was teaching. Had she been a regularly appointed teacher, she would have negotiated for more leeway to teach in the way she felt most competent.

Despite the opinion of some teachers, and regrettably, some principals, the specific goals for a group of children are best set by parents and teachers rather than by administrators. The administrator, who has knowledge of the overall goals for the community's school system, can serve as facilitator, and sometimes as negotiator, in goal setting that involves both parents and teacher.

Parents Play an Important Role.   When the teacher just described discovered that two of the children in her class were having serious problems in learning to read, she proposed meeting in conference with the parents. The principal said, "You can, but I wouldn't advise it." He seemed to disregard the important role that parents can and should play in goal setting and in assessment.

In Head Start and other federally funded early childhood programs, and in the California Early Childhood Plan, parents constitute at least 51 percent of the policy or advisory committee. Basing their recommendations on a needs assessment of their neighborhood and community, parents help in the setting of goals that are specific to their situations.

Close involvement in goal setting by parents seems especially important at the early childhood level. The parents are the ones who know their children best and can be most explicit about their aspirations for them.

The old notion that the primary function of schooling is to homogenize children so that all conform to a white middle-class model is beginning to give way. An effort to maintain and value the cultural diversity that is so characteristic of the people of the United States means that new goals must be set for early education. Such goal setting is, however, not without controversy and typically requires much negotiation.

The reason negotiation is necessary is suggested in a recent study of parents with Spanish speaking backgrounds.[3] Some wanted their children to learn English as soon as possible; some wanted a bilingual, bicultural program; others preferred to have their children instructed only in Spanish.

Another area that may divide parents, or more often parents and teachers, is the teaching of academic skills at an early age. The emphasis in the 1960s on the crucial importance of the early years to the child's eventual intellectual development, seems to have been accepted by many parents. They, however, translate "intellectual" into "academic" (as did certain early intervention programs of the 1960s) and place a heavy premium on evidence that their children are beginning to read. Considering the current extent of reading difficulties, their concern is understandable.

Teachers Play an Important Role.   More accurately, perhaps, teachers bear the brunt in the goal-setting process. They have to take into consideration not only what the parents want but what is realistic and feasible. Ideally, drawing on knowledge of child development and learning and of a variety of instructional methods, teachers discuss with the parents the appropriateness of the proposed goals to the children's levels of development, and what may be gained or lost in attempting to achieve the goals with the various methods available.

In actuality many teachers have not had a thorough grounding in child development and learning. Even when they are well informed they must acknowledge the tentativeness of some of the knowledge they use. We know, from scientific investigation, much more than we knew a decade or two ago. We can be guided by some well-established general principles, but it is not possible to say, "Given these children and these methods, we can guarantee these outcomes." Development is too complex and there are too many intervening variables for such prediction. Thus, even the best informed teacher probably relies at least as much on her clinical judgment as on her scientific knowledge.

It seems well to accept this fact. It would be interesting to see whether the necessary collaboration between parents and teachers could be enhanced if teachers more openly acknowledged the limitations of their own expertise. To do so would, of course, go against the typical panacea approach to education—"this new method, or this new textbook series, or these new games, will drastically improve children's reading ability," or "strengthen their moral development," or "release their creativity." But, in the long run, collaboration might help to restore parents' faith in the commitment of schools to the development and well-being of their children.

Children Give Clues. Traditionally the best interests of the child have been thought to be with the parents. The school or the center then functions *in loco parentis*. Recently, however, questions are being raised about children's rights. Should they not have a say about their own care and education? Debate continues on this issue and that of the age when the opinions of the child can be drawn out.

Although preschool children clearly cannot verbally opt for one kind of program in preference to another, their behaviors in a program give many clues about their feelings toward the program. The kind of assessment we propose provides opportunities for teachers and parents to take these clues into consideration as the assessment proceeds.

Older preschool children and elementary school children can participate actively in goal setting. Teachers and parents should guard against confusing their own goals for the child with the child's goal for himself or herself.

Setting Goals Is Ongoing

Most of the discussion so far has implied that goals for a program are set as it begins. While it is true that the opening of the school year is a propitious time for parents and teachers to work together on goals, the process is, in actuality, ongoing. Experience one year leads to revision another year, or even within the year. New parents who come into the class must be informed and, in turn, add their ideas. It is also important that the broad goals applicable to the entire class be broken into subgoals relevant to particular activities or experiences to be provided. Similar goals are set for and with individual children. New goals are set in the light of what has been accomplished.

Developmental Screening and Mainstreaming. Some appraisal of developmental functioning is essential if the goals set for children are to be reasonable. The earlier such appraisal is made, the more likely that the child can be helped to function as effectively as possible. Accordingly, programs for preschoolers, such as Head Start, have initiated developmental screening, while preschools and day-care centers that are privately operated require that each child be examined by a physician, usually prior to admission.[4]

Developmental screening procedures are intended to supplement the medical history, provide clues about the child's periodic health-care needs, and identify developmental delays, as well as serve as a guide for individualizing the curriculum. Since 1969, early and periodic screening, diagnosis and treatment (EPSDT) have been mandated as a part of the Medicaid program. However, for a variety of reasons, states have been slow in implementing the program. In many instances no provision has been made for providing treatment when anomalies are identified.

Screening procedures may be carried out by teachers or nonprofessional adults. Both require special training. However, a number of questions currently are being raised about the appropriateness and effectiveness of "screening" for young children, particularly when the procedures are carried out by individuals who do not know the child, or when the child is not familiar with the setting. The likelihood is great that a child who actually does well in normal situations may be labelled as functioning poorly. At the same time the screening may overlook serious but subtle anomalies.

Critics of developmental screening as it now operates suggest that a developmental review process be substituted. This is a profile of strengths and weaknesses, assets and liabilities; it describes the transactions between the child and the surrounding world in terms of the tasks required of him or her, and the significant people in particular settings at the time of every review. It assumes that each child and his or her environment (including significant care-givers) is a unit and not divisible. It involves a combination of methods and basically is concerned with competence— how the child has met and continues to meet the expectations set by society for children of comparable age. Such review is described as an assessment of functions rather than the diagnosis of a condition.[5] This view of developmental screening is compatible with the point of view on development and assessment taken in this book.

This kind of review should be particularly helpful to teachers who are working with children now being mainstreamed rather than placed in special education classes. It would assist them in seeing the child as a total person, rather than so exclusively as a child who is blind or has Down's syndrome. Accordingly, it would be easier to set appropriate goals for such children, planning for all areas of their development instead of concentrating exclusively on the areas of disability.

MONITORING PROGRESS

Along with assessment, we need to show how children progress toward the goals that have been set. To monitor progress, we keep and organize the evidence that comes from child study. How can this be accomplished in the most effective ways?

The Teacher's Records

At a minimum, all teachers keep attendance records on children. At first glance these seem to tell little about children's progress. On the other hand, every day missed deprives the child of whatever opportunities for growth the program presents. Days missed often reflect complications in the child's home life or a low level of physical functioning. Absence may also reflect the quality of the program. In a study of Follow Through programs, for example, children from highly structured programs absented themselves significantly more than did children from child-centered programs.[6]

Most teachers also keep checklists of various kinds, as we pointed out in chapter 2. They are particularly useful in keeping track of children's progress toward goals set for academic skills. A number of children may be checked on a single page. In this case a particular child's progress may be noted by comparing pages checked at different times. Or the teacher may have a checklist for each child with the checks made at different times showing progress.

Checklists may apply to observations in which the teacher, during the ongoing flow of the classroom, notes that a child performs in a way that exemplifies some aspect of a set goal. Checklists may also apply to more structured situations where the teacher asks the child to perform a task such as one involving eye-hand coordination or one based on Piaget's studies of children.

As suggested earlier, the checklist is a time-saver. Unless the teacher who uses it keeps clearly in view each child as a totality, however, it may not provide an adequate picture of progress.

Anecdotes about children, or more detailed observations of them, provide good pictures of the way they function. Such anecdotes and detailed observations (examples are given in chapter 2) are useful in monitoring progress toward such goals as taking responsibility for one's own learning or increasing understanding of the rights of others.

Sometimes a vignette is an apt way of assessing progress. A vignette of child activity is an account of a particularly meaningful event in children's interaction with other persons or with an environment in which children are free to be themselves. It may represent a typical or interesting event, or a developmental milestone. The choice of an event represents the teacher's judgment about the behavior that is significant for the child. Here is an example that illustrates the child's developing awareness of individual differences:

> "Sharon, a three-year old, and I worked together on a puzzle for about twenty minutes. She carried on a conversation about the puzzle and where the different parts should go. During this time I observed that she was looking at my face rather intently. All of a sudden she asked, "What is that?" and pointed in the direction of my face. Having an idea of what she might be thinking about I pointed to the freckles also on my hand and asked, "Do you mean these spots?" She looked at my hand and repeated, "What is that?" I told her simply, "They are freckles." She paused for a moment and then went back to working on her puzzle."[7]

The following vignette taken from observations of five-year-old Katie reveals her quick and smooth functioning in both cognitive and motor areas:

> Katie and Mary-Lou are on the playground each holding an end of a ten foot skipping rope stretched between them. Suddenly three girls racing from one end of the playground to the other run into the middle of the rope, and continue down the field pulling on the rope like charging horses, dragging Katie and Mary-Lou along after them. Mary-Lou digs in her heels and tries to pull back on the rope. In contrast, Katie almost instantaneously begins to run along beside the girls so that her end of the rope becomes shorter and shorter. Almost even with the girls, she dashes quickly around in front of them, and she and Mary-Lou return to their former position free of their interruption.

A plan for collecting anecdotes or vignettes helps to insure their representativeness. For example, each child might receive the attention of a detailed observation every week, or two weeks, perhaps with the place for observation specified, as during reading, or in the science center. Such planned observation need not rule out the collection of anecdotes, incidents that are worth recording because they are typical of a particular child, or indicative of the progress he or she is making, or perhaps of a problem in the making.

To collect and record anecdotes takes time. They are most useful to teachers when they have some scheme for organizing them. For example, a note might be made about the goal, or goals, to which the anecdote applies when the incident is recorded or filed. This will facilitate its use when needed to summarize progress over a particular period.

Most teachers find it essential to set aside a weekly block of time to file and think about a week's or two weeks' collection of anecdotes and other records. This should include time to plan for activities of individual children and for the collection of more material. As this process goes on— if possible, involving all of the teachers of a group of children—teachers usually find that their skill in recording improves along with their understanding of the children.

Other Ways of Documenting Progress

While the teacher usually takes responsibility for organizing the evidence that is gathered to document the progress the children make, not all of it comes from the teacher's pen or pencil. Parents sometimes assist and occasionally schools or centers designate a person to document progress in one or more classrooms.

Children who have some reading and writing ability can keep certain records of their own progress. Even younger children who are not yet reading can be taught to mark or use a chart if its symbols are ones they can recognize. For example, in one preschool where the teachers wanted to encourage the children in the four-year-old group to use the large equipment in the yard more extensively, they placed sketches of each of the pieces of equipment across the top of a board. On the side were the children's names (symbols could be used if the children had not yet learned to recognize their names). At the intersections of name and equipment the children could paste squares of colored paper, corresponding in color to the equipment sketch, to indicate their mastery of a particular skill.

In a classroom for older children, the teacher devised a system that enabled the children to keep records of their own activity which she would then transfer to a weekly or monthly record. Figure 8.2 provides an example of a weekly record. Each day, each child kept a record of his or her activity on a smaller sheet of paper, "What I Did Today," in which the activities were similarly listed. The children carried the small sheets in plastic holders around their necks. The teacher used these records to fill in the larger chart pictured in figure 8.2. The children could look at the charts to see how the days and weeks compared. Another variation the teacher used was to indicate on the "What I Did Today" record what she expected the child to do by putting a slash in the box following an activity. Her slashes slanted to the right **/**. When the child completed the

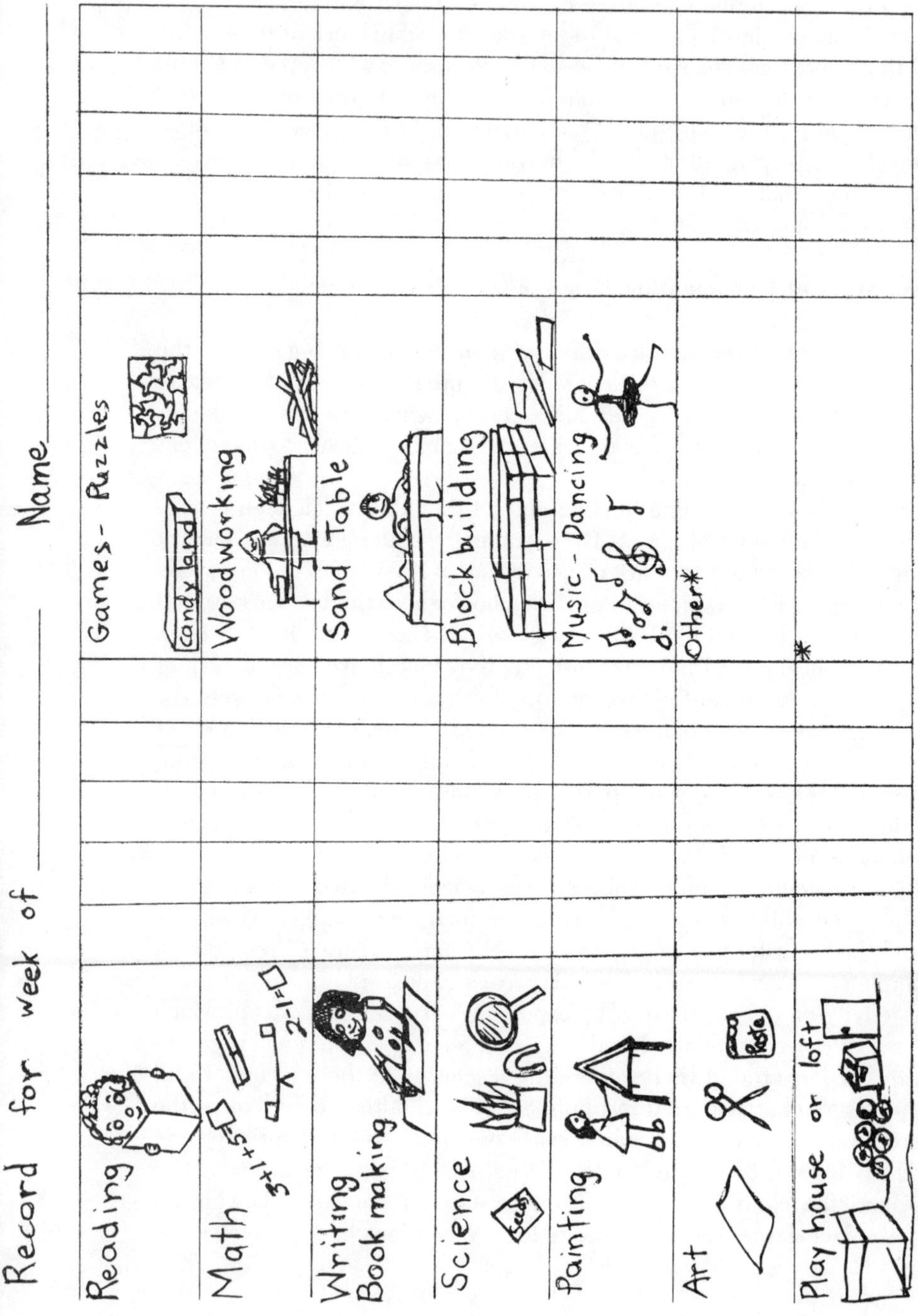

FIGURE 8.2. A WEEKLY RECORD   *The teacher checks the child's activities daily. Accumulation of the weekly records provides a continuing picture of the child's work.*

Reprinted, by permission, from Engel, *A Handbook on Documentation,* p. 44.

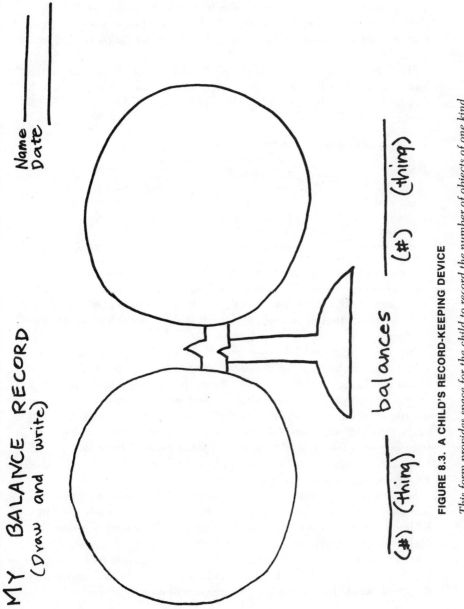

FIGURE 8.3. A CHILD'S RECORD-KEEPING DEVICE

This form provides space for the child to record the number of objects of one kind (for example, wooden cubes) needed to balance a number of objects of another kind (for example, unit building blocks).

activity, he or she would mark a slash to the left \ thus completing an **X**. A quick survey of the slash and **X** marks gave a picture of the child's functioning on a particular day.

Children's products such as their drawings and paintings, the stories and poems they dictate or write, the mathematics problems they complete, the maps they make—all provide documentation of their progress. Further, this is an aspect of assessment that allows for the participation of the child.

Here, for example, is a list of the words that appeared on cards in the folder of one boy in a kindergarten-second classroom. They are words that he learned as he dictated stories and accounts of his interests to his teacher.

Abbot and Costello	earthquake	play
Asia	fat Samantha	pretty
bat	full of people	robot
bit	gave	road runner
car wash	grand prix	seen
day	Great America	South
chubby	jaws	
doberman	park	

Figure 8.3 provides another example of an activity with a built-in record-keeping device. The child's activity with a balance and various collections of objects is self-recorded. Teachers do well to plan assessment and recording that is an inherent part of the curriculum, as in this instance.

Not everything the child does should go into the folder that is kept. When documentation is for the use of the teacher and parents, the issue of the child's right to privacy differs from that involved in documenting for more public use. Deciding what to insert and discussing the ways later insertions differ from earlier ones offer the child a chance for self-evaluation and reflection. Older children will participate more thoughtfully but even four-year-olds may gain some sense of their own growth when comparing, for example, an early scribble and a later drawing that they recognize as particularly their own.

Some children's products, the expansive block building, the clay sculpture, an episode in creative dramatics, cannot be neatly filed in a folder. Here the camera and tape recorder, if the school or center has such, can come into play.

As the planned curriculum depicted in the curriculum tree in Figure 2.1 evolved, photos of the children's sculpture and the bridges and houses they built would have provided good documentation.

Photographs or sketches of block buildings made at two different times make the increasing motor and cognitive competence of the child much more concrete and meaningful to parents as well as to the teachers. Pictures of the interest tables at different points in time should also show the evolution of the children's ideas. Tape recordings of discussions related to certain key concepts also would reveal progress.

Communicating with Parents

If parents, either as a group or as individuals, have been involved in goal setting, they are likely to anticipate reports of progress. When parents have not participated in that process, communication may be more difficult.

As suggested in the previous chapter, at the early childhood level, the conference seems the most effective way for parents and teacher to communicate. This holds particularly for those times when assessment of the child's progress is the matter at hand.

In cases where the conference is not feasible or where the parent requests a written report, or school custom requires it, much thought goes into the presentation of the child in a way that is both fair and clear. An example of a written report on Anthony, a second grader, can be found in the appendix.

Perhaps the most important message that the appended report conveys is the detailed information Anthony's teacher has about him. The handwritten comments on the checklist as well as the summary statement reveal this. One hopes, however, that the report and checklist formed the basis for a conference. Some parents, particularly those accustomed to more traditional schooling, might find the details overwhelming. Others might want to know more about the thinking and learning involved in some of the activities.

Anthony obviously has made good progress, but reporting on a child with uneven development or problems is more difficult. Again, the conference, whether with or without a written report, provides better opportunities for clarification, understanding, perhaps the setting of new goals.

Examples can be drawn from the kindergarten progress report a teacher made on Dan. Dan had a deteriorating bone condition that necessitated an orthopedic brace on hips and legs.

The kindergarten report cards used in Dan's school had been developed by the teachers. They included sections on prereading experience, number readiness, perceptual motor-skills, health and science, music, and conditions affecting learning. Each section included space for the teacher to check "yes," "improving," or "no" for the described characteristics for each of the two conferences held. Each section also had space for comments.

For the first fall conference the teacher added the following comments to the report.

> *Pre-reading.* Working on naming and forming letters. He expresses himself quite well orally and participates in class meetings.
>
> *Number readiness.* Dan has some difficulty manipulating a pencil and reverses many forms. He counts and matches 1-1 quite well.
>
> *Perceptual-motor skills.* Doing great with his brace. A tracing book would help fine motor coordination.
>
> *Art.* Dan's art work is done hastily and he seems embarrassed by his inability to draw as he would like. He is just beginning to enjoy easel painting.
>
> *Music.* Dan seems shy about singing with the group.
>
> *Conditions affecting learning.* Dan has been cheerful and courageous about his attempts to adjust to his brace. We have all learned some important lessons from him. He will try almost anything and find ways to get around the room and yard.

In the first conference with Dan's mother, the teacher described how Dan had responded to the other children's questions, demonstrating how the brace fastened. She also said that when teased in the yard by older children, not in his class, he had "maintained his cool." Fortunately some of the bigger children in his own class (which included first and second graders) had come to his rescue. Dan's mother said that some days when he returned from school he "fell apart" and cried from frustration.

At a midyear conference, the teacher noted that Dan's progress on the alphabet had about come to a halt. She had also observed that he often tore up his papers or forgot them when his mother came to pick him up. The teacher suggested that he might be experiencing too much pressure on academics at a time when so much of his energy was going into physical and psychological adjustment to the brace. He might not learn to read at this time. She and the mother talked about being sure to provide positive feedback for the paintings and block constructions that he seemed to enjoy.

A third conference was held in early spring. Dan had learned to climb steps and could ride the bus to school. The conference followed the second conference theme of lessening pressure on reading. Dan was, however, beginning to enjoy using manipulatives in math and his mother was encouraged to assist him in this at home. By now, too, Dan had overcome his shyness in music and was about to lead the chanting in a multicultural performance the school was having.

By the end of the year Dan had good control over his brace and had established his position as a respected member of the school. His prereading skills had improved. He dictated elaborate stories and could copy them with relatively few reversals.

Cumulative Records

How many of the details of Dan's progress should be put in the cumulative record? Should a report such as that on Anthony be included? The answer depends in part on the policy established in the school or center. Some would include the entire report. Others would omit the narrative report and comments and include only the checklists. Still others would include little more than a statement of completion of the kindergarten or second grade. In any event, whatever goes into the cumulative record must be available to the parent, and the records can be made available to individuals other than the child's teachers only at the parent's specific request.

THE USE OF TESTS

So far this chapter has barely mentioned the use of tests. We have postponed their discussion until the end of the chapter in order to highlight other means of assessing young children. That does not mean that tests are always ruled out, for there are certain kinds of tests that may serve useful functions in certain situations. But those who use tests must understand not only how they are to be used but also their built-in limitations, and especially the problems in using them with young children.

Tests of all kinds have proliferated rapidly during the last two decades. At the early childhood level, evaluators and researchers involved with programs like Head Start and Follow Through not only made use of available tests such as those for intelligence, readiness, and achievement, but also devised a number of new tests. The teacher who is interested in critiques of tests that are frequently used can consult the *Mental Measurements Yearbook.*[8] These yearbooks describe each new standardized test that is published and in addition include critical reviews of each test, along with related research references. In contrast to test manuals that mainly emphasize a test's strengths, the yearbook reviews also point out its weaknesses and indicate how it can be used best for certain purposes.

Unfortunately in too many school systems and in the evaluation of many federal programs, insufficient attention has been given to the inherent limitations of any standardized test. The sources of error are many and largely unavoidable. Some lie in the nature of that test as a measuring instrument. Its items are but samples from a domain of behaviors that represent a roughly defined concept such as "intelligence," "achievement," "personality," or "reading achievement." The significance of the answer the child gives to a particular item, and the score he or she gets when all his or her answers are pooled, depend largely on the performance of the group of children used in the standardization of the test.

Additional errors relate to the child at the time of the testing situation. Lack of experience in test-taking, boredom, distractibility, emotional concern, failure to understand the directions, physical discomfort—all these are factors that can lower the child's performance. Skilled psychologists giving individual tests to young children try to insure that such factors are minimized. Anyone who has tried to administer a group reading readiness or intelligence test to as small a group as six kindergarteners or first graders, however, knows how difficult it is to keep all children's attention focused on the test. One youngster's glance soon wanders to a companion's page while another becomes interested in blackening the pictures rather than marking the x's. The younger the child, the less likely that a testing situation will give a true picture of typical behavior or understanding. This is a significant reason for placing a major emphasis on observation of the child's performance in natural situations rather than on tests.

Young children in testing situations are often penalized not only by the test's format and their own unreliability but also by the content of the questions.[9] Take the child who is just learning to read, for example, who may have a sizeable sight vocabulary and a beginning ability to reason out the meaning of new words. The limited vocabulary of the test may not match the sight vocabulary the child has. Yet the child's attack may be good. One first grader, for example, confronting a reading test with a picture of several men with wind instruments and a drum, puzzled over four alternatives—hand, sand, band, and land. "It can't be any of these," he said, " 'cause that's an orchestra and orchestra is a long word."

A further penalty comes for the child when the tests are machine-scored so that teachers have no chance to go over them. Thus they have little opportunity to use the test diagnostically to find out what the child thought. They also miss the opportunity to spot those children who were more interested in making a pretty pattern than in answering correctly.

Children who come from minority groups, particularly when the children are poor, are often penalized by tests with content that is unfamiliar to them. Because of this, and concern over the general misuse of tests, some national educational organizations have called for a moratorium on testing. Group-administered IQ tests have been banned in California, Washington, D.C., and New York City.[10] In some instances, achievement tests are given on a sampling basis. One class gets one part of a test, another a different part. This procedure yields information about general performance in a particular school but it does not penalize a particular class or a particular child.

Despite current dissatisfaction with standardized testing, most teachers, particularly in public schools, probably will find that some testing will continue. They can guard against the hazards in testing young children by raising questions about the validity and the reliability of the tests as well as about the reliability of the young child. If tests must be given, teachers can make sure that the children have some preparation for the rules that apply in the testing situation. They can also monitor the testing to insure that all children are doing as well as they can. Teachers can examine the content of the tests, and the children's responses, to see where wrong answers may be given for good reasons. This does not mean changing standardized requirements. Rather, teachers are adding sophisticated knowledge to their interpretation of the results.

SUMMARY

This chapter has considered how the ways of studying young children that are described in the rest of the book can be used to assess children's development and to monitor their progress. We have chosen to emphasize assessment that takes account of the interrelated aspects of a child's development as a person. We have also considered assessment that mostly relies on behavioral objectives and standardized tests.

Assessment, as we see it, is most effective when parents are actively and continuously involved. Parents can assist teachers in setting goals that are appropriate for the children. If the children are to receive optimal support for their development and learning, and if problems are to be solved before they become insurmountable, ongoing communication between teachers and parents also is essential.

The assessment we prefer depends on the accumulation of reliable, valid, and sufficient evidence about each child. On the one hand, this evidence establishes what the child has learned, and to some extent how he or she has learned. On the other hand, this evidence helps the teacher to modify instruction so that it is more effectively paced to the child's individual style and interests.

Assessment that is geared to the development of the individual child and that is shared with parents places heavy responsibility on the teacher. To document children's progress adequately takes time, patience, and thoughtful reflection. Many teachers find that their investment in documentation pays off in greater satisfaction in their teaching and a heightened sense of professionalism.

NOTES

1. Ruth Ann Aldrich Olson, "Marcy Open School: Feeding Back to Decision Makers," in *Testing and Evaluation: New Views*, ed. Monroe Cohen, and coordinator Vito Perrone, p. 50. Reprinted by permission of the Association for Childhood Education International, 3615 Wisconsin Avenue, N.W., Washington, D.C. 20016. Copyright © 1975 by the Association.

2. Lucia Ann McSpadden, *Formative Evaluation: Parents and Staff Working Together to Build a Responsive Environment* (Washington, D.C.: Day Care and Child Development Council of America, n.d.) This pamphlet provides many excellent examples of procedures for child assessment and also of questionnaires and interview schedules for staff and parents.

3. Jane R. Mercer, "The Origin and Development of the Pluralistic Assessment Project," mimeographed (Riverside, Calif.: University of California, 1972).

4. Schools and centers do not always follow up recommendations that are made. Provisions for monitoring health and nutrition often are minimal. See A. Chang et al., "Health Services and Needs in Day Care Centers," *Child Welfare* 61, no. 7 (July 1977): 471-477.

5. U.S. Department of Health, Education and Welfare, Health Care Financing Administration and American Association of Pediatric Services for Children, *Development Review in the EPSDT* (Washington, D.C., 1977) HCFA 77-24537.

6. Jane Stallings, "Implementation and Child Effects of Teaching Practices in Follow Through Classrooms," Monographs of the Society for Research in Child Development, serial no. 163 (1975).

7. Sandra Anselmo, "Vignettes of Child Activity," *Childhood Education* 53, no. 1 (January 1977), pp. 133-136. Reprinted by permission of the Association for Childhood Education International, 3615 Wisconsin Ave. N.W., Washington, D.C. 20016. Copyright © by the Association 1977.

8. Oscar K. Buros, ed., *Mental Measurements Yearbook*, 7th ed. (Highland Park, N.J.: Gryphon Press, 1972).
9. See D. Meier on reading tests in *Testing and Evaluation: New Views*, ed. Cohen, pp. 32-36.
10. Edward B. Fiske, "Controversy over Testing Flares Again," *New York Times*, 1 May 1977.

SUGGESTED READING

Bloom B.S. et al. *Handbook on Formative and Summative Evaluation of Student Learning.* New York: McGraw-Hill, 1971. The ideas in this compendium undergirded much of the evaluation research related to early childhood intervention programs. Recommended for early childhood teachers are chapters by Kamii and Cazden. Kamii, in "Evaluation of Learning in Preschool Education Social-emotional, Perceptual-motor, Cognitive Development," contrasts Piagetian views of assessment with more traditional views. Although she now says that further study of Piagetian theory has modified some of her thinking, we think preschool teachers will find the distinctions she makes, and the many examples of assessment tasks she has given, helpful. Cazden's chapter "Evaluation of Learning in Preschool Education, Early Language Development" is rich with examples. It provides critiques of a number of commonly used tests, including some used in kindergarten, first and second grades. Cazden stresses the importance of observation of children in natural situations.

Carini, P. *Observation and Description: An Alternative Methodology for the Investigation of Human Phenomena.* Grand Forks, N. Dak.: University of North Dakota Press, 1975. This monograph combines analysis of the processes involved in documentation with some examples, drawn from several age groups. Carini examines the philosophical and logical underpinnings of the methods used.

Cohen, M., ed., and Perrone, V., coordinator. *Testing and Evaluation: New Views.* Washington, D.C.: Association for Childhood Education International, 1975. This small pamphlet includes several articles by members of the North Dakota Study Group on Evaluation (a group concerned with finding appropriate ways to evaluate open education) as well as articles by test publishers and users. It is one of the best references we have found.

Engel, B.S. *A Handbook on Documentation.* Grand Forks, N. Dak.: University of North Dakota Press, 1975. This monograph provides an overview of documentation processes, including purposes, content, and procedures. It includes some hundred pages illustrating different ways of documenting found in schools ranging from Vermont and Massachusetts to Minnesota, Iowa, and North Dakota. Perusing this should further the creative ideas of teachers seeking new ways to document progess.

Pederson, C.A. *Evaluation and Record Keeping.* Grand Forks, N. Dak.: Center for Teaching and Learning, July, 1977. This monograph contains materials used in Follow Through classrooms plus a number of articles useful in planning and record keeping. Several articles provide questions for teachers to ask themselves in preparing for conferences with children, in developing evaluation strategies, and in considering reading tests.

Perrone, V. et al. *Two Elementary Classrooms: Views from the Teachers, Children, and Parents.* Dubuque, Iowa: Kendall/Hunt Publishing Co., 1977. This monograph presents material from interviews relating to two public school classrooms. One is a second-grade class. The report provides a clear picture of the kind of information that can be gleaned from children and parents. Additionally it reveals the processes involved in "opening" a classroom.

Thorndike, R.L., and Hagen, E. *Measurement and Evaluation in Psychology and Education.* 4th ed., New York: John Wiley & Sons, 1977. This book gives a thorough consideration of the uses and limitations of various kinds of tests, along with a comprehensive discussion of the criteria for evaluating them.

U.S. Department of Health, Education and Welfare, Health Care Financing Administration and American Association of Psychiatric Services for Children. *Developmental Review in the EPSDT.* Washington, D.C., 1977 HCFA 77-24537. This small pamphlet integrates information from psychology and pediatrics. It describes how developmental assessment should be done and discusses possible hazards. An excellent resource for teachers.

9 GROWTH IN HUMAN UNDERSTANDING

Tremendous professional and personal rewards await us when we undertake a program of child study. Although we began this manual with a plea for realism about limitations, we would be most unrealistic if we did not also emphasize the benefits to be gained in studying children.

We have scattered many notes of caution through our descriptions of the various ways of studying children: consider all the interpretations; look for more evidence; don't press too hard; remember the limitations of the teacher's role. But when we are prudent in our use of child study we find in it adventure and challenge. It not only promotes the development of the children, it also enhances our own development as adults. Child study has to do with human beings, and human beings are inherently interesting.

As early childhood teachers, we have a great opportunity to influence the attitudes children develop toward learning and toward achievement. Depending on how we handle the classroom situation, the children we teach may acquire a realistic confidence in their own abilities, a perpetual expectation of defeat, or an anxiously competitive outlook. It is true that children's experiences outside the school or center have their own influence. These may incline each child toward greater or less resilience. Some children become more tough-skinned than others. Nevertheless, the teacher has real power to hurt or help.

Although children construct their own meanings, developing their own understanding, they need the teacher's assistance as they organize their learning, relate it to previous learning, and clear up their own confusions. When we are so cautious that we don't even try to sense the child's inner experience in the learning situation, or we are too obtuse to interpret his behavior in it, we deprive children of guidance they need.

205

Whether we are beginners or veterans in the teaching profession, we have a basic choice to make. We can teach mostly by rote or we can teach as meaningfully as possible. We can teach according to a prescribed formula, always in the same way, always expecting the same responses. We can make teaching a mechanical process, a matter of eliciting predetermined answers to predetermined questions. Of course children learn from such teaching, and they need to learn many responses that can be automatic. But when teaching of this sort predominates, children also learn to be bored and apathetic.

Perhaps teaching by rote sounds old-fashioned, a remnant of a bygone day. Unfortunately, however, it is not merely a thing of the past. Mechanical teaching can be seen in some well-equipped modern schools and in the work of some teachers with brand new certificates. Beautiful textbooks, fine science facilities, abundant audiovisual aids, plentiful material for art and music do not insure good teaching.

The alternative to mechanical teaching is teaching in which we are concerned both with the abilities the child brings to the learning situation and the probable meaning of the situation for the child. Our interest in the child's acquisition of certain knowledge is not less than it has ever been, but we also want to know how that knowledge is related to what he or she already knows. The moment we become aware of the child as a person who selects, rejects, and organizes the material that is taught, we are confronted with the need for child study.

Once we have understood that child study must be undertaken if our teaching is to have much meaning for children, we may as well commit ourselves to a systematic approach. If our study is based on the accumulation of evidence and an awareness of our own biases, the chances of our misinterpreting behavior are considerably lessened. We run less risk of doing harm to children than we might if we relied solely on our own intuition, useful though that may be.

While child study is essential to meaningful teaching, it is, of course, only one aspect of it. We have pointed out, for the early childhood teacher, the importance of working constructively with parents. Early childhood teachers also need to be knowledgeable people. Child study is no substitute for the teacher's knowledge of the physical and social world the young child encounters and tries to understand. Nor is child study a substitute for the teacher's command over a variety of teaching strategies. The child study that the teacher does with a particular group of children must also be illuminated by a broader knowledge of child development, derived from research and theory.

Nevertheless, child study can help the teacher to understand what is most appropriate for the children in his or her group. Child study may also help the teacher to deal more effectively with the pressures for the standardization of curriculum and of teaching strategies that are ever present in our society.

Child study, thoughtfully undertaken, not only enhances the teacher's professional skills but also has important personal implications for the teacher. To understand how a child learns, or more importantly what blocks learning, is to come to grips with what matters to the child. It is to face the child's interests, hates, and fears. As child study helps us to a deeper awareness of the child's inner life, it also helps us to such an awareness of ourselves. We cannot honestly study a child without noting the feelings within ourselves that are stirred by the child's problems.

To face our own turmoil, to learn to live with the frightened, or hostile, or yearning children we once were, is not a task easily undertaken or accomplished. But to embark on the process is to comprehend more fully the powerful interplay of emotions and intellect that characterizes most of human development and learning.

Once we seek to study children, the search has no end; this is true of most of the important things in life. We cannot "know" a child in any final sense. Often children change because we study them and gain new insights about how to help them learn. Often they change (or resist changing) in response to influences that are beyond our control.

The difficulties in knowing children are similar to those inherent in our attempts to know ourselves. We also have potentialities for growth; we also have things to learn.

The rather simple techniques this manual has described may lead us further into the field of human understanding.

INDEX

Academic skills; group facilitates acquisition of, 88-90, 112, 121-24; parents' expectations concerning, 178-79, 188

Accommodation, defined, 69

Action research, defined, 4

Activities: child's recording, 193-95, 196; group, planning, 87-88

Activity chart, 117-19

Administration, role of, 16, 169, 187

Anecdote, use of, 40-41, 171, 191, 192-93

Artwork: development reflected in, 55-57, 68-69, 145-49, 196, 197; as expressive activity, 130, 144-49

Assessment: developmental vs. behavioral, 183-86; goals setting in, 186-90 (*see also* Goal setting in assessment); Piagetian interviews in, 74; progress, monitoring, and, 191-99 (*see also* Progress, monitoring); standardized tests, use of, in, 199-201

Assimilation, defined, 69

Attendance records, use of, to monitor progress, 191

Behavior: assessing, 183, 184-85; cultural differences affect, 14, 53, 109-

10, 173 (*see also* Cultural differences); development, relating to, 22, 23-24, 34, 42 (*see also* Children's thinking; Social development, how groups foster); modifying, a teaching approach, 22-23; observation of (*see* Observation); thinking reflected in, 52

Bias, teacher's: towards children, 9, 35, 45, 110, 120; towards parents, 155, 168; reducing, 7-8, 169

Bilingual children, 94-96, 110, 188

Blank, Marion, dialogue approach of, 82-84

Case conference, 173-77

Casual conversations, 97-99

Checklists, use of, 45, 46, 191

Child development. *See* Development

Children: child study benefits, 205-6; cultural differences among (*see* Cultural differences); development of (*see* Development); feelings of (*see* Feelings, child's); individual (*see* Individual child); information about, recording (*see* Record keeping); information about, sources of (*see* Information about child, sources of);

209

APPENDIX

CAMBRIDGE ALTERNATIVE PUBLIC SCHOOL CONFERENCE REPORT

<u>ANTHONY TOWNE</u>, Second Grade   June, 1974

SOCIAL AND EMOTIONAL DEVELOPMENT

Anthony has matured in so many ways during the past two years. He has a positive self image and much more confidence in his ability to handle many different situations. He is a very sensitive and aware person who doesn't too openly show his feelings but enjoys closeness with others in a quiet undemonstrative way. Anthony places a high value on friendships and fairness with others. He has become very close with many of the other children and is able to work and play co-operatively with them in class and on the playground. Anthony is also friendly with many of the older children in the school and enjoys playing games of soccer and hockey with them. He has gained a special status in our class for this and has developed into a real leader in organizing those and other games for our children.

WORK HABITS

Anthony has good powers of concentration and a long attention span. He grasps new concepts quickly and with ease. Anthony's specialty continues to be math and he enjoys any kind of work involving it. He will often ask for extra or special work in math and will work independently at it. Generally, Anthony is conscientious about all of the assignments that he is given. He is showing more interest in all of the classroom activities and seldom finds that he has "nothing to do." I am very pleased with the way that he has used the room and its activities this past term.

LANGUAGE ARTS

Anthony has shown less interest in reading this past term, perhaps because so many other interests have emerged. He has spent long periods of time with hockey cards and magazines and is able to read much of them. He continues to read library books and should be encouraged to as much as possible during the summer to help improve his fluency and expression. He is presently reading at the ending second grade level, according to standardized tests, recently given.

Anthony likes to make labels and signs for drawings that he does. He writes good stories when encouraged to do so and has participated in some note writing that we did where children wrote to me and others.

Anthony continues to express himself clearly, using a mature vocabulary. He has become pretty good at handwriting and is beginning to spell well on his own. He has done many crossword puzzles which has helped. He is learning to use the dictionary and has done many alphabetizing exercises.

GENERAL COMMENTS

Anthony has been an interesting person to have in our class. He has been most co-operative and well behaved. I especially enjoy his sense of humor and that delightful quality that is "just Anthony." Needless to say I will very much miss having Anthony in our class.

(cont.)

MATH: SCOPE AND SEQUENCE

The following topics or skills are arranged in a _suggested_ order for children to learn. A child may follow the sequence through from beginning to end at a simple level and then go back to extend and get deeper into some of the skills. There are some skills that are definitely prerequisites for others; for example, learning the concept of what five is must preceed addition or subtraction combinations of five. Some skills such as telling time or graphing can be done as a child shows interest or as part of other projects. There are also many math skills in logic, spatial awareness, problem solving and other areas that are not listed, but are a part of every day activities and games in the classroom.

A. SETS
  ✓1. One to one correspondence. (Matching one object to another.)
  ✓2. Comparison of sets using vocabulary....greater than, less than, equal, not equal. (symbols not used yet)
  ✓3. Cardinal numbers of sets with 0-9 members.
  ✓4. Writes numerals 0-9.
  ✓5. Statements of equality and inequality for set with 0-9 members.

B. Cuisenaire Rods   (usually done along with early set work)
  ✓1. Free play
  ✓2. Classification
  ✓3. Seriation
  ✓4. Numerical values by sight and _feel_.

C. ADDITION

  ✓2. Oral use of concept using rods.
  ✓3. Written equations using facts to ten.
  ✓4. Missing addends, e.g. $3 + \_ = 8$
  ✓5. Commutative property of addition, e.g. $3 + 5 = 5 + 3$

D. SUBTRACTION
  ✓1. Using rods and sets, oral first, then written.
  ✓2. Subtraction facts to ten.
  ✓3. Missing addends, e.g. $8 - \_ = 3$

E. RELATED FACTS
  ✓1. "Family groups"....ways of adding and subtracting the same three numbers. e.g. $5 + 3 = 8; 3 + 5 = 8; 8 - 3 = 5; 8 - 5 = 3$
  ✓2. Children should understand the concept first and then put together the family groups on their own for most of the facts to ten.

F. COUNTING
  ✓1. Understanding of tens and ones beginning with teens and then the rest of the double digit numbers.
  ✓2. Writing the numerals to 100.
  ✓3. Place value to the hundreds place.
  ✓4. Counting by twos, threes, fives and tens.

G. ADDITION AND SUBTRACTION
  ✓1. Facts to twenty using sets and rods.
  ✓2. Missing addends
  ✓3. Commutative property of addition
  ✓4. Associative property of addition

(cont.)

H. NUMBER LINE ACTIVITIES AND GAMES

✓ 1. Hopping games
✓ 2. Logic games
✓ 3. Addition, subtraction, counting

I. MULTIPLICATION

✓ 1. Understanding of concept using rods.
✓ 2. Relationship to repeated addition
✓ 3. Discovery of time tables up to ten times table.
✓ 4. Commutative property of multiplication

J. FRACTIONS

✓ 1. Understanding fractions as portions of shapes, e.g. dividing
   a pie into halves, quarters, thirds, etc.
✓ 2. Writing fractions
✓ 3. Finding fractions of numbers, e.g. $\frac{1}{2}$ of 8 = 2, $\frac{1}{2}$ x 8 = 4
✓ **Also- adding fractions - finding common denominators.**

K. EQUALITIES AND INEQUALITIES USING SYMBOLS

✓ 1. Understanding the symbols: = (equals) and $\neq$ (not equal)
   $>$ (greater than), and $<$ (less than)
✓ 2. Using the symbols between two numerals: 6 = 6, 6 $\neq$ 7, 6 $>$ 3, 6 $<$ 9
✓ 3. Using the symbols in equations: 5 + 2 $>$ 4 + 1

L. GEOMETRY

✓ 1. Recognition of shapes
✓ 2. Finding perimeter and area, using rods.

Anthony discovered the formulae for area and perimeter. He did a great deal of work on this.

M. MEASUREMENT

✓ 1. Length in inches, feet, yards.
✓ 2. Beginning of metric units (rods are one centimeter square)
✓ 3. Volume in cups, pints, quarts, gallons.

N ✓ TELLING TIME - **A little uncertain of minutes before the hour.**

O. ODD AND EVEN NUMBERS

✓ 1. Concept
2. Number theory, e.g. O + O = E, O + E = O

P. ADDITION, SUBTRACTION AND MULTIPLICATION

✓ 1. Use of the three skills in more complex equations.
✓ 2. Word problems using the three skills.

Q. DIVISION

✓ 1. Understanding concept using rods
✓ 2. Discovery of division tables - **Not all of them done yet.**
✓ 3. Relationship to multiplication

R. PLACE VALUE TO 1,000

✓ 1. Understanding of place value.
✓ 2. Writing numerals to 1,000

*Note Anthony has an excellent math sense. He is very logical and creative in solving problems. He is excellent at math games.

S. ADDITION AND SUBTRACTION

✓ 1. Two digit without regrouping (carrying and borrowing)
✓ 2. Two and then three digit, with regrouping

U. FACTORING

1. Prime numbers
2. Composite numbers

(cont.)

To give you a better idea of what your child has been doing in school
during the last term, I have listed the major activities and projects.
Since integration of all subjects is our aim, it is difficult to list
all the incidental learning that happens. I have checked off those
areas where your child has shown interest and has participated actively.

SOCIAL STUDIES

✓Study of Kenya
✓Homes of other lands
✓Buildings and structures
✓Spain
✓Morocco
✓Our community - Good knowledge.
✓Maps - Good beginning skills.

Has participated actively in Social
Studies discussions and projects. Shows
expanding awareness of the world and
its people

SCIENCE

✓Electricity: batteries, bulbs
✓Experiments with magnets
✓Experiments with sound
✓Seeds, plants, planting
✓Pond life
Planning and making a bird feeder
Gerbils
✓Sea worms
Animals

Developing good inquiry skills. Very
interested in physical science activities
such as magnets, electricity, sound etc.

ARTS AND CRAFTS

Painting
✓Drawing
Weaving
✓Sewing - likes to make bean bags.
Woodworking
Collage work
✓3-D sculpture
✓Recycled "junk" creations
Finger knitting
✓Slide making
✓Marblized paper
✓Plaster of Paris
Crayon resist
✓Puppet making
✓Rubbings
✓Macaroni collages
✓Clay
✓Mural work
✓Print making
✓Color mixing
✓Cartoon making
✓Work with Claudia

OTHER

Music with Melody - doesn't like to
participate in music class
✓Gym with Ken - enjoys - is physically agile and
Creative drama   strong
Imaginative play
✓Sand play
✓Water play
✓Building blocks
✓Cooking
✓Grinding wheat into flour
✓Making peanut butter
✓Building things for the gerbils
✓Mixing food coloring
✓Jig saw puzzles
✓Chess
✓Checkers } enjoys very much
✓Card games
Other games

Making musical instruments
✓Using the encyclopaedia
✓Independent reading

Anthony shows interest in
many more activities than he
has in previous terms. He has
become much more involved
and active in participating.

Anthony's drawings are exceptionally
detailed. He enjoys making very small
fine drawings of "creatures" - also models
of them in clay. He has experimented
with many other materials and has
produced things which have good balance
and design and which he likes.

Appendix reprinted, by permission, from Engel, *A Handbook on Documentation*, pp. 11-14.